SUCCESSFUL READING

SUCCESSFUL READING

Key to Our
Dynamic Society
Third Edition

Maxwell H. Norman
Enid S. Kass Norman

Holt, Rinehart and Winston
New York Chicago San Francisco Atlanta Dallas

Library of Congress Cataloging in Publication Data

Norman, Maxwell H.
   Successful reading.

   1. Reading.   I. Norman, Enid Kass, joint author.
II. Title.
LB1050.N6   1980   428'.4'3   79-16779

ISBN 0-03-043126-3

ACKNOWLEDGMENTS

"The Man Who Wrote His Own Obituary," by Mark Waters, reprinted with permission from the July 1966 *Reader's Digest.*

"38 Who Saw Murder Didn't Call Police," by Martin Gansberg, © 1964 by the New York Times Company. Reprinted by permission.

"Deadly Game—Fishing for Killer Sharks," copyright 1966 by Newsweek, Inc. All rights reserved. Reprinted by permission.

"How to Read a Difficult Book," copyright © 1961, 1963 by Mortimer J. Adler. Reprinted by permission of Pocket Books, a Simon & Schuster division of Gulf & Western Corporation.

"Zip Out." Reprinted by permission from *Time*, the Weekly Newsmagazine. Copyright Time Inc.

"One in 100," copyright 1954 by Newsweek, Inc. All rights reserved. Reprinted by permission.

"Don't Wait Too Late to Play," by Arthur B. Peacock. Reprinted from *The Rotarian* Magazine for July 1977.

"Contexts," from *Language in Thought and Action*, Second Edition, by S. I. Hayakawa; copyright 1941, 1949, © 1963, 1964 by Harcourt Brace Jovanovich, Inc., and reprinted with their permission.

"Science No Barrier to 'Far-Out' Ideas," by Joanne Omang, *Los Angeles Times*, July 10, 1978. Reprinted from the *Washington Post.*

"Guns and Blackmail," from the *Washington Post*, July 6, 1963. Reprinted by permission.

"Living: Pushbutton Power," reprinted by permission from *Time*, the Weekly Newsmagazine; Copyright Time, Inc., 1978.

"Back Door: Death on the Comeback Trail," by Carll Tucker. © Saturday Review. All rights reserved.

(continued on p. xviii)

To the Instructor

Notes on the Third Edition

We have become increasingly aware, as the manuscript for this third edition comes into being, how eclectic is the whole process of writing a text. We have now had the advice and encouragement of three editors, 15 frank critiques from college reading teachers from all over the country, dozens of discussions with our former colleagues at Phoenix College, plus the important contributions of the university professors who instructed *us*—the procedures, textbooks, methods *they* used. To these contributions must be added, of course, the all-important reactions of our own students in the classroom.

It is all too easy to generalize about reactions, and "consensus" is a difficult approach to the "perfect" book. In trying to reach a consensus, therefore, we have been struck repeatedly by differences in opinion among those who have been asked to evaluate the manuscript. Reviewer A thinks highly of our technique (an original one, we believe) in teaching outlining, but reports that in his or her institution, vocabulary is handled in a separate word-study class. Reviewer B has no time to work on outlining in class, thinks highly of our approach to vocabulary, and advocates more such exercises. A third reviewer may approve of both techniques but wonders why the book is not reorganized so that the chapter sequence suits her or his particular approach!

Looking at (as well as beyond) these totally valid differences has been most helpful. Just as there are differences among teachers of college reading (or biology or math), there are differences among the students we are attempting to help. In this text as well as in our lower-division *How to Read and Study for Success in College*, every effort has been made to provide both instructor and student with a variety of ideas and exercises (again called Activities in this edition) as specific aids. In both texts, in all five editions, we continue our efforts to overcome what we feel is the key block to successful college reading—lack of motivation.

To this end, this third edition again hones the 12 Reading Techniques. Ten of the Reading Selections are new. In those areas in which individual students need help, twenty new exercises should prove useful. Again, in all Reading Techniques, the introductory and summary paragraphs have been italicized for extra emphasis and immediate recognition.

We hope we have been successful in retaining the flexibility of the original text. Much of the content of *Successful Reading: Key to Our Dynamic Society* can be handled by a student on his or her own; much more can be accomplished, we think, with the provocative interaction that comes from a motivated class.

Technology whirls us ever faster. In the first edition (1968), an Albert Rosenfeld article described the potential of both *in vitro* reproduction and cloning. A little over ten years later, as this volume goes to press, one of these procedures has been partially perfected; the second has created an international uproar. Supersonic transports race the sun; computers are faster, smaller, cheaper.

We cannot keep up with this explosion of knowledge with a half-hour television news program. And human knowledge *has* doubled in that decade plus. . . . Despite the declarations of far-out prophets of the sixties, the printed word is still our major learning tool.

We hope those words in this new edition are effective aids to college reading.

Leucadia, California
January 1980

E. S. K. N.

Why Bother?

Preface to the Third Edition

When the manuscript for the first edition of *Successful Reading* was sent to the publisher in late 1967, our editor raised her classic eyebrows in doubt at the statement that "pocket calculators capable of performing the four basic mathematical functions could be purchased for $49.95." A superb example of the headlong movement of our technology explosion is the fact that as this manuscript is revised for a third edition, a calculator which can handle *eight* functions—plus a full memory—can be bought for *less than seven dollars.* And this despite the rampant inflation which has beset our economy.

Along with technology, *the sum total of human knowledge has quadrupled since World War II, and is doubling every ten years.* New information is racing at us in such abundance that it threatens to be overwhelming. In a recent advertisement, the Xerox Corporation aims directly at the problem:

> With 72 billion pieces of information arriving yearly, how do you cope with it all? How do you gather it, edit it, disseminate it, store it and retrieve it?

In terms of technological advances, this is, perhaps, the most dynamic period in the history of humankind.

What has all this to do with reading successfully, reading effectively, *reading purposefully and willingly*? Interesting question, this. . . . Who is to make the decisions that will affect *your* future? Can an uninformed or apathetic public make decisions about population control, reproduction-without-sex? Or should we leave it to a few individuals in a smoke-filled room? If *you* were offered retirement *today* at age 47, with a livable income for life, would you know what to do with yourself? Would you know what paths to take to grow as a broader human being? Or would you simply start looking for another job to keep from being bored to death? More to the point as you select college courses: will you be re-trainable, after mastering drafting, when, as industrial engineers predict, 90 percent of that activity within the next decade will be done by computers?

We, all of us, must re-define the goals of education. Vocational training is still necessary, but is it enough? And for how long should "education" be a part of living? There is nothing in the Constitution of the United States that says education must end at 16 or 22; there is nothing in the by-laws of the Plumbers and Steamfitters Union which requires that the expert mechanic be culturally illiterate. . . .

And so we get back to reading, a key to growth as an individual, an open door to the immense treasury of human creativity. Psychobiologists tell us of the possibility of learning through electrical stimulation of the human brain. Molecular biologists have high hopes for the same end by means of chemical injections. But until these or similar technologies are perfected, the ability to read effectively—and the desire to use that ability—may well be the most important tool to an expanded mind, to a higher life-quality. And knowledge, gained basically through the printed word, will help you participate in the decision-making so vital in these next decades.

College textbooks cannot help being eclectic, a collection of ideas and procedures which reflects the experiences and education of the authors. And this is particularly true of new editions which have been criticized and evaluated by editors and by colleagues from many kinds of colleges and universities. We cannot begin to list all those who have been of help to us, but a few certainly deserve our deepest thanks. The late Dorothy Laurence MacDonald, founder and first director of the Reading and Study Skills Center at Phoenix College, was an ardent advocate of the philosophy of individual growth that forms the basis of our approach. Ms. Susan Katz, Associate Editor, English, of Holt, Rinehart and Winston, guided this edition through the many difficulties accompanying any new production.

Seth M. Norman, a budding writer (and our older son) contributed greatly in choosing and rating the new Reading Selections in this edition. We are grateful to the following for their help on this third edition: Professors Linda Wadleigh, El Camino College; D. W. Cummings, Central Washington University; Cheryl McKernan, Central Washington University; Nancy Wood, The University of Texas at El Paso; George Mather, The Loop College; Harry P. Hunt, American River College. And a final word of thanks to the several hundred of our own students who "worked the book over" with us in our own classrooms. They challenged, they analyzed, they evaluated, and, we hope, they became successful readers.

Leucadia, California   E. S. K. N.
January 1980

CONTENTS

*These sections are included in each chapter.

*These sections accompany each Appendix reading selection.

Reading as a Tool . . .
How To Use This Book

Reading is a tool, and good reading techniques can be mastered just as any skill can be mastered. Your reading success in using this book should not be measured by your ability to remember the various methods discussed, nor should you be satisfied by doing well in the self-testing devices. Full realization of your efforts will become apparent in your increased competence in the reading you do in other areas and in the enjoyment that reading can bring.

Each chapter consists of two reading units of approximately 1000 words. Each reading unit has its own vocabulary, testing device, and associated Activities. The first unit concerns reading techniques; the second unit is a selection of general interest.

PROCEDURE

1. On the first page of each chapter is a vocabulary list of words with which you may not be familiar. Page 1 of Chapter 1 notes the technique to be used.

2. Read the first chapter's Reading Technique on pages 2 and 3 as quickly as possible, remembering that you are to answer questions about it later. Use a stopwatch or any watch or clock with a second hand. Note the time it takes to complete the reading, in minutes and seconds, to the nearest 5 seconds.

3. Turn to the inside of the back cover. From the 1000-word Time-Rate Conversion on the left-hand page, find the words per minute (WPM) figure that corresponds to your time. This figure will be used to help complete the Progress Chart on the right-hand page. Look at the chart itself. Along the bottom you will see that the chart is divided into 36 columns, one for each timed reading. Two columns headed WPM go from 100 to 1000. To complete the rate portion for this reading, select the square opposite the WPM column to the closest 25 words, and fill in the block in the column above the timed selection.

4. For each timed reading—two in each chapter (totaling 24) and 12 in the Appendix—you will find a 10-question multiple-choice quiz. You can check your answers to the chapter quizzes by sliding back the quiz page about one inch. The correct answer is opposite each question on the exposed page below. Be sure to check any wrong answers. (Answers are not given for Appendix selection quizzes.)

5. If the quiz question deals with the *main idea* of the reading, its number is in a circle: ②. If the question is an inference question, one which requires you to draw a conclusion from the information given, its number is in a square: 9.

6. The Progress Chart includes two columns marked "Number of correct answers." Using these as a guide, place a *dot* in the center of the square opposite the number of right answers and in the same column as the rate block.

Note: The Reading Selections have been evaluated with the Reading Techniques in terms of difficulty. At the end of each selection, you will find a figure in parentheses (+50), (−25), which you should add to or subtract from your reading rate before entering it on the Progress Chart.

The steps noted above should be used for all 12 chapters; they will become mechanical after a few are completed. From Chapter 2 on, we will add two steps to the timed reading. They will be explained in Chapter 2.

The Progress Chart, accurately completed, will give you a clear picture of where you are going. It will show increases (as your reading "awareness" becomes heightened and as new habits replace old ones), "plateaus," even a sag or two. At a glance, diagnosis and technique changes will be obvious.

Note: Rate control may be accomplished without a watch or clock if special reading "pacers" are available. Settings for these machines may be determined from the information given in their accompanying booklets.

Following Chapter 12, you will find an Appendix which includes 12 varied readings. Each of these is accompanied by its own vocabulary preview and quiz. Because of the greater length of these readings, a 1500-word time-rate conversion chart has been provided at the bottom of page 232. Many of the quiz questions have been written to provide the groundwork for class discussions. (As mentioned, no answers are given for these questions.)

The Purpose of the Reading Résumé

The next two pages are titled "Reading Résumé." Fill in the blanks as honestly as you can and turn in the sheet to your instructor.

One of the facts about reading and studying that you will often find discussed in connection with many kinds of skills is that each student is an individual. Each person has a different background, different strengths and weaknesses, different ideas and attitudes. As a result, your instructor will make every effort to help you solve your own problems on a personal basis. As a starting point, this personal background sheet can be extremely useful in finding the areas in which you need the most help. You can answer some of the items without a second thought; others will call for a few minutes of honest self-judgment. The more accurate and honest you are in answering, the easier it will be for your instructor to help you identify your needs and plan your program.

Name _____ , _____ Class _____
           (Last)   (First)

READING RÉSUMÉ

Personal

Address _____ Phone _____

Age _____ Single _____ Married _____ No. of brothers/sisters _____

General Health Condition

Any special problems? _____ Explain: _____

Date of last *complete* eye exam? _____ Wear glasses? _____

Any hearing problems? _____ Headaches? often _____ seldom _____

Eye problems: Burning sensation? _____ Redness? _____ Tire easily? _____

Often wake up in the morning with patches of mucus in eye corners? _____

Allergies? _____ To what? _____

Suffer from any chronic illness? _____ Which? _____

Academic Background

What high school did you graduate from? _____ When? _____

Present class: Freshman ___ Sophomore ___ Now taking ___ semester hours.

Last grade average (last semester or senior high school year): _____

Subjects you like best: _____

Subjects you like least: _____

Participate in athletics? _____ Which sports? _____

Your present major: _____ Planning _____ yrs. college.

Active in student clubs or organizations? _____ Which? _____

Hobbies or special interests? _____ Which? _____

Reading Background

Read a daily newspaper? _____ Which? _____

Which sections do you read? _____

Do you regularly read a *news* magazine? _____ Which? _____

How many fiction books have you read in the last year? _____

Nonfiction? _____ Subject: _____

Read other magazines regularly? _____ Which? _____

Have a favorite place to read at home? _____ Where? _____

Where do you study? _____

Did you have any reading problems in elementary school? _____

Explain: _____

How would you describe your own reading ability? Excellent ____ Good ____

Fair ____ Poor ____ Do long reading assignments worry you? _____

Reading Skills

Grade yourself (as compared to other students) in the following:

	Excellent	Good	Fair	Poor
Speed				
Understanding				
Ability to find main ideas				
Ability to concentrate				
Ability to remember what I read				
Outlining skill				
Summarizing skill				

Possible Problem Areas You May Know About

Do you frequently go back over a word or a line (or two) because you're not sure of what you have read? _____ Do you often finish a reading assignment unsure of what you have read? _____

Please state, briefly and honestly, whether or not you like to read and why.

_____

_____

Are you employed? ____ Hours per week? ____ Doing what? _____

SUCCESSFUL READING

1
ARE YOU A SUCCESSFUL READER?

A Few Words on Words

At the beginning of each chapter, you will find a list of words, chosen from the reading units, with which you should be familiar before starting to read the selection. Often the fact that you may not know the meaning of *one word* may make a sentence, a paragraph, or even the whole article meaningless to you. Chapter 7 is devoted to the importance of vocabulary and some approaches you may find helpful in attacking new words. However, we will start "word-control" now in order to eliminate any problems in these early chapters.

Since most words have several meanings, you will find that each list contains the word as used in context—that is, with the words that surround or influence it. You may know many of the words included in these exercises. Be sure you understand them *in the context in which they are used.* If you have any doubt, use your dictionary. Remember that words are the keys to ideas, and that understanding ideas is the key to successful reading.

Vocabulary Preview

Reading Technique

In the space provided, write the meaning of the italicized word.

1. "the *intuition* of writers" _____

2. "the printed word provides, *vicariously*" _____

3. "reading that *transcends* the fact" _____

4. "*mediocre* jobs" _____

5. "this *attribute* has been placed last" _____

6. "study sessions *terminate* because" _____

7. "chances of real progress are *minute*" _____

8. "*Physiological* causes" _____

9. "an *integral* part of your home" _____

10. "the *neurology* of reading" _____

Reading Selection

The Reading Selection for Chapter 1 comes from *The Reader's Digest.* The vocabulary level of this article should present no problems. One word, "*emphysema*," may be new to you. In brief, it is a disease of the lungs caused by an accumulation of air which the normal body functions are not able to control.

1

Reading Technique

—begin timing—

Are You a Successful Reader?

c *In simple terms, a "successful reader" may be described as one who easily keeps abreast of his or her share of the billions of words printed each year. For the student, it may mean that reading a three-chapter assignment in General Psychology is not a disaster, but a normal process that can be mastered and put to use. A business administrator who reads well is not overwhelmed by the flood of memos that cross his or her desk daily, can read merchandising journals of value, and is still able to keep informed of the world's hap-*

b *penings.*

a ## I. THE SUCCESSFUL READER DEFINED

c In addition to these special groups, there are multitudes whose normal routine does not demand reading, but for whom a wide variety of books can provide escape from the monotony of everyday existence. Every human being can benefit from exposure to other lives, those long dead or contemporary, alike or alien, real or imagined. The active reader tastes the joys and frustrations of the laboratory and the creative thinking of great minds. He or she is

d moved by the intuition of writers who attempt to solve the infinite number of problems that affect each of us. The printed word provides, vicariously, a never-ending expanse of new scenes, ideas, solutions.

d If we analyze the term "successful reader," however, we find a number of definite characteristics. Primarily, he or she must have *purpose*, must have a reason for reading that transcends the fact that an assignment has been made. It is purpose that enables the reader to *concentrate*. The combination of these two characteristics leads us to that most important aspect of reading skill, *com-*

c *prehension*, without which the reader is simply exercising the eye muscles. This combination of purpose, concentration, and comprehension cannot help resulting in *retention*—remembering what you read.

To read well, without strain and irritation, the reader must have mastery of a solid *vocabulary*—and more: a method of attacking new words. Finally, he or

a she must be able to read rapidly, to cover large quantities of written material with *speed*. Note that this attribute of reading has been placed last on the list. There is no perfect rate to be set as a goal. A "whodunit" might be read at a rate of 100 pages per hour; two pages of Aristotle might require the same

b amount of time. The successful reader knows that varied materials call for varying speeds, and that rate is a totally individual characteristic.

b ## II. WHY READERS "FAIL"

Thousands of researchers and hundreds of programs have been devoted to the question of the "poor" reader. There are many contributing factors, and how each applies to the individual is still an unsolved problem. Several of the more important are worth a brief discussion.

A. Physiological Causes. When was the last time you had your eyes examined? After a long reading session, do your eyes smart? Do you wake up in the morning with little patches of white mucus in the corners of your eyes?

2

Do many of your study sessions terminate because of headaches that develop? Is it possible that poor eyesight has contributed to your low grades *for years*? Speaking bluntly, no effort you make can be successful if your need glasses, eye exercises, or other treatment. Good general health contributes to good reading; without good eye health, your chances of real progress are minute!

B. *Psychological Causes.* Have reading failures in the past given you a reading inferiority? Do you find yourself turning pages without any idea of what you have read? Do you honestly approach a reading assignment with a determination to master it? Have you grown up with books as an integral part of your home? Did your third-grade class laugh as you stumbled over new words, leaving you with a distaste for reading that remains with you today?

Frequently, these psychological causes of poor reading can color your entire existence. Secretly, you doubt your ability to hold your own with your classmates. You accept low grades, mediocre jobs, with an outward shrug of the shoulders, and an inner resentment toward those who appear to have keener intellects. Your daily activities may be tinged with feelings of guilt and failure. And since you doubt your own capacity, you make little effort to tackle the demands of new ideas—and the reading and thinking that must be used to investigate them. The result may be a psychological block to good reading based on *inadequate self-evaluation.*

C. *Intellectual Causes.* Facing the issue squarely, there is a small perentage of individuals whose verbal intelligence is not up to mastery of the printed word. Numerically, they are few. Moreover, intellectual limitations are frequently not those of intelligence at all, but are part of environmental influences. If the language spoken at home is not the English that is used in your text, you are obviously at a disadvantage. If the vocabulary of your friends and family is limited, yours may be too, and reading may be boring simply because you don't understand what has been written.

D. *Neurological Causes.* The neurology of reading is very complex, and our knowledge of it limited. There is one segment of reading specialists who believe that poor reading is primarily due to a malfunction of the delicate nerve chain that originates with the eye and ends in the billions of brain cells that make up the human brain. This hypothesis is under investigation.

III. READING HABITS: HOW ABOUT YOURS?

The above causes contribute to poor reading habits, the major source of difficulty in the field. This book is designed to point out these reading habits and to show you how to replace them with good ones. If you *want* to become a successful reader, you must *want* to establish good habits. And you must be willing to *practice, practice, practice* to keep the good ones.

A "successful reader" is one for whom reading is not a problem, but rather an opportunity to participate in the many aspects of a full life. That reader has purpose, the ability to concentrate, comprehend, remember. He or she has a good vocabulary and covers written material rapidly. Readers fail for physiological, psychological, intellectual, or neurological reasons which lead to poor reading habits. Overcoming these habits depends on purpose and practice.

—end timing—   (min___sec___)

Comprehension Quiz

Reading Technique

Instructions: For all of these quizzes, read each question and all answers. Select the letter of the correct answer and write it in the blank provided in the margin.

(___) 1. An acceptable title for this chapter could be:
    a) How to Read Efficiently
    b) Speed Reading Is An Art
    c) Factors That Affect Reading
    d) Causes of Reading Failure

(___) 2. The characteristic of the good reader that is described as "primary" is:
    a) the ability to comprehend
    b) a positive attitude
    c) the capacity to remember
    d) high speed

(___) 3. Good comprehension depends on:
    a) purpose and concentration
    b) purpose and retention
    c) concentration and speed
    d) speed and retention

(___) 4. To qualify as a "successful reader," says the chapter, you must be able to:
    a) read 100 pages per hour
    b) read 1,000 words per minute
    c) vary your reading rate
    d) triple your present speed

(___) 5. The principal physiological limitation mentioned is:
    a) low intelligence
    b) poor muscle tone
    c) headaches
    d) eye problems

(___) 6. Psychological causes that may contribute to reading difficulties:
    a) result from lack of books at home
    b) could have developed in the third grade
    c) could be the result of inadequate self-evaluation
    d) all of the above

(___) 7. Intellectual causes that contribute to poor reading:
    a) affect many people
    b) indicate poor general health
    c) may result from bilingual homes
    d) give you a feeling of security

(___) 8. Neurological causes of reading difficulties:
    a) are, today, only hypothetical
    b) result from heart trouble
    c) were described as inherited
    d) stem from poor eyesight

(___) 9. The major source of reading difficulties noted in the chapter is:
    a) the need for glasses
    b) poor reading habits
    c) intellectual limitations
    d) poor teaching methods

(___) 10. In general, from the material discussed in this first Reading Technique:
    a) the ability to read well is inherited
    b) you can read more effectively if you have the desire to improve
    c) by the end of this course, everyone should be reading at 800 WPM
    d) all of the above

As described in "Reading as a Tool," page xiii, check your answers by simply sliding the margin of this page back so that the left margin of page 2 is exposed. After completing your Progress Chart, find the correct answers to any questions you missed.

ACTIVITY 1-1
Getting the Ideas Down!

What did Reading Technique 1 really say? In Chapter 6, you will find a number of ideas on note-taking. Before you ger to that chapter, however, use exercises like this one to help you sum up the information you have just read. Reading Technique 1 is summarized below as an example.

A successful reader is one who can handle a wide variety of written materials without difficulty. He / she has purpose, can concentrate, understand and remember. He/she has a good vocabulary and reads as rapidly as the material allows. Poor reading may be caused by physiological, psychological or neurological problems. Poor reading habits can be over come by determination and practice.

Outlining: Unpleasant Job, or Important Study Help?

If you want to be sure that you are really "communicating" with the author of a book—and that's what reading is all about—you will be helped enormously if you see his or her "structure," the basic theme, the ideas that contribute to that theme, and the supporting facts, major and minor, that fit together to give you the whole picture. That means understanding the writer's outline—the basic structure which was enlarged to give you the finished chapter.

To show you how the outline relates to the finished material, each of these early chapters includes a partially completed outline which you can handle as a "fill-in-the-blanks" exercise. You should find this easy to do, but you must go one step further. Compare the finished outline with the Reading Technique, noting the relationships between the major and minor points. Outlining is such an important skill that each chapter has one for you to complete. Outlining, too, will be discussed in Chapter 6.

ACTIVITY 1-2
Outline: Are You A Successful Reader?

Main Idea: Discusses the importance of reading effectively in today's world, the characteristics of a good reader, and the factors that contribute to poor reading. Emphasizes developing good reading *habits*.

I. Definition of a successful reader
   A. One who is prepared to enjoy, vicariously, a multitude of experiences
   B. Characteristics of the successful reader
     1. Has purpose
     2. Can concentrate

     3. _____
     4. Retains-remembers—what he or she reads

     5. _____

     6. _____

II. Why readers fail
   A. Physiological causes
     1. Critical: condition of eyes

     2. Importance of good _____
   B. Psychological causes
     1. Feeling of inferiority

     2. Psychological blocks due to _____

     _____

   C. _____
     1. Percentage comparatively small

     2. Often related to _____ influences

   D. _____ causes
     1. Reading difficulties may be caused by _____.
     2. Due to limited knowledge, at present, this is only a hypothesis.

III. Importance of reading habits
   A. To replace poor habits with good ones requires:

     1. _____

     2. _____

ACTIVITY 1-3
Vocabulary Exercises

Reading Technique

Instructions: Substitute for the italicized words and phrases the correct word from the following list. (The form of the word as used in the sentence may not be the same as the one in the list.) Write the letter of the correct word in the blank provided.

a) intuition
b) vicariously
c) transcends
d) mediocre
e) attribute

f) terminate
g) minute
h) physiological
i) integral
j) neurology

1. The game would *come to an end* in just three minutes.   (__)
2. A knowledge of mathematics is an *essential* part of engineering.   (__)
3. An important *characteristic* of an opera singer is range.   (__)
4. Her ability to concentrate *goes far beyond* the ordinary.   (__)
5. *Through his friend's description* he experienced the dangers of the fire.   (__)
6. *The study of the brain and nervous sytem* is a specialized branch of medicine.   (__)
7. Sam's *quick insight* proved to be accurate.   (__)
8. Despite the cold, the sled dog's *physical* condition was good.   (__)
9. His chance of winning the first prize was *very small*.   (__)
10. Her tennis game was *ordinary*.   (__)

Instructions: Choose the correct word from the three listed below each sentence to make the sentence complete. Write its letter in the blank at the margin. (Note the effect of the word endings—the suffixes. See more in Chapter 7.)

1. In just a few minutes after he applied the powder, the wasps were
   _____.   (__)
   a) terminated   b) exterminated   c) interminable
2. The doctor decided that _____ tests were needed.   (__)
   a) neurologically   b) neurologist   c) neurological
3. At that time, she became interested in the science of _____.   (__)
   a) physiology   b) physiological   c) physiologically
4. Shrewdness was his outstanding _____.   (__)
   a) attribute   b) attributed   c) attribution
5. While she was hospitalized, her _____ pleasure came from books.   (__)
   a) vicariously   b) vicarious   c) vicariousness

Reading Selection

THE MAN WHO WROTE HIS OWN OBITUARY

by **Mark Waters**   (from *The Reader's Digest*, July, 1966)

—begin timing—

a   *Mark Waters, long a reporter for the* Honolulu Star-Bulletin, *started his last story January 27. "Run it as my obituary," he said on that day. "Maybe it will help someone." Four days later he made the final corrections in his copy. On the next day, February 1, in Queens Hospital, Honolulu, he died of lung cancer.*

b

Cigarettes were the death of me. I became acquainted with my killer when I was about 14 and began stealing several a day from my father's pack.

Inhaling caused some nausea at first, but persistence conquered.

d   I was born in a miniature Hell's Kitchen in Davenport, Iowa, on June 2, 1909.

At 16, I moved with my family, including two sisters, to Baltimore, a city that I loved and adopted as my hometown.

It was still no problem getting cigarettes.

c   I got odd jobs after school to buy them, and tried all sorts of queer brands, such as Melachrinos, Omars and English Ovals. I felt quite sophisticated, but I can't recall now that I enjoyed smoking them.

d   In 1928, the coming depression cast its shadow. With money scarce, my father began counting his Camels, so a chum and I took to picking butts off the street. We toasted the soggy tobacco in an oven, and rolled it into rice-paper cigarettes. They were horrible.

a   Jobs for youth were nil, so I decided to join the Navy—a mouth removed from the table, and I could send money home.

Now cigarettes were no problem. If you were at sea, they were 40 cents a carton. I smoked two packs a day, inhaling most of the smoke.

c   When my 20-year Navy career ended, I went to the University of North Carolina. After I graduated I got a job with the *San Diego Union*.

One night, while walking to my car, I had a slight stroke and staggered to the left. I had been smoking one cigarette after another that night, and I felt that that was what caused it.

My wife, Muriel, and I tried to quit. We lasted eight days.

d   It wasn't that I got any real pleasure out of smoking. Except for the first cigarette in the morning with my coffee, I never enjoyed it.

My mouth always tasted like a birdcage. Smoking took away my appetite. It brought on emphysema that made it hard to breathe. My chest colds were real dillies.

a   In 1956, smoking more than ever, I came to Honolulu to work for the *Star-Bulletin.*

In June 1965 my stomach began hurting, and I would get up every hour or half hour during the night to drink milk and smoke a cigarette.

b   In September 1965 I came down with a horrible cough. I was hoarse, and there was a nasty soreness in my left lung.

I went to my doctor. He listened to my chest and ordered an X-ray.

"You have a lung tumor," he said.

Four days later, the lung surgeon took out a left lobe.

A month later, I was back at work. I hadn't smoked since the day before my operation. It wan't hard to quit—for one simple reason. Motivation.

I came along fine, gained ten pounds and really felt good. Then, on January 3, I thought I had caught a cold.

I went to my surgeon, who tapped a quart of burgundy fluid from my left chest cavity.

I went back several times, and my surgeon said, "The time is drawing closer."

Later, my wife told me he had told her after the operation that I had less than a year to live. But she wouldn't believe it, and she didn't tell me. I find no fault with that.

There are four cell types of lung cancer. The type seems to have a lot to do with its rate of growth. My doctor told me this; he also said that out of every 20 lung-cancer cases only one survives. The other 19 die.

That's the survival rate for lung cancer, taking into consideration all available forms of treatment. There is no 50-50 chance—the figure for other cancers—for this type of cancer.

My doctor has understandable missionary zeal about getting people to quit cigarettes. He says that there's no question of the relationship between cigarette smoking and lung cancer. The statistics are overwhelming. It is estimated that one in every eight males who have been smoking heavily (20 cigarettes or more a day) for 20 years gets lung cancer.

The bad effect of cigarettes doesn't end with lung cancer. Smoking doubles the chances of death from coronary-artery disease, and the chances of dying from emphysema are 12 times greater. Then there's cancer of the mouth, larynx, esophagus and all the rest, too.

I think doctors get to feeling pretty helpless at times. They warn people like me, but all their warnings go unheeded.

And there's all that cigarette advertising. As my doctor says, "Millions of dollars are spent in all forms of advertising to give the public the impression that cigarettes can make up for a number of shortcomings."

In Italy and Great Britain, they have passed a ban against all cigarette advertisements on TV. I think that's a step in the right direction because, as the doctor says, the big effort should be to stop kids from getting started.

Whether this story will stop anyone from smoking, I don't know. I doubt it. Not a soul I've preached to has quit smoking—not a single, solitary soul.

You always think: "It will happen to the other guy; never to me."

But when you get your lung cancer—God help you.

All you need to see is that shadow on your chest X-ray. It's a real shocker. You can't do a thing.

At this point, I'm comfortable. The nurses give me something whenever there's pain.

I'm very short of breath. I can't take five steps without having to sit. The cancer has gone into my liver and I don't know where else.

I don't have a ghost of a chance.

It's too late for me.

It may not be for you.

(−50)   —end timing—   (min___sec___)

Comprehension Quiz

Reading Selection

Instructions: Read each question and all answer choices. Select the letter of the correct answer and write it in the blank at the left of the question.

(__) 1. Waters started to smoke at age:
      a) 14   c) 20
      b) 16   d) 24

(__) 2. During the Depression, Waters:
      a) stopped smoking   c) got a newspaper job
      b) joined the Navy   d) moved to Baltimore

(__) 3. Waters soon found that cigarette smoking:
      a) provided day-long pleas- c) helped his appetite
         ure
      b) freed him from chest colds d) made it hard to breathe

(__) 4. In 1956, he started to work for the *Star-Bulletin* in the city of:
      a) San Francisco   c) Honolulu
      b) Juneau   d) San Diego

(__) 5. In the year 1965, he was affected by:
      a) a bad cough   c) soreness in his lung
      b) stomach pain   d) all of the above

(__) 6. After the first examination, the doctor told Waters:
      a) he had a lung tumor   c) to gain weight
      b) he had emphysema   d) to go back to work

(__) 7. The doctor later stated that patients with lung cancer have:
      a) a 50–50 chance of recov- c) a 1 in 20 chance of survival
         ery
      b) a better-than-even chance d) no possibility of living

(__) 8. The article states that smoking can also contribute to:
      a) coronary-artery disease c) emphysema
      b) cancer of the mouth and d) all of the above
         larynx

(__) 9. Waters' past preaching against cigarette smoking was:
      a) completely unsuccessful c) moderately successful
      b) generally unsuccessful   d) not mentioned

(__) (10.) The general theme of this article is:
      a) lung cancer is deadly   c) lung cancer is curable
      b) cigarette smoking is dan- d) have a chest X-ray every
         gerous   year

(Slide back edge of page to check answers on margin of page 8.)

2
GET YOUR OARWET!

Vocabulary Preview

Reading Technique

1. "You have *envisaged*" _____
2. "*significantly* different" _____
3. "you look for it *intensively*" _____
4. "to locate the *topic sentence*" _____
5. "you now have, *fundamentally*" _____
6. "we *predetermine* the secondary points" _____
7. "a subject is extremely *complex*" _____
8. "*utilization* of an organized approach" _____
9. "we know what *specific* information" _____
10. "*Evaluate* the information" _____

Reading Selection

1. "their *chatter* interrupted him" _____
2. "*homicide* investigations" _____
3. "*recitation* of many murders" _____
4. "the slaying *baffles* him" _____
5. "voices *punctuated* the early-morning stillness" _____
6. "after much *deliberation*" _____
7. "he *sheepishly* told the police" _____
8. "a court *committed* him to a hospital" _____
9. "for *psychiatric* observation" _____
10. "*rattled* off an account" _____

2

Reading Technique
—begin timing—

Get Your OARWET!

c *For a comparatively small group of people, informational reading presents no problems. Textbooks, business magazines, instruction sheets can be handled by these lucky ones with ease. For most readers, however, the key to mastery of factual information is the utilization of an* organized approach.

I. THE IMPORTANCE OF A PLANNED STUDY APPROACH

c The importance of this tool cannot be overemphasized. It can mean the difference between success and failure in any area where reading is called for. This is, perhaps, the most important single chapter in this book; it may be the
b most important study unit you have ever read.

II. ONE STEP AT A TIME: OARWET
d
What, precisely, is an organized approach in the field of reading? Basically, it means that you formulate an over-all picture of the information you must master *before* you start to read it. You become aware of the main idea and have a sound picture of the secondary objects. You are not reading in a vacuum.
a You are prepared to tie in new information with previous experience. You concentrate better because you now look for new facts to complete the general picture you have already envisaged.

b There are no magic wands in successful reading, but if anything approaches one, pre-organization is it. OARWET is simply a catchword whose individual letters stand for six steps used in attacking factual material.

Using OARWET, the approach is significantly different:

A. **O**verview

b 1. Read the chapter *title*. Really read it! Let's assume that Chapter 8 discusses "Applied Psychology." If you are not sure what that term means, you raise a question. You know that one of the first things you must determine is
d the definition of the term itself. You look for it intensively in the first few paragraphs.

2. You then determine what main divisions the author will consider in the discussion. All this requires is thumbing through the chapter to *find the subheads*. While doing this, you become aware of pictures, maps, graphs, and
d charts. Without having done any "real" reading, you now have, fundamentally, the outline of the chapter.

3. In order to provide flesh for our chapter skeleton, we now do a little preliminary reading. We spend a few seconds reading the first two or three paragraphs to locate the *topic sentence*. (In this OARWET chapter, for example, the topic sentence is the last one in the first paragraph.) It provides us
b with a general idea of what the chapter will cover. You can check this by reading the *summary paragraph* at the end.

In brief, the author has told us, "This is what I will talk about and how I will break it down." Then, "This is what I have said."

B. **A**sk

Phase A has given us the general outline of the major divisions of the material contained in the chapter. How can we predetermine the secondary points made in each section?

1. Most modern textbooks contain questions covering the material. In many, these are found at the end of the chapter; some authors place them at the end of each subhead section. Read these questions immediately after the Overview. Read them intensively so that you will be looking for the answers as you read the chapter. Again, you know before you start reading what points the author considered important.

2. Some texts may not have questions. In that case, you must make up your own. This can be easy if you use the subheads. For example, let's suppose one subhead reads "Applications in Industry." Our question would be: What are the applications of applied psychology in industry? Practically, you need not spell out the questions completely—"Applic. in Ind.?" would probably give the information necessary to sharpen your thinking as you read that portion of the chapter. Many of your exam questions will come from this list.

C. Read

Only now do we start to read the chapter from beginning to end. We know its outline, we know what specific information the author considers important.

D. Write

For many people, note-taking is of great help in getting information *set*. Because this subject is discussed in Chapter 6, the main point to be made here is this: If you can *outline* a chapter which you have just finished reading, you *know* it!

E. Evaluate

What did all that material really mean? Does it make sense? Does it tally with your own background and experience? In your particular case, are you driving a supercharged super-eight because somebody used applied psychology on you?

F. Test

Let's go back to the questions at the end of those 38 assigned pages. Can you answer them without referring to the chapter? If not, locate the answers. The class quiz will be Tuesday, but if you have done a thorough job with OAR-WET, it will present no problems.

III. CAN YOU AFFORD THE TIME?

How much time are we talking about? Unless a subject is extremely complex, the *O*verview stage will consume only a few minutes. The *A*sk step might take a little longer, depending on how many questions there are; but again we are talking of minutes. Taking notes is essential. *T*esting will be easy. Moreover, the time spent in using OARWET will be made up when you review for examinations. Your reading rate should increase because you will have a good idea of what to look for. The question then becomes, "Can you afford *not* to use OARWET?"

OARWET is an extremely valuable organized approach to reading for information. Each of the six letters stands for a step in the mastery of a textbook. The Overview stage calls for intensive reading of the title, subheads, introductory and summary paragraphs. In stage two, Ask, you become familiar with the questions you should be able to answer after finishing the reading. With that background, you then Read, stage three. Stage four involves note-taking, an aid to memory, stage five has you "thinking through" what you have read. Finally, stage six helps you to check your mastery of the information. OARWET requires little time, but provides much help.

—end timing—   (min___sec___)

Comprehension Quiz

Reading Technique

Instructions: Read each question and all answer choices. Select the letter of the correct answer, and write it in the blank at the left of the question.

(__) **1.** The title of this chapter is:
- a) An Organized Approach to Reading
- b) A Planned Study Approach
- c) Get Your OARWET!
- d) How To Read for Information

(__) 2. The chapter contains _____ subheads:
- a) 1
- b) 2
- c) 3
- d) 4

(__) 3. The chapter says the OARWET technique is applied to:
- a) all reading
- b) factual reading
- c) relaxation reading
- d) only psychology texts

(__) 4. The "*O*" for *O*verview means:
- a) knowing the main idea
- b) knowing the secondary idea
- c) knowing the topic sentence
- d) all of the above

(__) 5. If there are no questions included in the text:
- a) make up your own
- b) disregard this step
- c) review is not necessary
- d) notes may be minimized

(__) 6. The "*R*" in OARWET stands for the *R*eading step. Because of *O*verview and *A*sk:
- a) the reading will take longer
- b) reading time should be less
- c) time should not be affected
- d) reading time was not mentioned

(__) 7. Under *W*rite, the one method of note-taking mentioned was:
- a) summarizing
- b) outlining
- c) underlining
- d) using index cards

(__) 8. To *E*valuate, as it is used in the OARWET process, means:
- a) to question the sense
- b) to determine the worth
- c) to tie in with your own experience
- d) all of the above

(__) 9. The *T*est section of OARWET refers to:
- a) your self-testing at the end
- b) the classroom quiz
- c) final examinations
- d) all of the above

(__) **10.** The main idea of this chapter is:
- a) Most good students do well because they are "natural" readers.
- b) Successful reading, in most cases, depends on an organized approach.
- c) OARWET should be applied by all readers to all reading.
- d) OARWET is a system used after informational reading is completed.

ACTIVITY 2-1
Outline: Get Your OARWET!

Main Idea: Emphasizes the importance of an *organized approach* to reading for information. Describes the procedures and importance of OARWET.

I. The importance of a planned approach to reading

II. The six steps of *O–A–R–W–E–T*
   A. *Overview*—getting the general picture *before* reading
      1. *Really* read the chapter _____.
      2. Read all subheads to get an _____ of the chapter.
      3. Read the first 2–3 paragraphs to find _____ of the chapter.

      Check this by reading the _____ paragraph at the end.
   B. _____ phase
      1. Look for questions in the text, usually found at end of chapter, and read them carefully so that you can look for answers.
      2. If the text has no questions, make them up, using

      _____.

   C. *Read* the chapter, knowing in advance the _____, the

   outline, and the _____.
   D. _____. Tie the information down.
   E. _____ the material read. Tie in with previous knowledge.
   F. *Test.* Can you _____?

III. _____

_____

_____

_____

ACTIVITY 2-2
Applying the Technique

Instructions: Use this form to Overview a textbook for another course.

1. Name of course _____Instructor _____

2. Title of textbook _____ Author _____

3. Number of chapters _____ Number of pages _____

4. Illustrations: pictures? _____ maps? _____ charts? _____

5. Preface? _____ Introduction? _____ Index? _____ Glossary?_____
   Bibliography? _____ (If yes, in each chapter or at end of book?) _____

6. Read the Preface. See if you can find the main thought or basic idea that the author presents in the book. Write it in your own words: _____
   _____
   _____

7. List the chapter subjects. Use your own words, or abbreviate if you like.

   1. _____   9. _____

   2. _____   10. _____

   3. _____   11. _____

   4. _____   12. _____

   5. _____   13. _____

   6. _____   14. _____

   7. _____   15. _____

   8. _____   16. _____

8. Does the author use introductory paragraphs? ____ Roman numerals? ____
   Do subsections stand out? _____ How? _____
   Are there questions included? _____ Where? _____
   Exercises? _____ Discussion questions? _____
   Are there summaries? _____

OARWET Instructions

To help you experience the value of an organized approach when reading for information, the chapters that follow have been set up for use with OAR-WET. For maximum effectiveness, proceed as follows:

Be sure of the vocabulary words on the preview pages.

1. *O*verview the chapter. Allow about one minute.

2. Spend another minute reading the questions, which now *precede* each reading. Read the possible answers if you have the time. *A*sk.

3. Go ahead with the timed reading and the quiz as in the previous chapters, noting the results on the Progress Chart. *R*ead.

4. Tie down the information! Outline the chapter. *W*rite.

5. *E*valuate the technique involved in terms of your own needs.

6. *T*est and test again by going over the questions before exams.

Test the whole technique in your reading for other subjects.

ACTIVITY 2-3
OARWET Review Exercise

Take a few minutes to apply OARWET to this textbook chapter, step by step, paying no attention to the time limits suggested on page 17.

Overview

1. Look again at the chapter title (page 12).
   Have you ever thought about "organizing your reading" before?
   Do you see how it can help you to understand textbooks?
   Can you see the reason for the use of the "word" OARWET in the title?
2. Leaf through the Reading Technique section and check the subheads.
   Does I show you that both "organized approach" and OARWET will be explained there? Underline the subhead to help you remember it.
   What does subhead II tell you?
   When you read about the six steps in II, you might have thought of the amount of time that the technique would take. Too much? It looks like III deals with that problem.
3. Now to the introductory paragraph in italic type. Which sentence tells you what this chapter is all about? Underline it.
4. Turn to the summary paragraph at the end, again in italic type. Read it carefully. Does it help to "firm up" the ideas that you have developed?

Ask

Read over the quiz questions on page 14 slowly and carefully. Underline words which seem important, to help fix the questions in your mind. (You may find that you can answer some questions just from Overview.)

Read

Because you have read the chapter and taken the quiz, there is no point in doing it again unless you're not sure of the steps of OARWET.

Write

A good set of notes is a "must." Note-taking is discussed at length in Chapter 6. In the following chapters, you should find note-taking simpler because of the method suggested in this chapter.

Evaluate

Now sit back and judge the suggestions made in this chapter for yourself. How have *you* read textbook chapters in the past? Are the claims made in this chapter for an "organized approach to reading" worth anything to you? Do you have doubts about the time it takes? Will it save time when you have to review? Can OARWET improve your grades? Is it worth a try?

Test

You will see how using the "know in advance" method helps you increase your own efficiency in reading this book. Test OARWET in other ways. Try it—honestly—in your next reading assignment in another class. See if it helps in recitation classes. Prove its value to yourself!

2

Comprehension Quiz

Reading Selection

Instructions: Write the letter of the correct answer in the blank provided.

1. Another good title for this article by Martin Gansberg might be:
   a) Murder in the Streets   c) Bar Manager Knifed   (___)
   b) Woman Killed in Queens   d) Nobody Gives a Damn!

2. The murder of Kitty Genovese took place:
   a) between 3:00 and 4:00   c) in the late afternoon   (___)
      A.M.
   b) at breakfast time   d) early in the evening

3. In the 35-minute period described, Miss Genovese was attacked:
   a) twice   c) five times   (___)
   b) three times   d) not mentioned

4. The first telephone call to the police was made:
   a) after the first attack   c) after the fatal attack   (___)
   b) after several knifings   d) before the killer left

5. The people of the neighborhood were awakened by:
   a) police sirens   c) the exhaust of the killer's   (___)
                                    car
   b) a man who shouted "Let   d) Miss Genovese's screams
      that girl alone!"

6. The killer:
   a) lived in one of the houses   c) arrived and left on foot   (___)
   b) drove away in a white car   d) walked with a limp

7. The neighborhood where the murder took place was:
   a) badly run-down   c) fairly well-to-do   (___)
   b) a shopping area   d) all apartments

8. When asked, the witnesses said they did not call the police because:
   a) they "were afraid"   c) "I didn't want to get   (___)
                                    involved"
   b) they "didn't know"   d) all of the above

9. The man who finally called the police did it:
   a) after asking a friend for   c) both a) and b)   (___)
      advice   d) as soon as he saw what
   b) from another apartment   happened

10. From the reporter's newspaper article, you gathered that:
    a) he was not surprised at   c) this was a typical news   (___)
       the lack of action by the   story
       "38"
    b) he was disturbed by the   d) he made no judgment
       inaction

Note to students: After scoring your quiz, be sure to return to the article and check on all wrong answers.

19

Reading Selection

38 WHO SAW MURDER DIDN'T CALL POLICE

by **Martin Gansberg**   (from *The New York Times*, March 27, 1964)

—begin timing—

For more than half an hour 38 respectable, law-abiding citizens in Queens watched a killer go after and stab a woman in three separate attacks in Kew Gardens.

Twice their chatter and the sudden glow of their bedroom lights interrupted him and frightened him off. Each time he returned, went after her, and stabbed her again. Not one person telephoned the police during the attack; one witness called after the woman was dead.

Good People. Still shocked is Assistant Chief Inspector Frederick M. Lussen, in charge of the borough's detectives and a veteran of 25 years of homicide investigations. He can give a matter-of-fact recitation of many murders. But the Kew Gardens slaying baffles him—not because it is a murder, but because the "good people" failed to call the police.

"As we have reconstructed the crime," he said, "the attacker had three chances to kill this woman during a 35-minute period. He returned twice to complete the job. If we had been called when he first attacked, the woman might not be dead now."

Murder with an Audience. At 3:20 A.M. twenty-eight-year-old Catherine Genovese, who was called Kitty by almost everyone in the neighborhood, was returning home from her job. She parked her red Fiat in a lot near the Kew Gardens Long Island Rail Road Station.

She turned off the lights of her car, locked the door, and started to walk the 100 feet to the entrance of her apartment at 82-70 Austin Street, which is in a building with stores on the first floor and apartments on the second.

The entrance to the apartment is in the rear of the building because the front is rented to retail stores.

Miss Genovese noticed a man at the far end of the lot, near a seven-story apartment house at 82-40 Austin Street. She halted. Then, nervously, she headed up Austin Street toward Lefferts Boulevard, where there is a call box to the 102nd Police Precinct in nearby Richmond Hill.

She got as far as a street light in front of a bookstore before the man grabbed her. She screamed. Lights went on in the 10-story apartment house at 82-67 Austin Street, which faces the bookstore. Windows slid open and voices punctuated the early-morning stillness.

Miss Genovese screamed: "Oh, my God, he stabbed me! Please help me! Please help me!"

From one of the upper windows in the apartment house, a man called down: "Let that girl alone!"

The attacker looked up at him, shrugged, and walked down Austin Street toward a white sedan parked a short distance away. Miss Genovese struggled to her feet.

Lights went out. The killer returned to Miss Genovese, now trying to make her way around the side of the building by the parking lot to get to her apartment. The assailant stabbed her again.

"I'm dying!" she shrieked. "I'm dying!"

Windows were opened again, and lights went on in many apartments. The assailant got into his car and drove away. Miss Genovese staggered to her feet. It was 3:35 A.M.

The assailant returned. By then, Miss Genovese had crawled to the back of the building, where the freshly painted brown doors to the apartment house held out hope for safety. At the second door, he saw her slumped on the floor at the foot of the stairs. He stabbed her a third time—killing her.

Police Are Called.   It was 3:50 by the time the police received their first call, from a man who was a neighbor of Miss Genovese. In two minutes they were at the scene. The neighbor, a 70-year-old woman, and another woman were the only persons on the street. Nobody else came forward.   **d**   **a**

The man explained that he had called the police after much deliberation. He had phoned a friend in Nassau County for advice and then he had crossed the roof of the building to the apartment of the elderly woman to get her to make the call.

"I didn't want to get involved," he sheepishly told the police.   **b**

Six days later, the police arrested Winston Moseley, a 29-year-old business-machine operator, and charged him with the homicide. Moseley had no police record. On Wednesday, a court committed him to Kings County Hospital for psychiatric observation.   **c**

The police repeated how simple it would have been to have gotten in touch with them. "A phone call," said one of the detectives, "would have done it."

Today witnesses from the neighborhood, which is made up of one-family homes in the $35,000 to $60,000 range with the exception of the two apart-ment houses near the railroad station, find it difficult to explain why they didn't call the police.   **d**

"We Were Afraid."   A housewife, knowingly if quite unexcited, said, "We thought it was a lover's quarrel." A husband and wife both said, "Frankly, we were afraid." They seemed to understand the fact that events might have been different. An upset woman, wiping her hands in her apron, said, "I didn't want my husband to get involved."   **b**

One couple, now willing to talk about that night, said they heard the first screams. The husband looked at the bookstore where the killer first grabbed Miss Genovese.   **c**

"We went to the window to see what was happening," he said, "but the light from our bedroom made it difficult to see the street." The wife, still worried, added: "I put out the light and we were able to see better."   **d**

Asked why they hadn't called the police, she shrugged and replied: "I don't know."

A man peeked out from a slight opening in the doorway to his apartment and rattled off an account of the killer's second attack. Why hadn't he called the police? "I was tired," he said calmly. "I went back to bed."   **c**

It was 4:25 A.M. when the ambulance arrived to take the body of Miss Genovese. It drove off. "Then," a solemn police detective said, "the people came out."

(—0—)   —end timing—   (min___sec___)   **b**

ACTIVITY 2-4
Summarizing

Instructions: In three or four sentences, and in your own words, write a paragraph that "sums up" the story. Details are not required; it is the general idea that you should try to get down. Summarizing as a method of note-taking will be described in more detail in Chapter 6. While it has its limitations, it is an excellent method of bringing into focus the theme of what you have read.

_____

_____

_____

_____

_____

_____

_____

_____

React to the story you have just read. Find it powerful? Why, why not?

_____

_____

_____

_____

_____

_____

_____

_____

_____

ACTIVITY 2-5
Vocabulary Exercises

Reading Technique

Instructions: Substitute for the italicized words and phrases the correct word from the following list. (The form of the word as used in the sentence may not be the same as the one in the list.) Write the letter of the correct word in the blank provided.

a) envisaged
b) intensively
c) significantly
d) complex
e) fundamentally

f) specific
g) topic sentence
h) predetermine
i) utilization
j) evaluate

1. The major idea of a paragraph is established in the *theme statement.* (__)

2. Learning to *make use of* athletic equipment in the proper way is part of a physical education course. (__)

3. He searched *very hard* for the lost mine. (__)

4. She eyed the legal papers *weightily.* (__)

5. He knew what the result would be; he had *planned it ahead of time.* (__)

6. The Board of Inquiry wanted *definite* answers to searching questions. (__)

7. Before voting, *determine the worth of* the candidates' positions. (__)

8. The engine of a racing car is specialized and *intricate.* (__)

9. From your voice I *pictured* you as older. (__)

10. *Basically*, your argument is correct.

Reading Selection

Instructions: Write the letter of the matching word in the blank provided. *Forms may differ in this and following sets of exercises.*

a) chatter
b) homicide
c) recitation
d) baffles
e) punctuated
f) deliberation
g) sheepishly
h) committed
i) psychiatric
j) rattled

1. dealing with mental illness (__)
2. shyly, self-consciously (__)
3. confuses, puzzles (__)
4. cut through, sounded (in air) (__)
5. jailed, locked up (__)
6. oral reply to a question (__)
7. much talk that says little (__)
8. considered thought (__)
9. killing, murder (__)
10. talked in noisy, quick way (__)

3
SPEED—
THE FLEXIBILITY FACTOR

Vocabulary Preview

Reading Technique

1. "there has been a *tendency*" _____
2. "escape from the *rigors* of the day" _____
3. "you identify with the *protagonist*" _____
4. "intense and *arduous* processes" _____
5. "feeling of *gratification*" _____
6. "the *excerpt*" from Aristotle _____
7. "when dealing with significant *concepts*" _____
8. "she *peruses* an important legal document" _____
9. "the reader develops *muted* activity" _____
10. "It is *imperative* that you be aware" _____

Reading Selection

1. "their *massive* jaws" _____
2. "have changed almost *imperceptibly*" _____
3. "the *mystique* of danger" _____
4. "tiger sharks, true *gourmands*" _____
5. "those *votaries* of swordfish" _____
6. "begins the *tedious* process" _____
7. "*surf-addicted populace*" _____
8. "they have held *legendary* terror" _____
9. "in the past few *decades*" _____
10. "cost . . . can be *prohibitive*" _____

Comprehension Quiz

Reading Technique

Instructions: Write the letter of the correct answer in the blank provided.

1. The main idea of this chapter is that a successful reader:
   - a) reads at 500 wpm
   - b) reads at 100 wpm
   - c) reads at 200 wpm
   - d) adjusts his or her rate to the material   (__)

2. The rate set by a good reader depends on:
   - a) the reader's purpose
   - b) the difficulty of the material
   - c) both a) and b)
   - d) neither a) nor b)   (__)

3. Lack of flexibility in reading rate may be the result of:
   - a) old, constant-speed habits
   - b) muscular problems of the eye
   - c) need of glasses
   - d) a poor vocabulary   (__)

4. Moving your lips limits your speed to approximately:
   - a) 100 wpm
   - b) 200 wpm
   - c) 500 wpm
   - d) 400 wpm   (__)

5. Lip-moving while reading may be stopped by:
   - a) total concentration
   - b) adjusting your reading rate
   - c) placing a pencil between the lips
   - d) reading the same material again   (__)

6. Vocalizing:
   - a) can be felt at the voice box
   - b) can be stopped by awareness
   - c) produces no audible sound
   - d) all of these   (__)

7. When reading material a second time:
   - a) your rate will increase
   - b) comprehension will increase
   - c) there should be no vocabulary problems
   - d) all of these   (__)

8. Reading in a familiar field usually results in:
   - a) a faster rate
   - b) a lesser comprehension
   - c) vocabulary problems
   - d) large quantities of new facts and ideas   (__)

9. The rate at which you read an article:
   - a) does not depend on your experience
   - b) should be the same for all readers
   - c) should be set by the individual reader
   - d) is independent of your knowledge of the field   (__)

10. The aspect of rate is discussed at this time because:
    - a) rate is the most important factor
    - b) bad rate habits are easiest to break
    - c) you must learn to move your eyes quickly as soon as possible
    - d) successful reading and speed reading are synonymous   (__)

3

Reading Technique
—begin timing—

Speed—The Flexibility Factor

There has been a tendency these last few years to talk about reading in terms of speed. Although the successful reader can cover printed matter quickly, the speed factor is meaningless when considered alone. Successful reading is determined by your ability to adjust to the material *with which you are concerned, your "flexibility factor."*

I. FLEXIBLE READING AND SPEED CONTROL

Consider your own reading. On a warm summer evening, after a demanding day, you sit down with a "cloak and dagger" adventure story. Your primary aim is relaxation; your immediate goal—escape from the rigors of the day. If the book suits your taste, you identify with the protagonist and dash through page after page to determine the twists of the plot. You become tense as disaster threatens, relax as hero overwhelms villain, and close the book with a feeling of gratification.

At another time, you might be reading an assignment for your philosophy course. It is a short assignment, pages 136–138 in Aristotle's *Ethics*. Suddenly, we have neither a hero nor a plot, and identification and understanding become intense and arduous processes.

Suppose it took the whole of an evening for each of the above readings: two hundred pages in the thriller, three pages with the great Greek thinker. Can we say that the first reading was successful, and that the second represented failure? Obviously not. These totally different selections simply indicate the flexibility demanded in any successful reading program. You must be able to adapt your rate to the material.

Two factors should provide the standards for *your* control of the speed at which you read. The first of these is your *purpose*. You read the adventure story because you wanted to relax. You read the philosophy text with the need to learn, to understand, to grow. Six months from the date of that first evening, the lightweight book may be little more than a vague, pleasant memory. Twenty years after you closed the cover on the excerpt, Aristotelian ethics may still be an important factor in many everyday decisions.

The second control factor is the *difficulty of the material*. If the subject matter is simple and its vocabulary easy, you should have no problem in reading rapidly. When dealing with significant concepts or large numbers of new words and ideas, the most capable minds must slow down.

The important idea is your recognition of these two points. You must control your own reading rate, with that control determined by these two factors: purpose and difficulty.

II. SLOW READING: POOR HABITS

In Chapter 1, speed was placed at the end of our list of characteristics of a good reader. The question of rate is presented early in this book because of the "habit" factor, also discussed in Chapter 1. There are four poor habits relating to speed that can seriously affect reading efficiency.

A. Do you habitually read everything at the same speed? Professional people frequently stumble into this rut because of the huge amount of material with which they must be familiar. The lawyer might read relaxation material at the same rate at which he or she peruses an important legal document; the biochemist might slow down all reading to the rate used with professional journals.

B. Poor habit number two is of concern to those people (and there are many) who, for all practical purposes, read aloud without making sounds. While reading silently, they move their lips to pronounce the words. Analyze this situation: a rapid speaker will occasionally talk at a rate of 200 words per minute. If your are "speaking silently" while reading, you limit your rate to this speed. Have a friend watch your lips as your read. If there is lip movement, you can easily stop it by placing a pencil or a finger between your lips. Not very sanitary, but quickly effective.

C. Habit three in this area also has to do with the oral effect. In this case, the reader develops "muted activity" in the vocal cords in the throat. Touching the voice box with your fingers will let you feel the vibrations that are taking place, even though no sound is heard. Awareness of this activity— "vocalization"—usually puts an end to it.

D. "Regressing" is the act of going back over a line—sometimes several— because you are uncertain of a word or the basic idea of the sentence. Sometimes this is sound and necessary. Often, however, *it is simply a bad habit* built up over the years. If your regressing is the result of habit, use every bit of willpower to stop it. Use a "pacing" machine if one is available.

Rate is emphasized at this time for this reason: of all the habits which limit your reading effectiveness, poor rate habits are the easiest to break. Once they are disposed of, progress should be rapid.

III. FAMILIARITY AND EXPERIENCE

Two subordinate factors affect rate. A second reading takes much less time than the first because you are acquainted with the material. Prove this to yourself by re-reading any of the timed selections in this book.

Moreover, reading in a familiar field can be accomplished more quickly. There will be little new vocabulary to slow you down, and many ideas or facts will already be known. Comprehension will be easier, too. Because rate is related to experience, it is obvious that there is no "standard" rate. No two individuals have the same background.

From the very start, it is imperative that you be aware of the necessity for deliberately controlling your reading speed. Purpose *and* difficulty of material *are the guides to rate-setting. Four poor habits can interefere with effective reading rate: "same-speed" reading; moving lips while reading; vocalizing; going back or regressing. Get rid of poor rate habits.*

—end timing—   (min___sec___)

d

c

a

b

c

d

d

a

c

b

27

ACTIVITY 3-1
Applying the Technique

In the section which you just read, an imagined assignment was noted as taken from Aristotle's *Ethics*. There is little question that this man was one of the great thinkers of all times. His ideas on ethics are incorporated in one of the world's great religions today. Let us quote two paragraphs from that assignment:

> For it is not every kind of Notion which the pleasant and the painful corrupt and pervert, as, for instance, that "the three angles of every rectilineal triangle are equal to two right angles," but only those bearing on moral action.
>
> For the Principles of the matters of moral action are the final cause of them: now to the man who has been corrupted by reason of pleasure or pain does he see that it is his duty to choose and act in each instance with a view to this final cause and by reason of it: for viciousness has a tendency to destroy the moral Principle: and so Practical Wisdom must be "a state conjoined with reason, true, having human good for its object, and apt to do."

Obviously, racing through material of this nature would be foolhardy. If you examine the paragraphs carefully, you will find few words, perhaps, which are beyond your vocabulary. It is the nature of the material itself, the grammatical structure, and the need to think through the concepts involved that slow us down.

Now let us look at the other end of the flexibility line. The following excerpt is from Ian Fleming's *Moonraker*, a book you might read for excitement and enjoyment:

> He gave his head a shake and when he turned towards her she could see that his eyes were feverish with triumph.
>
> He nodded towards the desk. "The lighter," he said urgently. "I had to try and make him forget it. Follow me. I'll show you." He started to rock the light steel chair inch by inch towards the desk. "For God's sake don't tip over or we've had it. But make it fast, or the blowlamp'll get cold."
>
> Uncomprehendingly, and feeling almost as if they were playing some ghastly children's game, Gala carefully rocked her way across the floor in his wake.
>
> Seconds later, Bond told her to stop beside the desk while he went rocking on around to Drax's chair. Then he maneuvered himself into position opposite his target and with a sudden lurch heaved himself and the chair forward so that his head came down.

These examples are extreme. The question is, in your everyday reading, do you face similar extremes? Check the reading you do every day—and see.

ACTIVITY 3-2
Outline: Speed—the Flexibility Factor

Main Idea; _____

_____

_____

I. Reading Rate: Two factors which determine it

   A. _____

   B. Difficulty of the material

II. _____

   A. Reading everything at the same speed

   B. _____

  * C. *Vocalizing*—making muted sounds in the voice box (Use fingertip test.)

  * D. _____

   E. Poor rate habits are _____

III. _____

   A. A second reading of the same material goes faster.

   B. _____

*Use a symbol such as this one to remind yourself of a new word so that you can check yourself when reviewing.

ACTIVITY 3-3
Vocabulary Exercises

Reading Technique

Instructions: Write the letter of the matching word in the blank provided.

a) muted	1. short passage from larger writing	(__)
b) imperative	2. ideas, thoughts, opinions	(__)
c) tendency	3. urgently necessary	(__)
d) arduous	4. state of being satisfied	(__)
e) rigors	5. difficult	(__)
f) gratification	6. leading character	(__)
g) protagonist	7. hardships, severity	(__)
h) peruses	8. trend, inclination	(__)
i) concepts	9. muffled or deadened (sound)	(__)
j) excerpt	10. examines, scrutinizes	(__)

Reading Selection

Instructions: Write the letter of the matching word in the blank provided.

a) massive	1. periods of ten years	(__)
b) imperceptibly	2. eaters of everything	(__)
c) mystique	3. of great bulk and weight	(__)
d) gourmands	4. mythical status surrounding person or thing	(__)
e) votaries	5. based on story popularly believed	(__)
f) tedious	6. tending to prevent	(__)
g) surf-addicted	7. strong enthusiasts for something	(__)
h) legendary	8. barely noticeably	(__)
i) decades	9. people dedicated to the ocean's waves	(__)
j) prohibitive	10. boring, tiresome	(__)

3

Comprehension Quiz

Reading Selection

Instructions: Write the letter of the correct answer in the blank provided.

1. The main idea of this article is that:
   - a) sharks are mankillers
   - b) Mundus is a successful fisherman
   - c) shark fishing is expensive
   - d) shark fishing is a growing sport

   (__)

2. Shark fishing, as an accepted sport, originated:
   - a) off the Florida Coast
   - b) off Montauk Point
   - c) in South Africa
   - d) in Australia

   (__)

3. A shark may live to the age of:
   - a) 50 years
   - b) 100 years
   - c) 10,000 years
   - d) an unknown number of years

   (__)

4. As a sport, shark fishing dates back to:
   - a) 1900
   - b) 1920
   - c) 1951
   - d) not mentioned

   (__)

5. The biggest shark ever taken on rod and reel weighed about:
   - a) 1000 pounds
   - b) 1800 pounds
   - c) 2650 pounds
   - d) 4500 pounds

   (__)

6. Many sharks are taken in Australian waters because:
   - a) the water temperature is high
   - b) there are thousands of shark fishermen
   - c) both of these
   - d) Australians like to eat them

   (__)

7. The monster Mundus harpooned was caught off:
   - a) Montauk Point
   - b) the Florida Coast
   - c) the South Australian coast
   - d) the California coast

   (__)

8. Mundus' method of attracting sharks is called:
   - a) trolling
   - b) bait-casting
   - c) chumming
   - d) all of the above

   (__)

9. Shark meat, when cooked, tastes much like:
   - a) sea-bass filets
   - b) salmon steaks
   - c) porpoise meat
   - d) swordfish steaks

   (__)

10. As a sport, shark fishing has an attraction that might be compared to:
    - a) bullfighting
    - b) gliding
    - c) football
    - d) horse racing

    (__)

31

3

Reading Selection

DEADLY GAME—FISHING FOR KILLER SHARKS

(from *Newsweek*, July 11, 1966)

—begin timing—

Sharks are among the few living animals with the size, power and inclination to eat a man alive. They have been called "the most vicious killers in the world" and, even less flatteringly, "the garbage dumps of the deep." They grow to 40 feet in length—without a bone in their bodies. Their massive jaws contain as many as five rows of teeth—sharp as razors and some the size of horseshoe nails. In 10 million years, they have changed almost imperceptibly. No one knows how long they can live. Since man first began to sail the oceans, they have held legendary terror and fascination. But for all that, it is only in the past few decades that sharks have become the object of man's sporting instinct. Now from Australia to South Africa, from Miami to Cape Cod, anglers are discovering that the world's biggest fish may be the world's best game fish.

Catching Killers. On a line, shark can combine the best of all big-game fish: the mystique of danger. Fights of up to nine hours to land a big one are common. Mako sharks, which run over 1000 pounds and are considered by some fishermen to be the best fighters in the world, have jumped or "tail-walked" into the cockpit of a boat, slashed crewmen and torn off the transom, leaving the angler with a limp line and grateful he's still alive. Big white sharks have attacked boats and inflicted severe damage. And tiger sharks, true gourmands, have been caught with stomachs containing everything from a roll of tarpaper to beer cans to human remains.

Shark fishing began as a sport in Australia in the early 1920's and, since then, Australians have set almost all existing records. (The biggest ever taken on rod and reel was a 2,644-pound white shark caught on a 130-pound test-line off Southern Australia in 1959. The fish was 16 feet 10 inches long, and measured 9 feet 6 inches around.) There are sixteen Australian big-game-fishing clubs whose 15,000 members catch about 1,800 sharks a year.

Costly Fishing. Australia's advantages for sharking include its year-round mild climate, warm water and surf-addicted populace. Also, sharks come so close inshore in Australia that they can be caught from small boats. To insure good sharking in the U.S.—where the fever came later—fishermen must go offshore—sometimes up to 50 or 60 miles. A charter boat charges $100 to $150 per day for deep-sea fishing, and the cost of outfitting a private (35–45-foot) boat can be prohibitive.

A fully equipped Rybovich sport fisherman can run $150,000. Penn Senator reels big enough for big game cost $95, and Fiberglas rods go for $125. Tackle is expensive, and a dedicated deep-water sportsman can spend more than $50 a day on gas alone.

But spend it they do. An Ohio golf-course owner named Erlo Cookman, 48, travels to Florida for five months each year and charters a boat for $100 a day to go out after sharks. Last year he got sixteen, all more than 200 pounds. One Floridian fishes only on weekends and has caught 91 in three years.

Professional Monster Hunter. Frank Mundus, one of the U.S.'s few professional shark fishermen, sails out of Montauk, N.Y. and he got into the trade almost by accident. In 1950, the tall angular Mundus was a charter-boat captain. On days off, he went out for sharks and called the pastime "monster fishing." So many people asked to go along that in 1951 he decided to make a career of fishing for monsters.

Mundus travels offshore as far as necessary—depending on water temperature and the type of shark he is after (the rare whites are usually closer to shore, makos further out). He then cuts his engine, and begins the tedious process called "chumming" for sharks. Ladle by ladle, the mate scoops a smelly mixture of ground bunker fish, porpoise meat, and black-fish whale over the side, creating an appetizing slick for sharks to follow. Lines are set out in the slick, baited with bunkers, cod or other tasties. When a shark hits a line, Mundus gives him enough line to swallow the bait, set the hooks, and the fight is on. $\quad$ **d**

One day in June 1964 a customer was fighting a porbeagle near the boat, when the mate spotted a big white shark nearby. "The mate followed him around back," recalls Mundus. "Then I seen him freeze up. His eyes looked like boiled onions." The big shark was staring up at the mate, mouth open, about three feet of his head out of the water. Mundus tried to bait him, but the shark refused. Finally, he harpooned the shark five times, fought him for five hours and dragged him ashore. He was too big for all the scales in Montauk, but at 17½ feet long with a girth of 13 feet, experts settled on a probable weight of 4500 pounds. $\quad$ **d**

d

The Fight's the Thing. Of the more than 200 species of shark, only about 25 are considered dangerous, and the International Game Fish Association lists six of those as game fish—blue, mako, white (also called man-eater), porbeagle, thresher and tiger. Most prized of all is the mako. $\quad$ **b**

Sharks are still despised by many fishermen, especially those votaries of swordfish, marlin, tarpon, wahoo and other hard fighters, because they steal fish off lines, cut leaders and clear out fertile grounds. The flesh is prized in Australia, but in the U.S., makos, porbeagles and whites are eaten mainly by unwary diners who think they are being served slightly oily swordfish. $\quad$ **c**

The appeal of the sport is in the fight of the elemental content. "You get a thousand-pound killer mako on a line," says Australian Peter Boadby, 37, who is one of the world's top shark hunters, "and it's brute against brute. They take everything you can pitch up—and toss it back with a bonus." $\quad$ **c**

(—0—) $\qquad$ —end timing— $\qquad$ (min__sec__)

a

c

d

a

ACTIVITY 3-4
Summarizing

Instructions: Write a one-paragraph summary of the Reading Selection.

_____
_____
_____
_____
_____
_____
_____
_____
_____
_____
_____
_____

What were your reactions?

_____
_____
_____
_____
_____
_____
_____
_____
_____
_____
_____
_____
_____

ACTIVITY 3-5
High-Speed Comparison of Phrases

Instructions: In the two columns below are short phrases which are either exactly alike or slightly different. Compare the similar phrases as fast as you can. If the two phrases are exactly alike, put a check mark in the space to the right. If they are at all different, do not write anything.

from the beginning	in the beginning	___ 1
into the circle	into the circle	___ 2
down the street	down the streets	___ 3
completely favorable	completely flavorless	___ 4
not yet ready	not yet ready	___ 5
really good progress	really good process	___ 6
rather loud sound	rather lewd sound	___ 7
under the car	under a car	___ 8
silently stealing	stealing silently	___ 9
a controlling factor	a controlled factor	___ 10
a moral person	amoral person	___ 11
slow acceleration	slow deceleration	___ 12
acute eyesight	acute eyesight	___ 13
student rights	student's right	___ 14
theoretically correct	theoretically correct	___ 15
amazingly simple	amazing sample	___ 16
a horizontal range	a horizontal rung	___ 17
beautiful angle	beautiful angel	___ 18
an aged great	an aged grate	___ 19
clear glass	clean glass	___ 20

4
SPECIALIZED TECHNIQUES
Vocabulary Preview

Reading Technique

1. "which *inhibit* good reading" _____
2. "Making their *predictions*" _____
3. "the *millisecond* 'fixation' stop" _____
4. "will expand your *peripheral* vision" _____
5. "freedom from every *distraction*" _____
6. "as do any *intermittent* noises" _____
7. "an *atmosphere* for concentration" _____
8. "*inadequate* lighting can cause" _____
9. "*minimize* eyestrain" _____
10. "calls for *extensive* reading" _____

Reading Selection

1. "*incisive* description" _____
2. "we *esteem* as precious" _____
3. "great books *seminars*" _____
4. "*undeterred* by footnotes" _____
5. "break the *crust* of a book" _____
6. "see their true *perspective*" _____
7. "over the *terrain*" _____
8. "from *vantage* points" _____
9. "drift *passively*" _____
10. "helps to *sustain* this attitude" _____

4

Comprehension Quiz

Reading Technique

Instructions: Write the letter of the correct answer in the blank provided.

1. This chapter is mainly concerned with:
   a) the elimination of poor habits
   b) a description of helpful techniques
   c) "no-message" words
   d) positioning the book
   (___)

2. No-message words include:
   a) "the," "a"
   b) "therefore"
   c) "however"
   d) all of the above
   (___)

3. The successful reader:
   a) "fixes" his or her eyes on each word
   b) moves the eyes smoothly
   c) "fixes" once per idea-phrase
   d) "fixes" twice per line
   (___)

4. Expansion of peripheral vision:
   a) is of little value
   b) is difficult for athletes
   c) can be accomplished through exercise
   d) is not mentioned
   (___)

5. A good "reading environment" means:
   a) freedom from aural and visual distractions
   b) an available writing surface
   c) adequate lighting
   d) all of the above
   (___)

6. Permanent damage to the eyes can be caused by:
   a) insufficient light
   b) too much light
   c) both a) and b)
   d) neither a) nor b)
   (___)

7. Taking a three-minute break every half hour:
   a) rests the eyes and helps concentration
   b) breaks your study mood
   c) makes you sleepy
   d) all of the above
   (___)

8. The sentence "The happy child ran quickly up the stairs" has how many idea-phrases?
   a) one
   b) two
   c) three
   d) four
   (___)

9. For most people, which of the following would be likely to provide the best reading environment? Assume all are well-lighted.
   a) a desk in the family room
   b) the living-room sofa
   c) a table in the library
   d) a desk in your bedroom
   (___)

10. Concentration:
    a) is an inborn trait
    b) is unaffected by personal problems
    c) is aided by a good reading environment
    d) cannot be learned
    (___)

4

Reading Technique

—begin timing—

Specialized Techniques

In Chapter 3, a number of habits were discussed which inhibit good reading. In this chapter, you will find a number of techniques which should be mastered to the extent that they become *habits.* Replacing poor procedures with good ones demands practice and desire, *but you will find the results gratifying.*

I. ELIMINATING "NO-MESSAGE" WORDS

The grammar of many languages often includes words which do not contribute meaning to the ideas being communicated. English is no exception. Two specific examples of words of this kind are "the" and "a." Frequently, other words in a sentence may be eliminated without losing any of the meaning. Forms of the verb "to be" often need little attention. Compare the following:

It is easy to be entirely wrong about the future. Even the experts are sometimes in error when making their predictions.

.... easy .... wrong about .... future. Even ... experts .... sometimes ... error .. making ...... predictions

Obviously, a good many of the words in the first column could have been omitted without affecting the meaning of the sentence. But how do you choose? The answer to that question is found by considering the thoughts of the author writing the sentence. You must become aware of *idea-phrases.*

II. PHRASE READING: EYE MOVEMENTS AND THE READING FIXATION

If you examine the eye movements of someone who is reading, you will find that reading consists of a series of "move-stop" jerks across the line of print. Current belief is that the longer "stop" period—a "fixation"—constitutes the actual learning activity. The swift movement of the pupil of the eye is only a preparation for the millisecond fixation stop, the period of information transfer. Some readers—poor ones—fixate on every word.

How many fixations per line should you make? The answer is simple, although not easy to accomplish. Your fixations should parallel the author's writing: you should fixate on each idea-phrase. This relates closely to the elimination of no-message words. This procedure is complicated by printing methods. Idea-phrases are sometimes split into two lines, or a key word may be broken up at the end of a line. Note the slash marks in the following sentence: *Reading in idea-phrases/ with a minimum number/ of fixations per line/ is a characteristic/ of the successful reader.*

III. EYE EXERCISES: YOU HAVE MUSCLES!

If you have limited your eye movements when reading by examining each word, you can practice a few exercises which will expand your peripheral vision. One of these you will find in Activity 4–1 for this chapter. Here are two others:

1. With your head level, fix your eyes on a point 10 or 15 feet away. Raise both outstretched arms until they are parallel with the floor, and bring your hands together in front of you at shoulder level. Start snapping the fingers of both hands. Move your arms back slowly, making sure you can see the snapping fingers of both hands without moving your eyes from the original point. After a few weeks of practice for only a minute or two a day, you will find yourself able to see both hands with your arms almost straight out to the sides.

2. This one will hurt! Lock your head in a level position, with the body upright and your eyes looking straight ahead. Look up at the ceiling. Pull the eye focus-point back until you are looking at the ceiling as close to your head as possible. Try to see your own eyebrows. Roll your eyes in a clockwise direction, looking for your right shoulder. Continue the rotation, keeping the focus "pulled in," looking for your nose, then your left shoulder. Continue the rotation back to the ceiling, again trying to see your eyebrows. Reverse the movement to a counterclockwise direction.

These exercises will not only help to widen your visual span, but may help to correct other eye muscle difficulties. (Football and basketball coaches, please note!)

IV. SELECTING THE RIGHT READING ENVIRONMENT

Successful reading demands concentration, and for most people this means freedom from every distraction that can be eliminated. Radio and television broadcasts detract from your reading efficiency, as do any intermittent noises. Moving objects in your line of sight claim a share of your attention. Inadequate lighting can cause permanent damage, as can reading in bright sunlight. Note-taking for serious reading calls for a suitable writing surface. Studying in the right place at the same time every day can actually develop an atmosphere for concentration.

V. POSITIONING: YOU AND THE BOOK

If your eyesight is normal, a comfortable distance from your eyes to the line of print should be about 15 inches. It is apparent that if the book is flat on a desk top, the distance from the eyes to the top of the page is greater than it is to the bottom of the same page. To minimize eyestrain, the book should be held at a slant. If your program calls for extensive reading, you may find it worthwhile to purchase an inexpensive book-holder, adjustable to the slant-angle you need.

VI. REST YOUR EYES, REST YOUR MIND

If your evening schedule calls for several hours of reading, it is wise to plan for "breaks" every half hour. To relax the eye muscles, change the focal distance by looking at a more distant point for a minute. You can help maintain concentration, too, by using the break period deliberately to change your activity for two or three minutes. Get up and walk around the room; raid the refrigerator. The time will not be wasted; you will return relaxed and refreshed, ready again for total concentration.

Eliminating words which do not contribute to meaning, reading in idea-phrases, training the eye muscles, controlling the environment are all contributors to effective reading. Proper book/eye positioning reduces fatigue. A short rest period, scheduled regularly every half hour, controls mental and muscle tiredness. Make these techniques a part of your reading technique.

—end timing—   (min___sec___)

ACTIVITY 4-1
Applying the Technique

1. Read through Sections II and III on pages 38–39 as quickly as you can, drawing a line through the no-message words which can be eliminated without losing the meaning.

2. Read through Sections IV and V on page 39 as quickly as you can, using short vertical lines to divide the sentences into idea-phrases.

3. The lines below contain short black dashes broken with a single-digit number. You can practice fast, positive eye movements by shifting your eyes across the lines from dash to dash as rapidly as possible.

4 Now, try it again, this time adding the numbers in one quick eye-sweep of each line. *Do not go back to pick up a number!* If you have a tendency to go back, you may be "regressing"!

ACTIVITY 4-2
Outline: Specialized Techniques

Main Idea: _____

_____

_____

I. Eliminating "no-message" words

   A. Slide over words like _____, _____, _____.

   B. Follow author's writing, read in _____.

II. _____

* A. Eyes, reading, move in jerks; "stop" period called _____.

   B. You should fixate on each _____.

III. _____

   A. _____

   B. _____

IV. A good reading environment includes:

   A. _____

   B. Good lighting

   C. _____

   D. _____

V. Positioning the book

   A. Normal vision, about _____ from the eyes.

   B. _____

VI. Taking break periods every half hour rests:

   A. _____

   B. _____

ACTIVITY 4-3
Vocabulary Exercises

Reading Technique

Instructions: Write the letter of the correct word in the blank provided. (The form of the word as used in the sentence may not be the same as the one in the list.)

a) inhibit
b) atmosphere
c) predictions
d) inadequate
e) millisecond

f) minimize
g) peripheral
h) extensive
i) distraction
j) intermittent

1. The measurement of the boundary which the surveyor required was on the _____ of the lot.   (__)

2. The astrologer and the fortune teller both claimed I would become famous; they both made the same _____.   (__)

3. Because so much of the city had been bombed, the news reports stated the damage was _____.   (__)

4. The Dean's excessive praise of the student served to _____ her behavior; she felt uncomfortable.   (__)

5. My check bounced! Stamped "Insufficient Funds," it obviously meant my bank balance was _____.   (__)

6. As soon as the ex-convict entered the room, the whole _____ changed and became unusually tense.   (__)

7. Don't _____ your past education and training when job-hunting; list each as fully as possible.   (__)

8. The _____ ringing disturbed the concentration of people taking a difficult examination.   (__)

9. Any serious _____ can cause a driving accident.   (__)

10. From the flash of the explosion to the shock wave was a matter of _____.   (__)

Reading Selection

Instructions: Write the letter of the matching word in the blank provided.

a) incisive
b) esteem
c) seminar
d) undeterred
e) crust
f) perspective
g) terrain
h) vantage
i) passively
j) sustain

1. rate highly   (__)
2. region, territory   (__)
3. not prevented or discouraged   (__)
4. relationship, over-all picture   (__)
5. research class for advanced students   (__)
6. sharp, keen, penetrating   (__)
7. keep up, maintain   (__)
8. favorable position   (__)
9. without action   (__)
10. hard, crisp surface   (__)

4

Comprehension Quiz

Reading Selection

Instructions: Write the letter of the correct answer in the blank provided.

1. William Benton describes Adler as an "anti-expert." By that he means one who:
   a) opposes scientific specialization
   c) denies human equality   (__)
   b) favors continual questioning
   d) all of the above

2. Adler feels strongly that faith in reason and reasoning:
   a) are essential to democracy
   c) are old-fashioned approaches   (__)
   b) are nonscientific
   d) eliminate the need for experts

3. When Adler says we may have to defend our right to live "humanly or reasonably," he probably refers to the danger of:
   a) our tendency toward conformity
   c) thought control in mass communications   (__)
   b) the cybernetic revolution
   d) all of the above

4. His fundamental suggestion concerning difficult reading is to:
   a) be sure of the vocabulary
   c) check references   (__)
   b) qualify footnotes
   d) read right through the book

5. To understand difficult literature, you must first:
   a) grasp the over-all plan
   c) study each section   (__)
   b) study the footnotes
   d) study philosophy

6. Many students develop a dislike for the classics because:
   a) they never see the whole picture
   c) the plots are too familiar   (__)
   b) the themes do not apply today
   d) they read the book too quickly

7. A quick first reading of a difficult book allows you to:
   a) drift passively through it
   c) understand the details   (__)
   b) make a complete outline
   d) see the structure

8. Reading through without stopping will actually:
   a) save time
   c) make careful study easier   (__)
   b) eliminate the need for further reading
   d) all of the above

9. From this essay, one might reason that:
   a) great books are difficult
   c) both a) and b)   (__)
   b) difficult books are great
   d) neither a) nor b)

10. Adler's suggestion in this essay closely parallels:
    a) relaxation reading rules
    c) the purpose of *Overview*   (__)
    b) reading idea-phrases
    d) OARWET

4

Reading Selection
—begin timing—

Great Ideas, Great Books, Great Teacher

"For the greater part of his life as a student, teacher and author, Mortimer J. Adler's name has been linked with the great books. He was a student in the first great books class taught by John Erskine at Columbia in the twenties. After teaching the great books there, Adler went to the University of Chicago, where, with Robert M. Hutchins, he developed a great books program in the college there. . . . Dr. Adler left the University in 1952 to become Director of the Institute for Philosophical Research." So reads the biographical note preceding Dr. Adler's Great Ideas from the Great Books.

In William Benton's introduction to the same book, we find this incisive description of Adler's remarkable abilities: "We Americans esteem as precious the right to think for ourselves. But as the world becomes more complex we permit more and more of our thinking to be done for us by alleged experts.

"Mortimer Adler is an anti-expert. He is persuaded that freedom cannot withstand the free man's willingness to surrender his problems to somebody else. Every man is born to be free, and the free man should make his own decisions. Faith in reason—and faith in reasoning—becomes identical with faith in democracy. In a democracy, you and you and you must be the Answer Man."

In a second work, How To Read a Book, *Dr. Adler's evaluation of the importance of reading is stated succinctly.*

"Reading—as explained (and defended) in this book—is a basic tool in the living of a good life. I need not defend the goodness of living humanly or reasonably, though it looks like we might have to defend our right to do so."

The brief dialogue that follows is from Great Ideas from the Great Books.

HOW TO READ A DIFFICULT BOOK

by Mortimer J. Adler

Dear Dr. Adler,
  To tell you the truth, I find the so-called great books very difficult to read. I am willing to take your word for it that they are great. But how am I to appreciate the greatness in them if they are too hard for me to read? Can you give me some helpful hints on how to read a hard book?

           I.C.

Dear I. C.,
  The most important rule about reading is one I have told my great books seminars again and again: In reading a difficult book for the first time, read the book through without stopping. Pay attention to what you can understand, and don't be stopped by what you can't immediately grasp. Keep on this way. Read the book through undeterred by the paragraphs, footnotes, arguments, and references that escape you. If you stop at any of these stumbling blocks, if you let yourself get stalled, you are lost. In most cases you won't be able to puzzle the thing out by sticking to it. You have a much better chance of understanding it on a second reading, but that requires you to read the book *through* for the first time.

This is the most practical method I know to break the crust of a book, to get the feel and general sense of it, and to come to terms with its structure as quickly and as easily as possible. The longer you delay in getting some sense of the over-all plan of a book, the longer you are in understanding it. You simply must have some grasp of the whole before you can see the parts in their true perspective—or often in any perspective at all.

Shakespeare was spoiled for generations of high-school students who were forced to go through *Julius Caesar, Hamlet,* or *Macbeth* scene by scene, to look up all the words that were new to them, and to study all the scholarly foot-notes. As a result, they never actually read the play. Instead, they were dragged through it, bit by bit, over a period of many weeks. By the time they got to the end of the play, they had surely forgotten the beginning. They should have been encouraged to read the play in one sitting. Only then would they have understood enough of it to make it possible for them to understand more.

b

What you understand by reading a book through to the end—even if it is only fifty per cent or less—will help you later in making the additional effort to go back to places you passed by on your first reading. Actually you will be proceeding like any traveler in unknown parts. Having been over the terrain once, you will be able to explore it again from vantage points you could not have known about before. You will be less likely to mistake the side roads for the main highway. You won't be deceived by the shadows at high noon, be-cause you will remember how they looked at sunset. And the mental map you have fashioned will show better how the valleys and mountains are all part of one landscape.

a

There is nothing magical about a first quick reading. It cannot work won-ders and should certainly never be thought of as a substitute for the careful reading that a good book deserves. But a first quick reading makes the careful study much easier.

d

This practice helps you to keep alert in going at a book. How many times have you daydreamed your way through pages and pages only to wake up with no idea of the ground you have been over? That can't help happening if you let yourself drift passively through a book. No one ever understands much that way. You must have a way of getting a general thread to hold onto.

d

A good reader is active in his efforts to understand. Any book is a problem, a puzzle. The reader's attitude is that of a detective looking for clues to its basic ideas and alert for anything that will make them clearer. The rule about a first quick reading helps to sustain this attitude. If you follow it you will be surprised how much time you will save, how much more you will grasp, and how much easier it will be.

a

a

(—0—)   —end timing—   (min___sec___)

d

c

a

c

ACTIVITY 4-4
Summarizing

Instructions: Write a one-paragraph summary of the Reading Selection.

_____

_____

_____

_____

_____

_____

_____

_____

_____

_____

_____

What were your reactions?

_____

_____

_____

_____

_____

_____

_____

_____

_____

_____

_____

_____

_____

_____

ACTIVITY 4-5
"No-Message" Words

Instructions: In the paragraph below, cross out every word which does not directly contribute to the "sense" of the idea which the author is writing about. The first line has been done for you.

~~Here is a~~ man ~~being~~ admitted to ~~a~~ local hospital. ~~He~~ shows ~~his~~ Blue Cross card to the admissions clerk. She types an inquiry on an electronic teleprinter, which cuts it into punched tape. The tape then transmits it by wire to the Blue Cross computer in another city. The computer unprotestingly interrupts whatever it is doing and searches its memory unit for the patient's record. In *just two seconds*, the coded record is transmitted back to the hospital, allowing the clerk to complete her business with the new patient in less than three minutes. It used to take from two to four days when the inquiry was sent by mail. If the patient came in only for his annual checkup, he might have been discharged, under the old system, before his Blue Cross record was cleared. Observe that there is no multiplying and dividing in this case of data process.

—Stuart Chase, *The Most Probable World*

ACTIVITY 4-6
Practice in Reading Idea-Phrases

Instructions: In the paragraph below, using slash marks (/), break up each sentence into what seem to you to be logical idea phrases. The first line has been done for you.

The night was hot,/ and it seemed/ even hotter/ because of the fires/ against the sky, but the younger of the two girls Mr. Tanimoto and the priests had rescued complained to Father Kleinsorge that she was cold. He covered her with his jacket. She and her older sister had been in the salt water of the river for a couple of hours before being rescued. The younger one had huge, raw flesh burns on her body; the salt water must have been excruciatingly painful to her. She began to shiver heavily, and again said it was cold. Father Kleinsorge borrowed a blanket from someone nearby and wrapped her up, but she shook more and more, and said again, "I am so cold," and then suddenly stopped shivering and was dead.

—John Hersey, *Hiroshima*

ACTIVITY 4-7
Practice in Reading Idea-Phrases

Instructions: In the following paragraph, the sentences have been broken into idea-phrases by the use of two different kinds of type, roman (regular) and **boldface.** Read through the paragraph as quickly as you can, trying to read all the words in each type group *at one glance* (not one word at a time). If you have difficulty, read the paragraph again several times.

Recently **Dr. E. S. Hafez,** an Egyptian-born **experimental biologist** at Washington State University, **asked a scientist friend** from Germany **to bring him** a hundred head **of prize sheep.** The entire herd **is to be delivered** to Dr. Hafez **in a neat package** he can carry **in one hand.** It will be a **ventilated box** and inside will be **a female rabbit.** Inside the rabbit **will be** 100 possible rams and ewes, **all of them embryos** only a few days old, **growing as if** still in their natural mother. **Then,** following a procedure **already well established** in Europe, **he will implant** each embryo **in an ewe** where it will grow, **and in a few months,** be born. **Dr. Hafez,** whose research support **includes over $160,000** supplied by **the National Institute** of Health alone, **sees no reason** why his method **would not work** just as well **with people.**

—Albert Rosenfeld, *Life*

ACTIVITY 4-8
More on Idea-Phrases

Instructions: In the paragraph below, using slash marks (/), break up each sentence into what seem to you to be logical idea phrases. The first line has been done for you.

At first,/ he snarled/ and tried/ to fight;/ but he was very young,/ and this was only his first day in the world, and his snarl became a whimper, his fight a struggle to escape. The weasel never relaxed her hold. She hung on, striving to press down with her teeth to the great vein where his life-blood bubbled. The weasel was a drinker of blood, and it was ever her preference to drink from the throat of life itself. The gray cub would have died, and there would have been no story to write about him, had not the she-wolf come bounding through the bushes. The weasel let go the cub, and flashed at the she-wolf's throat, missing but getting a hold on the jaw instead. The she-wolf flirted her head like the snap of a whip, breaking the weasel's hold and flinging it high in the air. And still in the air, the she-wolf's jaws closed on the lean, yellow body, and the weasel knew death between the crunching teeth.

—Jack London, *White Fang*

ACTIVITY 4-9
High-Speed Comparison of Phrases

Instructions: In the two columns below are short phrases which are either exactly alike or slightly different. Put a check in the space to the right if the phrases are exactly the same; if they are different, do not write anything. *Try to complete the exercise in 15 seconds.*

a racing bike	a racing bike	___ 1
the snarling tiger	the snarling tiger	___ 2
steel belt	steal belt	___ 3
rigid wheel	rigged wheel	___ 4
a felt hat	felt a hat	___ 5
several days	several days	___ 6
first bass	first base	___ 7
baseball bat	baseball hat	___ 8
round sound	sound round	___ 9
dark color	dirk color	___ 10
lovely beer	lovely bier	___ 11
angry look	angry book	___ 12
extreme tension	extreme tension	___ 13
wretched snack	wretched shack	___ 14
probably shale	probably shall	___ 15
hard hat	hard heart	___ 16
glorious son	glorious sun	___ 17
darkened skies	darkened skies	___ 18
curious claws	curious clause	___ 19
special shears	special spears	___ 20

5
READING TO LEARN
Vocabulary Preview

Reading Technique

1. "may be *absurdly* simple" _____
2. "*pragmatically*" _____
3. "the *mundane* principle" _____
4. "create a *reservoir*" _____
5. "added some, *discarded* others" _____
6. "*Indicators* to main ideas" _____
7. "locating *salient* ideas" _____
8. "a specific idea is *critical*" _____
9. "if they are *unique*" _____
10. "*typography* to emphasize it" _____

Reading Selection

1. "dead-black *graphite* bricks" _____
2. "squatted black and *menacing*" _____
3. "*tethered* by another rope" _____
4. _____

   "to *douse* (4) *mutinous* (5) neutrons" _____
5. _____
6. "the *transmutation* of the elements" _____
7. "at a highly *opportune* moment" _____
8. "Mussolini *promulgated* laws" _____
9. "award for *meritorious* contributions" _____
10. "operation had been *futile*" _____

5

Comprehension Quiz

Reading Technique

Instructions: Write the letter of the correct answer in the blank provided.

1. The main idea of this chapter is:
   a) the importance of knowledge
   b) the sequence of steps in learning
   c) the importance of learning
   d) all of the above
   (__)

2. Purpose can be established by:
   a) developing genuine interest
   b) self-discipline
   c) recognizing long-range values
   d) all of the above
   (__)

3. OARWET fits into learning sequences by providing:
   a) predetermination of the main idea
   b) an outline of the material to be mastered
   c) both a) and b)
   d) neither a) nor b)
   (__)

4. In a handwritten letter to a friend, which typographical aid would you use to emphasize a point?
   a) italics
   b) boldface type
   c) gothic letters
   d) underlining
   (__)

5. Which of the following is not a pointer-word or phrase?
   a) "pleasant"
   b) "as a result"
   c) "in short"
   d) "because"

6. Which of the following would you be most likely to remember?
   a) The bomb is about to go off.
   b) The bomb is about to go off?
   c) The bomb is about to go off!
   d) none of the above
   (__)

7. A graph showing the variation in the relationship between gross income and "take-home" pay would most likely be found in:
   a) a science textbook
   b) a mathematics textbook
   c) an economics textbook
   d) a psychology textbook
   (__)

8. The fastest way to determine a main idea concerning the relationship between education and income in a sociology textbook would be to:
   a) read the topic sentence
   b) read the summary paragraph
   c) find the appropriate subhead
   d) examine a graph on the subject
   (__)

9. A sentence preceded by "For example" would alert the reader to:
   a) use the material that follows to clarify a preceding idea
   b) be prepared to sift the material that follows
   c) both a) and b)
   d) a point that must be memorized
   (__)

10. Relating new material to your own knowledge:
    a) provides a bridge between learning and memory
    b) is helped by *purpose*
    c) helps to make new information meaningful
    d) all of the above
    (__)

5

Reading Technique

—begin timing—

Reading To Learn

In these first chapters, the prime emphasis is on mastery of textbook information. For most people, "learning" does not just "happen"; it is the result of a deliberate procedure. How many of the following steps do you use?

I. LET'S EXAMINE YOUR ATTITUDE: THE PURPOSE OF "PURPOSE"

Is your reading "purposeful"? Examples of learning that have genuine purpose might center on your hobbies. Know a great deal about customizing cars? Or are you an expert on feminine fashions? In either field, you may have accumulated considerable information, easily and enjoyably. Then why do you dread a long reading assignment? The answer may be absurdly simple. For textbook reading you lack *purpose*. Yet, for successful reading, you must establish meaningful value for the material you are studying.

There is more than one approach to this idea of purpose. Pragmatically, there is the mundane principle that effective learning is essential in order to get good grades or a good job.

Purposeful learning, however, can mean more than dollar signs. It can provide great returns in self-satisfaction. It helps create a reservoir of information from which you may draw conclusions affecting every phase of your life. Those chapters in sociology may give you the background for understanding the society in which you live, may help you adjust to the society of tomorrow. Discipline yourself to "think through" the long-range results. Once you provide *meaning* to learning, *purpose* is established. How long did it take you to learn your telephone number? Necessity gave you purpose; mastery was a matter of minutes.

Your attitude—your purpose—is the first step toward learning.

II. ESTABLISHING A STARTING POINT: OARWET AND THE MAIN IDEA

With purpose established, the mechanics of "reading to learn" revolve around the organized framework of OARWET. Bring to every information unit—a full text, a chapter, a paragraph, a sentence—recognition of the fact that the fundamental task is to determine the *main idea*. OARWET's first step, *O*verview, is aimed at providing you with that base. When you "overview," you are using the same technique the author uses in his or her writing. His first procedure as he outlines his book is to select the important ideas he wants to present, chapter by chapter. After he has assembled main ideas, sorted them, sifted them, added some, discarded others, he ends up with an outline which appears as a Table of Contents. This is *his* sequence of main ideas.

The same procedure applies to subheads. Consider the author's approach again. Once she has a chapter idea set, she divides it into the important contributing facts, all major facets of the basic theme. Each of these contributing facts is broken down in the subchapters, this time into a series of points distributed throughout the smaller unit, paragraph by paragraph. If you bear this structure in mind, the "skeleton" is obvious, and the relationship of parts-to-the-whole is clearly seen.

III. OTHER CLUES TO MAIN IDEAS: TYPOGRAPHY, "POINTER-WORDS," PUNCTUATION, GRAPHICS

Indicators to main ideas are found throughout a text. Four common "clues" are noted below:

A. If the author feels a specific idea is critical, he may use typography to emphasize it. For example, in this text you have already seen a number of words and phrases set in *italics*. Other typographical clues are underlining, **boldface** type, or the use of CAPITALS. Sometimes, the whole structure of a unit is clearly outlined by the use of Roman numerals.

B. "Pointer-words" frequently provide clues to important information. Be **b** particularly alert for words or phrases like *therefore, except, however, to sum up, in addition. Nevertheless* can change the entire slant of a series of preliminary statements. *Moreover* strengthens previous arguments; *especially* singles out one of a number of items; *despite this* is a clue indicating change of direction. Awareness of these pointer-words is of tremendous help in locating salient **d** ideas and their relationships to each other.

C. It is easy to overlook punctuation, but frequently it is the key to the author's meaning. "I need help." "I need help?" "I need help!" Your imagination can provide you with totally different pictures from these short sentences. Train yourself to notice punctuation marks! **c**

D. Graphics, or more formally the "graphic arts," are visual representations such as charts, pictures, or graphs which are used to clarify ideas expressed in the text. A complex relationship between changing factors may be easier to understand if those changes and relationships are seen on a graph. Many textbook authors use carefully selected pictures to sharpen your images of an endless variety of subjects. Make use of them. **d**

IV. MUST YOU KNOW EVERYTHING?

The more difficult an idea or theme is, the more examples an author may use to make it clear. Discussion of a complex issue may require many times the **a** amount of space needed to make the basic statement. Recognize examples for what they are: devices included to make the key idea understandable. Remember them only if they are unique.

You need not "know everything." Screen the information you read: retain what is valuable, discard what is not. **c**

V. REMEMBERING: PURPOSE + MAIN IDEA + EXPERIENCE

"Reading to learn" means remembering as well as understanding. For both of these facets of reading, *purposefulness* is the starting point. Once you *want* to **c** learn, the next step is to use an organized structure into which you can fit the main ideas and selected facts. The final step is to *relate the new information to your own background*, to tie it in with your previous experience and knowledge. If you master this procedure—and use it—you will find that *remembering* and *learning* become almost automatic. **d**

"Learning" is the result of organization–of purpose, of grasping the overall picture, of locating main ideas, of relating new information to old. Use every clue the author provides–typography, pointer-words, punctuation, and graphics–to help determine main ideas. Establishing this pattern as habit *must be your major goal.*

—end timing— (min___sec___) **c**

d

53

ACTIVITY 5-1
Applying the Technique

1. Underline the main idea of this chapter. Note its position.

2. Underline the topic sentence of the second paragraph. Note its position. What would you expect to follow? What is the pointer-word here? _____ Will it help in outlining?

3. What is the *personal* item mentioned in the fourth paragraph that is used to tie in "purpose" with your *own* experience?

4. How is section I summarized? Write the sentence below.

5. How does *O*verview parallel the author's approach?

6. List the typographical aids noted in section III. Can you think of another obvious one? How many are used in this chapter?

7. Skim rapidly through this chapter, circling all the words which you feel could be classified as pointer-words.

8. What examples were used to connect the information in this chapter with your possible previous experiences or interests? Should you remember them?

9. How is the main point in section V emphasized?

10. *E*valuate your own informational reading in other subjects. How many of these ideas do *you* use?

ACTIVITY 5-2
Outline: Reading To Learn

Main Idea: _____
_____
_____

I. Attitude and Purpose

    A. _____

    B. Factors that help establish meaningful value

        1. _____

        2. self-satisfaction

        3. establish a basic reservoir of knowledge

        4. _____

II. _____

    A. Overview helps to determine author's approach through:

        1. pre-determining chapter and subchapter organization

    B. _____

III. _____

    A. Typography includes such items as _____.

    B. _____

    C. _____

    D. Graphic aids include _____.

IV. _____

V. Remembering what you read depends on:

    A. _____

    B. _____

    C. Relating of new information to previous knowledge

ACTIVITY 5-3
Vocabulary Exercises

Reading Technique

Instructions: Write in the blank provided the letter of the word with the same meaning as the given word or phrase.

1. ridiculously: a) obscurely   b) absurdly   c) rigorously   (__)

2. style or appearance of printed matter: a) typography
   b) hypocrisy   c) graphics   (__)

3. related to study of events, stressing cause and effect:
   a) pragmatic   b) psychosomatic   c) phlegmatic   (__)

4. extra supply or store: a) restitution   b) reservoir
   c) redundance   (__)

5. rejected, dismissed: a) deterred   b) discarded   c) distracted   (__)

6. routine, ordinary: a) minute   b) myriad   c) mundane   (__)

7. standing out prominently, striking feature: a) sacrosanct
   b) strident   c) salient   (__)

8. of extreme importance: a) critical   b) clinging
   c) contemporaneous   (__)

9. without like or equal: a) unified   b) unique   c) unilinear   (__)

10. signifier, pointer: a) indigenous   b) ingenious   c) indicator   (__)

Reading Selection

Instructions: Write the letter of the matching word in the blank provided.

a) graphite   1. fastened or confined   (__)
b) menacing   2. put into effect officially   (__)
c) tethered   3. rebellious   (__)
d) douse   4. deserving of praise or reward   (__)
e) mutinous   5. threatening   (__)
f) transmutation   6. a variety of carbon   (__)
g) opportune   7. useless   (__)
h) promulgated   8. drench with liquid   (__)
i) meritorious   9. occurring at the right moment   (__)
j) futile   10. change of one element into another   (__)

5

Comprehension Quiz

Reading Selection

Instructions: Write the letter of the correct answer in the blank provided.

1. The world's first nuclear chain reaction took place at:
   a) Los Alamos   c) Chicago   (__)
   b) Hiroshima   d) Stockholm

2. The first "pile" consisted of graphite bricks with small cubes of:
   a) uranium   c) cadmium   (__)
   b) heavy water   d) balloon cloth

3. The Nobel Prize winner who headed the scientific team was an expert:
   a) experimental physicist   c) mathematician   (__)
   b) theoretical physicist   d) all of the above

4. The pile was kept from reacting by rods inserted into holes in the bricks. They were plated with:
   a) neutrons   c) cadmium   (__)
   b) Geiger counters   d) a cadmium-salt solution

5. The activity of the pile was measured by:
   a) the clicking of Geiger counters   c) both a) and b)   (__)
   b) the neutron curve   d) the cadmium-salt solution

6. The heading "Zip" referred to:
   a) the motor-controlled rods   c) the emergency rod   (__)
   b) the hand-controlled rods   d) all of the above

7. Fermi left Italy because of:
   a) Mussolini's racial laws   c) his trip to Stockholm   (__)
   b) his dislike of Fascism   d) all of the above

8. Dr. Compton's coded message about the Italian navigator meant:
   a) Fermi had escaped from Italy   c) Fermi's experiment was successful   (__)
   b) Fermi had won the Nobel Prize   d) all of the above

9. The first nuclear chain reaction resulted in:
   a) an immensely powerful weapon   c) the quick surrender of Japan   (__)
   b) a new source of power   d) all of the above

10. From the *Time* article, there are indications that the scientists were:
    a) sure of a successful result   c) very unhappy   (__)
    b) unsure of what would happen   d) all of the above

5

Reading Selection
—begin timing—
ZIP OUT

(from *Time*, December 9, 1946)

In a squash court under the stands of the University of Chicago's football stadium, a curious structure had grown, watched by the hopeful nervous eyes of some of the world's best physicists. It was built of dead-black graphite bricks with small cubes of uranium or uranium oxide embedded in some of their corners.

This was the world's first uranium pile. Within it, if all went well, would rage the first nuclear chain reaction. Physicist Enrico Fermi, Italian-born Nobel Prize winner, was sure that all would go well. He had figured every smallest detail, advancing through theory and mathematics far into the unknown.

On December 2, 1942, a small group of physicists gathered in the squash court for the final test. Partly shrouded in balloon cloth, the pile squatted black and menacing. Within it, all knew or hoped, a monstrous giant sat chained. Control rods, plated with cadmium (which readily absorbs neutrons), had been thrust into holes in the graphite.

When the control rods were removed, Fermi had calculated, the chain reaction would start spontaneously, and the giant would be free.

One of the rods was automatic, controlled by a motor which could shoot it back into the pile when instruments warned that neutrons were getting too thick. Another (called "Zip") was attached to a heavy weight by a rope running over a pulley. When in the "withdrawn" position, it was tethered by another rope; a man with an ax stood ready to cut it free, send it zipping into the pile if anything went wrong. The last rod, marked in feet and inches, was to be worked by hand.

But all the physicists knew that they were in dangerous, unknown territory. So above the pile was stationed a "liquid-control squad" to douse mutinous neutrons with cadmium-salt solution.

Into the Unknown. Fermi ran the test. At 9:54 a.m. he gave an order. A whining motor withdrew the automatic control rod. The Geiger counters on the instrument panel clicked a little faster; a pen drew a slightly higher curve on a strip of paper.

"Pull it to 13 feet, George," commanded Fermi. Physicist George Weil drew the final control rod part way out of the pile. Faster clicked the counters. He drew it out another foot; then another six inches.

At 11:35, the counters were clicking furiously. The physicists watched fascinated as the curve climbed steadily upward. Then, Wham! With a clang, the automatic control rod (which had been set for too low a neutron count) slammed back into the pile. "I'm hungry," said Fermi calmly. "Let's go to lunch." The other rods were inserted, the pile quieted down.

Neutrons Away. At 2 o'clock the physicists gathered again in the squash court. One by one, on Fermi's orders, the control rods were withdrawn, the counters clicked faster. The pile was alive with neutrons now; the giant was straining his bonds. But it was not quite a chain reaction. The neutron curve moved up, leveled off.

At 3:25 Fermi ordered the control rod out another foot. "This is going to do it," he said. "The curve will . . . not level off." Now the counters were roaring, not clicking, the graph curve was climbing upward. Fermi studied the instruments, grinned broadly: "The reaction is self-sustaining."

For 28 minutes the physicists watched as the curve climbed sharply upward. The giant was flexing his muscles.

"O.K." said Fermi. "Zip in." The Zip rod shot into the pile. The counters slowed their clicking. The graph curve sagged. But the world outside the squash court would not be the same again.

ONE IN 100

(from *Newsweek*, December 6, 1954)

"The Italian navigator has landed; the natives are friendly," Compton said.　　c

The Fermis had picked a miserable day to give a party—guests were scientists from the University of Chicago. Each greeted Enrico Fermi in exactly the same way: "Congratulations." Mrs. Fermi kept asking them what they were congratulating him for. "Ask your husband," she was told; or "Don't get excited. You'll find out sometime." It was December 2, 1942.　　a

Not until almost three years later did Laura Fermi find out what her husband had really done, a deed first announced by Dr. Karl Compton's famous telephone code message. That December afternoon on a squash court at the University of Chicago, the Italian-born scientist, then still an enemy alien, had directed the experiment that started the first self-sustaining atomic reaction in history.　　d

The American Branch. Even then his colleagues acknowledged that Dr. Fermi was "the world's outstanding nuclear physicist." Unlike most of them, he was both an experimental and a theoretical physicist. He was also a first-class administrator, and a great teacher.　　c

He was born in Rome on September 29, 1901. By the age of 13, he already had displayed an unusual flair for mathematics. He was still in his 20s when he made his first great contribution to science. At 37, he won the Nobel Prize for Physics for creating fission of uranium by neutron bombardment. This amounted to the transmutation of the elements.　　c

The Nobel Prize came to him at a highly opportune moment. He received notice of the award from Stockholm on the very day that Mussolini promulgated the second set of Fascist racial laws. Since his wife, Laura, was Jewish and he had never liked Fascism, when he went to Stockholm to receive the prize he continued on to New York.　　c

Mesons and Merit. It was a fortunate event for the United States. Fermi's achievement made the A-bomb possible, and he worked through the war at the Los Alamos laboratory. Since 1945, still a consultant to the Atomic Energy Commission, he had gone on with other valuable research projects in his Chicago laboratory.　　d

Two weeks ago, Enrico Fermi received the AEC's first $25,000 award for "meritorious contributions." He was already dying. He had been operated on for cancer more than a month before, but the operation had been futile.　　c

The great Italian navigator died this week. Said Dr. I. I. Rabi, a fellow physicist and chair of the AEC's General Advisory Committee: "We won't see his like in 100 years."　　d

(+50)　　　　　　　—end timing—　　　　　　(min__sec__)　　b

Name_____ Class_____

ACTIVITY 5-4
Summarizing

Instructions: Write a one-paragraph summary of the Reading Selection.

_____

_____

_____

_____

_____

_____

_____

_____

_____

_____

_____

_____

What were your reactions?

_____

_____

_____

_____

_____

_____

_____

_____

_____

_____

_____

_____

ACTIVITY 5-5
Pointer-Words and Pointer-Phrases

Instructions: Read the paragraph below quickly and carefully, paying close attention to the pointer-words printed in boldface type. Just as you should give a minimum amount of concentration to no-message words, you should train yourself to spot pointer-words and give them your fullest attention.

If you are not very good at telling jokes, **perhaps** there is value for you in attaining this skill. **Instead of** accepting the limitation upon your communicative abilities, work at this particular weakness **until** you do improve. **Similarly,** you may have trouble in organizing your ideas clearly, **or** in making effective summaries as your talks progress from one point to another, **or** in using questions that genuinely arouse listeners to a sense of active participation. Your **first two or three** talks presented to the class should serve a diagnostic purpose, **as** you and your instructor discover **what kinds of** problems you **in particular** need to solve. **When** this is determined, you should try successively in every speech **thereafter** to make substantial progress in mastering those problems. **What** you can do well you naturally most enjoy doing; **but** what you do poorly is **what** you most need to concentrate upon.

—adapted from Oliver, Zelko and Holtzman,
Communicative Speaking and Listening

ACTIVITY 5-6
More on Pointer-Words

Instructions: Read through the paragraph below as quickly as you can, underlining every pointer-word or pointer-phrase you find.

But the Allied Command did not take advantage of its complete command of the sea, which permitted it to make landings almost anywhere on both coasts of Italy. Nor did it push its great air superiority, as the Germans had feared. Moreover, no effort seems to have been made by Eisenhower's Command to try to use the large Italian forces together with his own, especially the five divisions near Rome. Had Eisenhower done so—at least this was the argument of both Kesselring and his chief of staff, General Siegfried Westphal, later—the troubles of the Germans would have become hopeless. It was simply beyond their powers, they declared, to fight off Montgomery's army advancing up the peninsula from the "boot," throw back General Mark Clark's invasion force, wherever it landed, and deal with the large Italian armed formations in their midst and in their rear.

—adapted from William L. Shirer, *The Rise and Fall of the Third Reich*

ACTIVITY 5-7
Study Area Checklist

Instructions: Analyze the place in which you do most of your studying. If you don't make a practice of studying at the same place, choose one now and start using it regularly.

	Excellent	Good	Fair	Poor
Lighting				
Freedom from distractions				
Writing surface				
Regular study hours				

If any of your answers are in the "fair" or "poor" columns, do everything you can to improve the situation.

ACTIVITY 5-8
Fixation Check

Instructions: How many fixations do you make per line? This activity will require the help of a fellow student. Remove this page from the book. With a pencil or ball-point pen, punch a hole through the page at the small circle at the end of this activity. Hold the page at eye level, with the print about 15" from your eyes.

Have the other student carefully watch one of your eyes through the hole in the sheet as you read one of the paragraphs. Your partner will soon be able to count the number of fixations you make for each line, and after checking a few lines, will be able to give you a good average. In turn, you observe the movements of your partner's eyes. Be alert for any quick reverses in the middle of a line. What do they indicate?

ACTIVITY 5-9
Preliminary Eye Check

Instructions: Sit upright with an open book held in both hands at a good reading angle. (If you normally use reading glasses, put them on.) Move the book fairly close to your eyes—about 10 inches—and then slowly away from you until your arms are almost fully extended. As you do this, carefully focus on the print. Find the distance from your eyes to the book where the words seem to be sharpest and most readable. Have a fellow student measure the distance. If it is less than 14 inches or more than 16 inches, it indicates that you should get a professional eye examination now! This is a rough test at best, so the fact that your eyes might be most comfortable within the 14"–16" area does *not* mean that you don't need to have them checked once a year.

ACTIVITY 5-10
No-Message Words

Instructions: Read the following paragraph as quickly as you possibly can. Concentrate on the words in regular type, and slide over the no-message words which are in italics. If you find this difficult, try it several more times and see if it becomes easier.

Commander Towers stayed *at* Yap *for* six days while *the* news, *such as it was,* grew steadily worse. *They did* not succeed *in* making contact *with* any station *in the* United States *or* Europe, *but* for *the first* two days *or so they were* able *to* pick up news broadcasts *from* Mexico City, *and that* news *was just about as* bad *as it* could be. *Then the* station went off *the* air, *and they could* only get Panama, Bogota, and Valparaiso, *who* knew *practically* nothing *about* what *was* going on *up in the* northern continent. *They* made contact *with a* few ships *of the* U.S. Navy *in the* South Pacific, most *of them as* short of fuel as *they were* themselves. *The* Captain of *the* cruiser at Yap proved *to be the* senior officer *of* all *these* ships; *he* made *the* decision *to* sail all U.S. ships *into* Australian waters *and to* place *his* forces under Australian command. *He* made signals *to* all ships *to* rendezvous *with him* at Brisbane. They congregated *there a* fortnight later, eleven ships *of the* U.S. Navy, all out *of* bunker fuel *and with very* little hope *of* getting *any* more. *That was a* year ago; *they were* there still.

—Nevil Shute, *On the Beach*

ACTIVITY 5-11
More on No-Message Words

Instructions: In the paragraph below, cross out every word which does not directly contribute to the "sense" of the idea which the author is writing about.

He could not have known the hopelessness of this action. Binoculars were worthless to see into that town and uncover its secrets. He would have been astonished to learn that the men who finally succeeded used instruments a million times more powerful than binoculars. There is something sad, foolish, and human in the image of Shawn leaning against a boulder, propping his arms on it, and holding the binoculars to his eyes. Though clumsy, the binoculars would at least feel comfortable and familiar in his hands. It would be one of the last familiar sensations before his death.

—adapted from Michael Crichton, *The Andromeda Strain*

These exercises do not suggest that you cross out no-message words before you read anything. They are aimed at making you realize that your full powers of concentration need not be wasted on many of the words that make up a typical paragraph. The word-by-word reader wastes time and effort.

6

MORE ON LEARNING:
Understanding Paragraphs, Taking Notes

Vocabulary Preview

Reading Technique

1. "a clear *exposition* of the material" _____
2. "it is a *transitional* unit" _____
3. "If it is an *inference*" _____
4. "does it lack *continuity*" _____
5. "develop a broad *spectrum*" _____
6. "to *dissipate* problems" _____
7. "use of *succinct* sentences" _____
8. "to *synthesize* the picture" _____
9. "helps you *solidify*" _____
10. "*amplification* of the chapter title" _____

Reading Selection

1. "*taut* with anxiety" _____
2. "a number of *revisions*" _____
3. "remembered that *admonition*" _____
4. "a monthly *annuity*" _____
5. "friends were *aghast*" _____
6. "the *proverbial* rainy day" _____
7. "nor do I *advocate*" _____
8. "*frittering* away" _____
9. "a *promissory* note" _____
10. "these *random* thoughts" _____

Comprehension Quiz

Reading Technique

Instructions: Write the letter of the correct answer in the blank provided

1. The main idea of this chapter is:
   a) more techniques for learning
   b) understanding paragraphs
   c) how to write a summary
   d) the importance of outlining
   (___)

2. The topic sentence of a paragraph may be located:
   a) at the beginning
   b) in the middle
   c) at the end
   d) any of the above
   (___)

3. A topic paragraph is usually:
   a) at the end of the chapter
   b) a single sentence
   c) the first or second paragraph
   d) none of the above
   (___)

4. To help determine the meaning of an unusually complex sentence:
   a) use the OARWET technique
   b) outline it
   c) increase your reading rate
   d) find the subject, verb, object
   (___)

5. Note-taking can help you read more efficiently because:
   a) it helps you to memorize
   b) it can be used for review
   c) it helps clarify chapter organization
   d) all of the above
   (___)

6. For a permanent record of the material in a library book, the best method of note-taking is:
   a) underlining
   b) using margins
   c) summarizing
   d) the combination method
   (___)

7. You know an upcoming test on a chapter will include many details. Your best method of taking notes is:
   a) using 3″ × 5″ cards
   b) using margins
   c) summarizing
   d) outlining
   (___)

8. You are primarily interested in a permanent record of the main ideas in each chapter of an important textbook. Which method of note-taking?
   a) underlining
   b) summarizing
   c) using margins
   d) outlining
   (___)

9. According to the chapter, the most helpful method of note-taking to be used for reviewing for a final examination is:
   a) underlining
   b) outlining
   c) summarizing
   d) index cards
   (___)

10. Reading to *learn* starts with:
    a) finding the main idea
    b) a good set of notes
    c) purpose
    d) summarizing the author's thinking
    (___)

6

Reading Technique
—begin timing—

More on Learning:
Understanding Paragraphs, Taking Notes

Chapter 5 discussed the method a writer uses to break down the information he or she wants to convey into specialized sections. These sections, the main ideas, placed in logical order, become the table of contents, the chapters, essentially the outline of the book. He or she then breaks down each chapter into subchapters, again with the ideas arranged in sequence. To communicate individual points, the author "fleshes out" this new outline by means of sentences and paragraphs. As a reader, your job is to reverse this procedure. Overview gives you the broad picture; understanding paragraphs gives you the contributing details.

I. LOCATING TOPIC PARAGRAPHS AND SENTENCES

As was mentioned, a paragraph is a group of related sentences centered on one idea or "topic." The sentence (or sentences) which states that single idea is called a "topic sentence." Remember that *current practice allows the topic sentence to be placed anywhere in the paragraph.*

To some extent, placement depends on the nature of the paragraph itself. If it is a *transitional* unit, you frequently will find the topic in the first sentence. If the paragraph is *descriptive*, the writer may indicate the direction in the first sentence, or wait until the last one in order to synthesize the picture he or she has drawn. If the primary object is to provide a *definition*, the word or concept is usually clarified in the very beginning. If it is an *inference* you are asked to make, the most likely placement of the topic sentence is at the end. No fixed rule applies. (And don't forget that writers are human—their efforts are subject to error. You may find paragraphs with more than one topic sentence; you may find an occasional one with none at all.)

There is, however, one basic guide: Look for the person—or thing—which is described, modified, traced historically, defined, or referred to by the other sentences in the paragraph. If you remove that *one* sentence, will the others lack meaning? Or continuity? That one is the topic sentence!

On a higher level, the topic sentence also performs a major function as far as larger ideas are concerned. In order for a chapter to flow smoothly, the author must state the main theme as close to the beginning as possible. This theme, expressed in a sentence which is usually an amplification of the chapter title, becomes the key sentence for the entire chapter, and the paragraph which includes it is called the *topic paragraph.* Sometimes, the first paragraph will include this general statement. Occasionally, the author may feel the need of an introductory paragraph to smooth the approach, or just to arouse interest. In general, you will find the main idea presented in either the first or second paragraph of each chapter and of each major subhead.

II. SENTENCE MEANING, OR HOW TO WRITE A TELEGRAM

Long, complicated sentences demand careful analysis to insure understanding. When you run into prose written this way, first admit the difficulty level and adjust your reading rate accordingly. Then adopt the "telegram-writing" technique: eliminate all words or phrases except those which carry the basic message. Actually, you are finding the subject, verb, and object (if any). Once you have these, fit in the modifying words, phrases, and clauses to their related basic words.

III. HOW ABOUT NOTES?

There are a number of note-taking procedures which you may find valuable. The very act of writing things down makes them easier to remember. The *Write* phase of OARWET helps you see the organization underlying what you are reading, helps you solidify it in terms of concrete items, and provides you with an excellent source of review material.   **a**

There are several methods for keeping written records. Try them all and select the one that is most effective for you.

A. Underlining (or Drawing Through).   Authorities disagree as to the total effectiveness of underlining significant ideas and facts. See if it works for you.

B. Using margins for notes.   This method can be efficient, but depends on your handwriting—and the size of the margins.   **d**

C. Index cards.   Ranging in size from 3″ × 5″ to 5″ × 8″, index cards are commonly used for research. Use one for each key idea. (They're easily lost!)

D. Combinations.   A most helpful and efficient means of keeping a written record is used for less important reading: combine underlining, margin notes, and outlining—see V below.   **c**

(See the illustrations that follow.)

IV. KNOWING YOU KNOW: THE SUMMARY   **d**

Want to walk into the classroom *knowing* you know the material to be discussed or tested? Spend a few minutes, when you have completed your review, stating aloud the most important ideas, then writing them down in your own words. Try doing it without the book. Then check your summary   **d** with the author's. Include each idea he thought deserved a subhead. If you elect to use this method of "knowing you know," you will find it worthwhile to develop a broad spectrum of abbreviations and short-cut symbols. $(+, -, =, \therefore$ borrowed from math courses are good.) Don't overdo these; you will have to be able to read them at a later date. Remember that a summary covers main ideas only; it does not include details.   **c**

V. KNOWING YOU KNOW: THE OUTLINE

There is no substitute for a good outline. It is difficult to imagine a success-   **d** ful student who cannot outline written and oral material—and do it well. Outlining may be brief or detailed, and lends itself to the use of succinct sentences, phrases, or key words. Take full advantage of the outlining practice provided in this book. It will pay off—in any course.

The ideas noted in Chapters 5 and 6 are extensions of the OARWET approach, coupled with the basic requirement of purpose. *Learning, essentially, consists of mastering ideas. You will find them in textbook prefaces, topic paragraphs (sometimes called* **d** *thesis statements) and topic sentences. Once you are sure of them, tie in new ideas with your own knowledge and "fix" them in your memory with a good set of notes.*

—end timing—   (min___sec___) **b**

                                                                                 c

analogies to European history and opponents tend to view the Viet Cong as 20th-century versions of Robin Hood?

The point is this: Adults often like to pretend the real world doesn't exist. Kids can't. We might want to *escape* from it, but we can't *forget* about it. And we know the difference between the world we're taught and the world we experience. And if we blame you for trying to put something over on us, it's only because we're taught what, alas, most Americans seem to think. If the school is trying to turn its back on reality, it only represents an America that's doing the same thing. And that's what really worries us.

Figure 6-1   Underlining by drawing through (*adapted from* Steven Kelman, *You Force Kids to Rebel*)

Computers, whose basic concept goes back to Blaise Pascal, were developed in their electronic form during World War II to help guns hit their targets more efficiently. There are two basic types – the analog and digital computer. The former operates ... as ... a kind of electronic slide rule able to apply higher mathematics to problems of rates of change in various flows. However fast it might have been, for the engineer, mathematician, and operations researcher it was not fast enough. So the digital computer was devised, a machine that employs the binary number system and consequently can only add and subtract. This is no impediment, for like an electronic abacus, the digital computer sends its impulses forward at an unbelievable speed, giving it a marked advantage over the analog machine. Moreover, digital computers have "memory" drums in which data can ... The electrical ... in a digital com-

[margin notes: Origin: Pascal / WW II / electronics / analog too / slow — / digital / binary / (abacus) / Very high speed. / memory drums]

Figure 6-2   Using margins for notes (Ben B. Seligman, *Man, Work and the Automated Feast*)

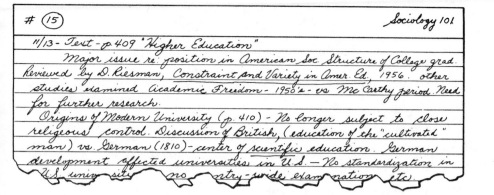

Figure 6-3   5″ × 8″ Card—Detailed notes

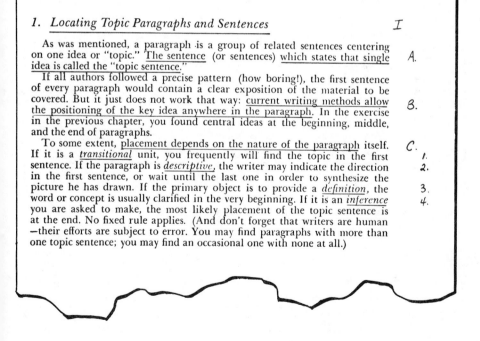

1. Locating Topic Paragraphs and Sentences   *I*

As was mentioned, a paragraph is a group of related sentences centering on one idea or "topic." <u>The sentence</u> (or sentences) <u>which states that single idea is called the "topic sentence."</u>   *A.*

If all authors followed a precise pattern (how boring!), the first sentence of every paragraph would contain a clear exposition of the material to be covered. But it just does not work that way: <u>current writing methods allow the positioning of the key idea anywhere in the paragraph.</u> In the exercise in the previous chapter, you found central ideas at the beginning, middle, and the end of paragraphs.   *B.*

To some extent, <u>placement depends on the nature of the paragraph</u> itself. If it is a *transitional* unit, you frequently will find the topic in the first sentence. If the paragraph is *descriptive,* the writer may indicate the direction in the first sentence, or wait until the last one in order to synthesize the picture he has drawn. If the primary object is to provide a *definition,* the word or concept is usually clarified in the very beginning. If it is an *inference* you are asked to make, the most likely placement of the topic sentence is at the end. No fixed rule applies. (And don't forget that writers are human —their efforts are subject to error. You may find paragraphs with more than one topic sentence; you may find an occasional one with none at all.)   *C.*
     1.
     2.
     3.
     4.

Figure 6-4   Combined note-taking techniques

ACTIVITY 6-1
Applying the Technique

1. Underline the main idea of this chapter, preferably using a ballpoint pen in a bright, sharply contrasting color. (Or draw through with a light-colored felt-tip.)

2. Underline the topic sentence in each paragraph.

3. Underline the secondary ideas and contributing details in pencil or in another ballpoint color.

4. Try note-taking in the left-hand margins of both pages of the chapter. Will it work for you?

5. Using the underlining you have done in 1, 2, and 3, outline the chapter in the right-hand margin, using the combination method suggested in section III. Compare this with the outline you complete on page 55.

6. Write below a one-paragraph summary covering the basic ideas of Chapter 6.

7. In the outline, how many words will be needed for expressing the main ideas for IV and V?

8. Do these 1000-word chapters lend themselves to the use of 3″ × 5″ cards for note-taking? Would larger cards be more useful? Worth a try?

Summary: _____

_____

_____

_____

_____

_____

_____

_____

_____

_____

_____

_____

_____

_____

9. Compare the amount of information available in this summary to the information in the outline that follows.

ACTIVITY 6-2
Outline: More on Learning

Main Idea: _____

_____

I. _____

  * A. _____

    B. Located _____

    C. _____

       1. _____ 3. definition

       2. _____ 4. _____

  * D. Topic paragraph contains _____.

       1. _____

II. Understanding sentences

    A. Locate _____, _____, _____

    B. Attach _____, _____, _____ to
    above.

III. _____. Find one most suitable.

    A. _____ C. Index cards

    B. _____ D. _____

IV. Summarizing

  * A. _____

    B. Abbreviate as much as possible, using own symbols.

V. _____

    A. Essential to sound learning technique

    B. _____

ACTIVITY 6-3
Vocabulary Exercises

Reading Technique

Instructions: From the list that follows, select the letter of the word that correctly completes the sentence and write it in the blank provided.

a) exposition
b) transitional
c) inference
d) continuity
e) spectrum

f) dissipate
g) succinct
h) synthesize
i) solidify
j) amplification

1. When the sleek sports car sped by, my roommate made a(n) _____ comment: she whistled in admiration. (__)
2. It's a good idea to _____ your class notes, research papers, and other study aids before exam time. (__)
3. A restful night's sleep helps greatly to _____ one's fears about the next day's problems. (__)
4. The always-bored person has a limited emotional _____. (__)
5. The politician's speech was more than an explanation of foreign policy; it was a(n) _____ of his own point of view. (__)
6. In a famous story, a man discovers a dead baby and a dog with a bloody mouth; his automatic _____ is that the animal attacked and killed the child. (__)
7. For many students, the junior college provides an excellent _____ education between the high school curriculum and the last two years of university work. (__)
8. His speech was poorly organized. It lacked _____. (__)
9. She provided ten minutes for a broad _____ of his main theme. (__)
10. With all the summer job opportunities offered the talented young man, he found it hard to _____ his plans. (__)

Reading Selection

Instructions: Write the letter of the matching word in the blank provided.

a) proverbial
b) random
c) taut
d) admonition
e) promissory
f) annuity
g) aghast
h) advocate
i) frittering
j) revisions

1. advice, warning (__)
2. shocked (__)
3. improvements, changes (__)
4. like a brief popular saying (__)
5. sum paid regularly (__)
6. wasting time on trifles (__)
7. without definite aim or course (__)
8. written statement to pay on demand (__)
9. to maintain a cause, plead (__)
10. tight, tightly drawn (__)

6

Comprehension Quiz

Reading Selection

Instructions: Write the letter of the correct answer in the blank provided.

1. The basic argument advocated by Dr. Peacock is:
   a) avoid demanding tasks   c) enjoy life today   (__)
   b) forget "rainy days"   d) travel is enlightening

2. George Howard, the first casualty, had been a(n):
   a) doctor   c) minister   (__)
   b) educator   d) not mentioned

3. His sudden death was probably the result of:
   a) a stroke or brain   c) cancer   (__)
      hemorrhage
   b) a heart attack   d) can't be determined

4. Howard died:
   a) at home   c) in an ambulance   (__)
   b) in the hospital   d) at the doctor's office

5. In order to travel, Carolyn, the doctor's sister, got money from:
   a) her bank   c) her pension fund   (__)
   b) the teacher's credit union   d) wasn't mentioned

6. Some of Carolyn's friends and relatives:
   a) lent her money   c) disapproved of her action   (__)
   b) were delighted at her trip   d) lent her a car

7. Carolyn died of cancer:
   a) a few years later   c) on the trip   (__)
   b) four months later   d) was not mentioned

8. The principle of "saving for a rainy day":
   a) may come from parents   c) is taught in school   (__)
   b) is well known in our   d) all of these
      society

9. Peacock is:
   a) a young physician   c) retired   (__)
   b) a practicing doctor   d) an educator

10. The economic problems of retirees today are minimized by:
    a) Social Security   c) help from children   (__)
    b) part-time work   d) none of these

6

Reading Selection

DON'T WAIT TOO LATE TO PLAY

by Arthur B. Peacock, M.D.   (from *The Rotarian*, July 1977)

—begin timing—

The call came at the end of a busy day, just as I as settling down to a late dinner.

"Doctor, it's Sarah Howard"—the voice on the telephone was taut with anxiety. "Something terrible has happened to George. Please come quickly!"

I was a young physician then, and had only been established in my first practice for a short while. But I knew that a person like Sarah Howard would not make such an urgent call except in a real emergency. So I grabbed my bag, dashed out to my waiting Ford, and started speeding along the four-kilometre drive to the Howards' country place.

As I drove, I reviewed what I knew about this interesting couple. Now in their late 60's, they had lived for many years in New York City, where George had enjoyed a distinguished career as an educator. They came to our southern New Jersey community for occasional holidays.

George was the author of a widely used textbook, and now that he was retiring he had promised his publishers to prepare a second edition with a number of revisions, which was soon due to go to press. The last time I had talked with him, he had told me that once he met the publisher's deadline, he and Sarah planned to start doing some of the things they had never found time for during his busy years. In short, they were going to forget all about work and just *play* a little. They were both looking forward to happy years of retirement ahead.

I turned in the driveway, pulled up to the door, and jumped out.

"Upstairs, Doctor!" Sarah's voice called urgently as I ran into the house.

I took the stairs two at a time and bounded into the bedroom, where I found George lying in a crumpled heap just outside the door to the adjoining bath. Kneeling beside him, I reached for his pulse.

"He had worked all day on the book revision," Sarah was saying numbly, "and he had looked so tired when he finally finished. He thought he'd take a shower before dinner . . . then all of a sudden, I heard him call 'Sarah . . . my head . . . my head!' And when I got here. . . ." Her voice trailed off and ended in a suppressed sob.

For a long moment there was silence. What could I say to her, I wondered, as I knelt there beside her lifeless husband? Despite my years of medical training and hospital internship, I felt helplessly young in the presence of something as old as death. But Sarah spoke first.

"There's nothing you can do for him, is there, Doctor?" she asked with quiet resignation.

I looked up at her and said simply, "I'm sorry. Even if I had been here when it happened, it would have made no difference. It was evidently a massive thing."

I rose and turned to her. Impulsively, she reached for my hand and clung to it.

"Doctor," she said earnestly, grief and wisdom mingling in her voice, "don't wait too late to play!"

I have often remembered that admonition as time has passed. It was brought home to me most forcibly some years ago when my sister Carolyn, who had been teaching in a junior college, resigned her post and accepted another position. She had accumulated a nice little pension fund, and she was given the option of taking it out in a lump sum or leaving it to earn interest until such time as she would formally retire (when it would be paid to her as a monthly annuity). Her eldest son was soon to be married in California, and she was determined that the entire family should attend the gala event. But where was the money coming from for such a trip?

Carolyn had the answer. Without a moment's hesitation she took her pension fund in its entirety, bought a new car, packed the family in, and proceeded to drive from the Atlantic coast to the Pacific and back again—enjoying every minute of the journey and seeing parts of the United States she had never seen before. Some of her relatives and friends were aghast. **c** Imagine blowing one's entire pension fund on a car and a single trip! What if she really *needed* the money when she retired? Didn't everyone have an obligation to try to provide for that season of life known as "old age"?

But Carolyn never had the experience of growing old. A few years later, a **b** rapidly spreading malignancy claimed her life just four months after it was diagnosed. Thank God, she hadn't waited too late to play! The pension fund she would never need had given her and her family a lump sum of happiness. **a**

* * *

Now, I don't mean to imply . . . that one shouldn't save something for the proverbial "rainy day." Nor do I advocate frittering away the summertime of life, like the grasshopper in the fable, without taking into account the winter **a** that may follow. What I *am* saying is that life is shorter than we realize. We are gloriously young one day. Then some morning, we awake and discover that we have suddenly grown old. The years between are precious few, all too **c** fleeting.

* * *

I can't state my case too strongly, but it is simply this: If you have something **c** you really want to do, do it *now!* If you have a yen to visit some far-off place, don't wait—call your travel agent *today* and start making plans! If some seemingly impossible dream has been kicking around in your head for a while, don't suppress it. Give it a chance to come true! It will, if you'll only let **b** it. I was idly turning the leaves on my desk calendar the other day when I came across this quotation from Kay Lyons at the top of a page: "Yesterday is a canceled check; tomorrow is a promissory note; today is ready cash—*use* it." **d**

The years have come and gone, and I am now retired. But as I sit here setting down these random thoughts, memory plays a trick on me and I am a young physician again—standing in a quiet, grief-filled room, while a voice old with wisdom is saying earnestly, "Doctor, don't wait too late to play!"

c

(—0—)   —end timing—   (min__sec__)

d

ACTIVITY 6-4
Summarizing

Instructions: Write a one-paragraph summary of the Reading Selection.

_____

_____

_____

_____

_____

_____

_____

_____

_____

_____

_____

_____

What were your reactions?

_____

_____

_____

_____

_____

_____

_____

_____

_____

_____

_____

_____

_____

_____

ACTIVITY 6-5
Finding Main Ideas

Instructions: After you have finished reading the paragraph below, choose from the four possible answers the one which you think *most clearly* states the main idea.

> In one such study, six girls appeared twice before high school classes. One girl was dressed alike on the two occasions. On the second occasion, which was approximately three weeks after the first, the classes were told that some of them had misunderstood the instructions the first time and that therefore the test needed to be repeated. The classes were not informed that the models had changed their clothing. Both times the students rated the models on various personal characteristics. The girl who was dressed alike on the two occasions was judged to have the same personal characteristics both times, while those who were wearing different clothing were judged differently. ... The changed ratings for the girls who were dressed differently indicates that the ratings on personality traits were influenced by the subjects' clothing.
>
> —adapted from Mary Shaw Ryan, *Clothing, A Study in Human Behavior*

1. A person's personality changes as he or she changes clothing. (__)

2. In a research study, six girls appeared before a group twice with one girl wearing the same clothes the second time. (__)

3. People are judged solely by their clothes. (__)

4. According to one study many people judge personality traits on the basis of clothing. (__)

Answer number 1 has some interesting possibilities, but it is not correct in terms of the experiment described in the paragraph. In the study described, the author was making the point that it was the *audience*, which rated the models' personality traits, that changed.

The second answer is true in both content and detail. However, what we are looking for is not a specific fact, but the *main idea* of the whole paragraph. This answer is too narrow, and is only a supporting fact. Answer 3 is entirely too broad. It takes the conclusions of this single study and balloons them into what is called a "generalization," a sweeping statement which is subject to question by anyone who thinks about it.

Answer 4, then, is the correct one, and re-states the main idea expressed in the topic sentence. If you go back and check each sentence in the paragraph, you will see how each contributes to the "topic" stated at the end.

Write the first and last word of the topic sentence:

_____

_____

7

VOCABULARY
AND THE VICIOUS CYCLE

Vocabulary Preview

Reading Technique

1. "is not an *esoteric* activity" _____
2. "a high *correlation* between" _____
3. "interest in reading *flags*" _____
4. "*root-affix* system" _____
5. "growth *decelerates* rapidly" _____
6. "*idiomatic* expressions" _____
7. "a better *tactic*" _____
8. "*apathy*" _____
9. "*empathy*" _____
10. "*pathetic*" _____

Reading Selection

1. "a public *personage*" _____
2. "powerful piece of *propaganda*" _____
3. "*remonstrated* with the editor" _____
4. "Lincoln had been *maligned*" _____
5. "*unanimous* decisions" _____
6. "we can *infer*" _____
7. "*Mother* formed in the bottle" _____
8. "an *invaluable* guide" _____
9. "the *extensional* events" _____
10. "meanings *denoted* by the words" _____

7

Comprehension Quiz

Reading Technique

Instructions: Write the letter of the correct answer in the blank provided.

1. According to Chapter 7, a broad vocabulary will:
   a) help you to communicate
   b) add to reading enjoyment
   c) aid concentration when reading
   d) all of the above   (__)

2. Large corporations frequently include vocabulary tests for job applicants:
   a) as a measure of intelligence
   b) to check letter-writing ability
   c) to rate personality
   d) not mentioned   (__)

3. A limited vocabulary may often be the result of:
   a) poor spelling ability
   b) an old-fashioned dictionary
   c) a general dislike of reading
   d) lack of a college education   (__)

4. The vocabulary of most adults:
   a) increases about 5,000 words yearly
   b) equals that of a tenth-grader
   c) increases through conversation
   d) is increased by television   (__)

5. Learning the meaning of a word from "context" is:
   a) limited to esoteric words
   b) the main source of the average vocabulary
   c) dependent on knowing Latin
   d) based on the use of a dictionary   (__)

6. The word *skip* means:
   a) to be jumped a class in school
   b) to scale a flat stone over water
   c) to leave town in a hurry
   d) all of the above   (__)

7. To use the "building-block" system of learning new words, you must:
   a) have a knowledge of Latin
   b) examine the context in which the word is used
   c) compare parts of new words with familiar ones
   d) all of the above   (__)

8. From this chapter, you would gather that many adults:
   a) do little reading
   b) read avidly
   c) carry a pocket dictionary
   d) seek out many new words   (__)

9. A good vocabulary could be independent of:
   a) a college education
   b) a financially deprived home
   c) a very high income
   d) all of the above   (__)

10. Using the right word at the right time:
    a) may save many words
    b) indicates learning
    c) helps communication
    d) all of the above   (__)

7

Reading Technique
—begin timing—

Vocabulary and the Vicious Cycle

Until extrasensory perception is perfected, human communication will have to depend, basically, on words. Your ability to communicate–and be communicated with– depends on your control of vocabulary. And if you have been plagued with "boring" books, if you "just can't concentrate," the chances are good that you don't understand the meaning of too many important words. What you don't understand, you don't like.

I. VOCABULARY: RELEVANT?

Developing a solid vocabulary is not an esoteric activity. There is an amazingly high correlation between current intelligence tests and standardized vocabulary tests. Many big corporations use this correlation when testing job applicants.

From another point of view—has a poor vocabulary denied you the pleasure of "relaxation reading"? Problems involving reading and vocabulary create a vicious cycle: poor vocabulary skill leads to a dislike of reading. But most of our knowledge of words comes from reading: no reading, poor vocabulary. Poor vocabulary, dislike of reading. Stalemate!

II. HOW DID YOU LEARN THE WORDS YOU KNOW?

The average adult is familiar with about 50,000 words. (In everyday conversation we use only about 10 percent of that number.) Where did that familiarity come from? How many *thousands* of words have *you* looked up in a dictionary?

Most people learn new words from communication, oral or written. A child of six or seven gulps down new words at the rate of about 5,000 a year. He or she learns by asking, touching, tasting, trying. Unfortunately, as he grows older, self-consciousness sets in and the urge to know is inhibited by the fear of appearing ignorant. If interest in reading flags, vocabulary growth decelerates rapidly. Many adults have vocabularies only slightly larger than that of a tenth-grader. Television writers know this: their guidelines are rigid!

The constant reader has a broad vocabulary; two methods enlarge it.

III. TACKLING A NEW WORD: USE ITS CONTEXT

How to determine the meaning of a word from the context in which it is used can be explained by examples. From the next three sentences, pinpoint the meaning of *trobert*. 1. *When the motor started to run unevenly, he carefully adjusted the carburetor with a trobert.* 2. *Knowing his brother's enthusiasm for mechanics, Tom bought him a six-inch chrome trobert for his birthday.* 3. *From the untidy garage floor, he picked up a rusty trobert.* What is a *trobert*? It seems quite obvious that it is a metal tool of some kind, probably steel, comes in various sizes, can be used with engines as an adjusting device. While this description leaves something to be desired, it gives you a pretty good idea of a *trobert's* function and a vague picture of its physical characteristics. And the next time you come across the word, you won't be at a complete loss. (That may be a long time, because *trobert* was invented for this example.)

How a word is uséd in context can be very important. Consider the word *acute*. You are familiar with this one from its usage in geometry—an acute angle is one which measures less than 90 degrees. How would you fit that meaning into this sentence? *Her eyesight was so acute that she was able to spot a movement in the brush long before any of the team.* Certainly you are not dealing with an angle here. The person described has exceptional eyesight. Your definition from geometry will not fit, but the context gives you a new meaning. A good dictionary may have dozens of definitions for many common words, some closely related, some widely varied. In your college dictionary the word *stand*, for instance, has well over 20 meanings without including idiomatic expressions. Note the difference between these few: to stand up; to stand six feet tall; to stand aside; to take a stand; to stand first in the class; to stand for election; a stand of wheat; to stand and fight.

d

Too many people have developed the negative habit of simply skipping over any new word. A better tactic, on seeing an unfamiliar word the first time, is to *guess* at its meaning. Usually the accuracy of this guess depends on the surrounding words which affect it. This is using context in a meaningful manner. The next time you see (or hear) the word, its new context will strengthen your first impression. This procedure, repeated often enough, has expanded your vocabulary in the past. Use it deliberately in the future.

a

c

IV. TACKLING A NEW WORD: TAKE IT APART

The prefixes, suffixes, and roots we have inherited from Latin and Greek can be valuable to you despite the fact that you have studied neither language. Many of these "building-blocks" are familiar to you through words you already know. Suppose your next test in European History contains an essay question that reads: "Many Frenchmen have a violent antipathy toward Germany. Explain." The word *antipathy* is meaningless to you. Context here might not help. Taking the word apart is the solution. A natural division point seems to be between the *i* and *p*. We now have *anti-* and *pathy. Anti-* is not much of a problem—anti-war, anti-communist. *Anti-* obviously means "against." *Pathy* is a little more difficult. What words do you know which contain those five letters, or what might be a variation of them? How about *sympathy*? Do you know *apathy*? Or *empathy*? *Pathetic*? All of these words have one thing in common— they involve human feelings. Try it: *anti-* against; *pathy* feeling. And we have it: a "feeling against."

b

b

d

In Activity 7–1 for this chapter (page 82), you will find a list of prefixes, roots, and suffixes which you should know. Although they are only a small portion of those used in our language, you will be amazed at the number of words they will help you understand. Try this "building-block" method—the root-affix system—the next time you cannot work out the meaning of a new word from context.

c

Vocabulary is basic to communication. Increase yours by making contexts and the root-affix system work for you.

—end timing—   (min___sec___) **a**

d

d

ACTIVITY 7-1
Applying the Technique

Here are three lists of frequently used "building-blocks"—prefixes, roots, and suffixes. Check your knowledge of them by using each in a word which you know. If you cannot remember a word, consult a dictionary. The letters in parentheses tell the language of origin: L-Latin; G-Greek; OE-Ole English.

PREFIXES

Of Position:

1. ab- (L) from
2. ad- (L) to
3. circum- (L) around
4. com- (L) with, together
5. de- (L) away
6. dis- (L) apart
7. ex- (L) out
8. in- (L) into
9. inter- (L) between
10. sub- (L) under
11. trans- (L) across

Of Number:
1. uni- (L) one
2. mono- (G) one
3. duo- (L) two
4. bi- (G) two
5. multi- (L) many, several
6. poly- (G) many, several
7. mil-, mille- (L) thousand
8. meg- (G) million
9. semi- (L) half

Of Time:

1. pre- (L) before
2. ante- (L) before
3. post- (L) after
4. retro- (L) backward

Of Negation:
1. a- (G) not
2. in- (L) not
3. non- (L) not
4. un- (OE) not

Of Opinion:
1. anti- (G) against
2. contra- (L) against
3. ob- (L) against
4. pro- (L) for, before

Of Degree:
1. extra- (L) beyond
2. ultra- (L) beyond
3. hyper- (G) over
4. hypo- (G) under

ROOTS

1. fac, fact (L) do, make
2. aud, audit (L) hear
3. ced, cess (L) go, give up
4. cred, credit (L) believe
5. demos (G) people
6. dic, dit (L) speak
7. mit, miss (L) send
8. port (L) carry
9. spec (L) see
10. voc (L) call
11. pathy (G) feeling
12. logy (G) knowledge
13. gynos (G) woman
14. anthropo (G) man
15. phob (G) fear
16. graphy (G) writing, record

SUFFIXES

1. *one who:* -er, -or, -ist
2. *state of:* -ancy, -tion, -ation, -dom, -ness
3. meaning *resembling:* -il, -ile
4. meaning *to make:* -age, -en, -fy

ACTIVITY 7-2
Outline: Vocabulary and the Vicious Cycle

Main Idea: _____

_____

_____

I. Vocabulary: Relevant?
   A. High correlation between _____
   B. Poor vocabulary can cause a dislike of reading, but _____

   _____

II. _____
   A. _____
   B. _____

III. _____
   A. Your understanding of most of the words you know comes from
      your having read them in context
   B. Procedure for _____
      1. _____
      2. _____

IV. _____
   A. _____
   B. _____

ACTIVITY 7-3
Vocabulary Exercises

Reading Technique

Instructions: Write the letter of the word that correctly completes the sentence in the blank provided.

a) affix
b) tactics
c) correlate
d) apathetic
e) flagged

f) deceleration
g) empathy
h) idiomatic
i) esoteric
j) pathetic

1. Imagining herself in the boy's place, she felt _____ for him.　(__)

2. A(n) _____ can precede or follow a word's root or stem.　(__)

3. The bank's figures and your checkbook ought to _____ exactly.　(__)

4. Too many people don't vote because they are _____.　(__)

5. _____ of reading speed can be caused by fatigue.　(__)

6. The judges felt the painting was too _____ for most people to understand.　(__)

7. He was a master of jungle pursuit _____.　(__)

8. Every language has its own _____ phrases which are difficult to translate.　(__)

9. The ragged, crying child was a(n) _____ sight.　(__)

10. Overcome by fatigue, her interest _____.　(__)

Reading Selection

Instructions: Write the letter of the matching word in the blank provided.

a) personage
b) propaganda
c) remonstrated
d) malign
e) unanimous
f) infer
g) mother

h) invaluable
i) extensional
j) denoted

1. deduce, accept from evidence　(__)
2. priceless　(__)
3. speak badly of　(__)
4. going beyond or continuing from　(__)
5. important individual　(__)
6. in total agreement　(__)
7. a slimy film used in producing vinegar　(__)
8. pointed out in protest or opposition　(__)
9. indicated, designated　(__)
10. scheme for supporting program, ideas, attitudes, and so forth

7

Comprehension Quiz

Reading Selection

Instructions: Write the letter of the correct answer in the blank provided.

1. According to Hayakawa, to ignore the context of a word is:
   a) stupid
   b) possibly vicious
   c) both (a) and (b)
   d) neither (a) nor (b)
   (__)

2. The Veterans Day speaker used the word *propaganda* to mean:
   a) agitating against war
   b) a misleading account
   c) pro-war talk
   d) explaining the moral purpose of war
   (__)

3. The newspaper editor was accurate in stating that the speaker had:
   a) called the Gettysburg Address *propaganda*
   b) insulted Lincoln
   c) used *propaganda* in its popular meaning
   d) none of these
   (__)

4. We can understand better what others are saying if we:
   a) examine contexts
   b) depend on our own definitions
   c) avoid controversial words
   d) not mentioned
   (__)

5. The historical" and "cultural" contexts of a word:
   a) have little significance
   b) confuse meaning
   c) clarify meaning
   d) lack accuracy
   (__)

6. Words used by the writers of the Constitution:
   a) have the same meanings today
   b) had a different context then
   c) cannot be interpreted
   d) none of these
   (__)

7. Hayakawa indicates that a dictionary meaning of a word helps explain:
   a) the word itself
   b) the probable meaning in context
   c) the rest of a sentence
   d) all of the above
   (__)

8. A dictionary is:
   a) a stable record
   b) a historical work
   c) more important than context
   d) all of these
   (__)

9. A dictionary meaning of a word:
   a) gives its context
   b) gives a single correct meaning
   c) avoids "areas of meaning"
   d) is a guide to interpretation
   (__)

10. From Hayakawa's general theme, you can infer that propaganda:
    a) generally surrounds us in various forms
    b) is anti-war
    c) only refers to war
    d) is moral
    (__)

7

Reading Selection
—begin timing—
CONTEXTS

by S. I. Hayakawa   (from *Language in Thought and Action*)

IGNORING CONTEXTS

The ignoring of contexts in any act of interpretation is at best a stupid practice. At its worst, it can be a vicious practice. A common example is the sensational newspaper story in which a few words by a public personage are torn out of their context and made the basis of a completely misleading account.

A Veterans Day speaker, a university teacher, declared before a high-school assembly that the Gettysburg Address was "a powerful piece of propaganda." The context clearly revealed that "propaganda" was being used, not according to its popular meaning, but rather, as the speaker himself stated, to mean "explaining the moral purposes of a war." The context also revealed that the speaker was an admirer of Lincoln. However, the local newspaper, ignoring the context, presented the account so as to suggest that the speaker had called Lincoln a liar. On this basis, the newspaper began a campaign against the instructor. The speaker remonstrated with the editor of the newspaper, who replied, in effect, "I don't care what else you said. You said the Gettysburg Address was propaganda, didn't you?" This appeared to the editor complete proof that Lincoln had been maligned and that the speaker deserved to be discharged from his position at the university. Similar practices may be found in advertisements. A reviewer may be quoted on the jacket of a book as having said, "A brilliant work," while reading of the context may reveal that what he really said was, "It just falls short of being a brilliant work." There are some people who will always be able to find a defense for such a practice in saying, "But he did use the words, 'a brilliant work,' didn't he?"

People in the course of argument frequently complain about words meaning different things to different people. Instead of complaining, they should accept such differences as a matter of course. It would be startling indeed if the word "justice," for example, were to have the same meaning to each of the nine justices of the United States Supreme Court; we should get nothing but unanimous decisions. It would be even more startling if "justice" meant the same to President Kennedy as to Nikita Khrushchev. If we can get deeply into our consciousness the principle that no word ever has the same meaning twice, we will develop the habit of automatically examining contexts, and this will enable us to understand better what others are saying. As it is, however, we are all too likely, when a word sounds familiar, to assume that we understand it even when we don't. In this way we read into people's remarks meanings that were never intended. Then we waste energy in angrily accusing people of "intellectual dishonesty" or "abuse of words," when their own sin is that they use words in ways unlike our own, as they can hardly help doing, especially if their background has been widely different from ours. There are cases of intellectual dishonesty and the abuse of words, of course, but they do not always occur in the places where people think they do.

In the study of history or of cultures other than our own, contexts take on special importance. To say, "There was no running water or electricity in the house," does not condemn an English house in 1570, but says a great deal against a house in Chicago in 1963. Again, if we wish to understand the Constitution of the United States, it is not enough, as our historians now tell us, merely to look up all the words in the dictionary and to read the interpretations written by Supreme Court justices. We must see the Constitution in its historical context: the conditions of life, the state of the arts and industries and transportation, the current ideas of the time—all of which helped to determine what words went into the Constitution and what those words meant to those who wrote them. After all, the words "United States of America" stood for quite a different-sized nation and a different culture in 1790 from what they stand for today. When it comes to very big subjects, the range of contexts to be examined—verbal, social, and historical—may become very large indeed.

c

In personal relations, furthermore, those who ignore psychological contexts often make the mistake of interpreting as insults remarks that are only intended in jest.

d

THE INTERACTION OF WORDS

All this is not to say, however, that the reader might just as well throw away his dictionary, simply because contexts are so important. Any word in a sentence—any sentence in a paragraph, any paragraph in a larger unit—whose meaning is revealed by its context, is itself part of the context of the rest of the text. To look up a word in a dictionary, therefore, frequently explains not only the word itself, but the rest of the sentence, paragraph, conversation, or essay in which it is found. All words within a given context interact upon one another.

a

a

Realizing, then, that a dictionary is a historical work, we should understand the dictionary thus: "The word *mother* has most frequently been used in the past among English-speakinng people to indicate a female parent." From this we can safely infer, "If that is how it has been used, that is what it *probably* means in the sentence I am trying to understand." This is what we normally do, of course; after we look up a word in the dictionary, we re-examine the context to see if the definition fits. If the context reads, "Mother began to form in the bottle," one may have to look at the dictionary more carefully.

c

b

A dictionary definition, therefore, is an invaluable guide to interpretation. Words do not have a single "correct meaning"; they apply to *groups* of similar situations, which might be called *areas of meaning*. It is for defining these areas of meaning that a dictionary is useful. In each use of any word, we examine the particular context and the extensional events denoted (if possible) to discover the *point* intended within the area of meaning.

d

(+100)   —end timing—   (min___sec___)

b

d

a

ACTIVITY 7-4
Summarizing

Instructions: Write a one-paragraph summary of the Reading Selection.

_____

_____

_____

_____

_____

_____

_____

_____

ACTIVITY 7-5
More on Main Ideas

Instructions: After reading the paragraph below, fill in the blanks with MI (main idea), N (too narrow), B (too broad), or NS (incorrect or not stated).

Rembrandt's social career was as successful as his professional one. In 1634, he married Saskia van Uylenborch, an heiress who brought him a handsome dowry. They bought a fine house on the Bree street (now a museum). Rembrandt organized a group of students and assistants, most of whom paid well for the privilege. His means now permitted him to purchase the most expensive pictures and objects, and he accumulated one of the finest collections north of the Alps. The familiar self-portrait in Dresden shows him at this time with Saskia on his knee, a sword at his belt, a plume in his hat, and a glass in his upraised hand. It is an emphatically carefree picture, if a vulgar one. The way of life was high and wide, and became a subject for gossip. In 1638, Rembrandt and Saskia sued for libel two persons who had accused the young couple of wasting her rich inheritance.

—adapted from John Ives Sewall, *A History of Western Art*

1. Rembrandt married a countess.   (___)

2. Rembrandt was accused of wasting his wife's dowry.   (___)

3. The young couple led a gay and carefree life.   (___)

4. Rembrandt was a famous painter and a social success.   (___)

ACTIVITY 7-6

Guessing Word Meaning from Context

Instructions: The words in italics are words that often are used in actual sentences typical of current texts or novels. Choose the correct synonym (word with the same meaning) for each from the four words listed. When necessary, guess!

1. The one thing she could not forgive was his *duplicity*. To her, his regular practice of saying one thing and doing another was unforgivable.
   a) sloppiness   b) double-dealing   c) lack of faith   d) ease   (__)

2. The first mate was always *irascible*. He roared orders at the stewards, scolded the cooks, and, at the slightest problem, attacked every other officer but the captain.
   a) gentle   b) rational   c) hot-tempered   d) unpleasant   (__)

3. When he was elected president, he felt that he had reached the *pinnacle* in his profession, and even while enjoying the many congratulations he received, he dimly realized that there was nothing greater he could aim for.
   a) high point   b) end   c) first step   d) danger point   (__)

4. When the going was particularly rough, they would sit across a table in the dining hall and *commiserate* with each other. Just having someone to talk to made things easier.
   a) sympathize   b) argue   c) tease   d) flirt   (__)

5. Before she was 18, she had the reputation of being a *shrew*. She lost friend after friend, and men rarely dated her a second time.
   a) scholar   b) wise person   c) nervous person   d) scold   (__)

6. After an hour, the *clamor* was more than he could stand. He closed all the windows, pulled the drapes, and retreated to the back of the house but still could not concentrate on his work.
   a) loud noise   b) destruction   c) dance music   d) hatred   (__)

7. The government, he decided, was *putrid*. Everywhere he looked he saw evidence of dishonesty, deception, and dictatorship.
   a) all-powerful   b) logical   c) rotten   d) admired   (__)

8. Their whole program was *stultified* by the fact that Dr. Walker was such a poor speaker. Instead of being aroused to take action against pollution, the listeners stirred restlessly, laughed at Walker's statements, and giggled at the way he presented some of the strongest arguments.
   a) aided   b) made to look foolish   c) helped   d) begun   (__)

9. After months of back-breaking labor, they left Zanesville and *vegetated* at an abandoned camp for almost three weeks. Seth did little more than lie in a hammock most of the day, lazily flicking at an occasional fly. Tod spent most of his time in an old rocking chair watching the leaves fluttering in the soft breeze.
   a) lived like vegetables   b) kept busy   c) cried   d) slept   (__)

ACTIVITY 7-7
Guessing Word Meaning From Context

Instructions: In each of the sentences or paragraphs below there is a made-up word printed in italics. Guess its meaning from the four possibilities listed below each sentence. The first one has been completed as an example.

1. He picked up the heavy *dogjib*, carefully inserted it between the tire and the rim, and after throwing his full weight against the tool managed to break the tight seal. (*C*)
   a) a hammer-like tool   b) a knife   c) a tire-iron   d) a saw

2. His rage was so great, his face became twisted with anger and his cheeks turned *rorten*. (__)
   a) down   b) red   c) frosty   d) scraggly

3. The wild dogs, roaming the forest in packs of twenty or more, savagely *ruggered* the stray sheep, leaving the uneaten carcasses to rot. (__)
   a) killed   b) chased   c) surrounded   d) collected

4. With her only source of income gone, she became *altute*, refusing to buy anything but the most necessary items of food. (__)
   a) lazy   b) panicky   c) greedy   d) shoddy

5. With less than three minutes to play, the quarterback, behind by three points, decided to go to a passing game, using every *garot* he knew to make one more touchdown. (__)
   a) trick   b) play   c) player   d) theory

6. The play would have been more enjoyable if the actors had spoken more *pogily*; it was almost impossible to hear them past the fifth row. (__)
   a) clearly   b) sharply   c) softly   d) loudly

7. Because the speaker for that evening was so *abacent*, the auditorium was completely filled, with many people unable to get in. (__)
   a) boring   b) disliked   c) famous   d) uninformed

8. The lawyer asked the court for an *imperandum* since her client had been involved in an automobile accident and was in a hospital. (__)
   a) judgment   b) indictment   c) conviction   d) delay

9. The sky darkened and the wind came up with increasing *bonhole*; there was no question about it, they were in for a rough one. (__)
   a) force   b) direction   c) humidity   d) clouds

10. Since they were early for their *partilite*, the driver drove slowly, pointing out colorful rock formations on the way. (__)
    a) rising   b) meeting   c) midnight dinner   d) decision

11. Williamson had been arrested as he attempted to pass a microfilm to a known enemy agent. He was charged with *drilltor*, and disappeared from sight for 24 hours. (__)
    a) murder   b) kidnapping   c) a felony   d) spying

ACTIVITY 7-8
OARWET Check

Instructions: Is OARWET becoming a habit? Remember you have to practice a habit to make it automatic. Don't let yourself become too casual in the steps involved. Check the job you did with the Skill Section by seeing how many of these questions you can fill in without rereading the section.

1. What is the chapter title? _____

2. How many sub-heads are there? _____ List as many of them as you can remember, trying to keep them in order.

_____   _____

_____   _____

_____   _____

3. Briefly state the main idea of the Skill Section. _____

_____

4. How many of the quiz question ideas can you remember? Write them down.

_____

_____

_____

The big question is, are you using OARWET with your other subjects?

ACTIVITY 7-9
More On Idea Phrases

Instructions: The short paragraph that follows has been printed with triple spaces between idea phrases. Try to "grasp" each whole phrase with one fixation.

Then he noticed   that Isaac   and that Jebb fellow   were coming out of the cave mouth.   The TV fellow   was talking   to them. What Isaac told   the TV fellow   made him jump   like he had sat on a hot griddle.   He started motioning   to people   to do this   and to do that.   They began swinging   the camera   and things.   They were bringing   one closer   over this way.

—Robert Penn Warren, *The Cave*

91

8
EFFECTIVE SEMI-READING: Skimming and Scanning
Vocabulary Preview

Reading Technique

1. "a *minimum* expenditure" _____
2. "to *delve* deeply into" _____
3. "*orient* your thinking" _____
4. "look for *successive* words" _____
5. "*couched* in different words" _____
6. "quickly *gauges* the interest level" _____
7. "to get a *cursory* overview" _____
8. "*assessing* the contents" _____
9. "*applicability* to your need" _____
10. "in its *entirety*" _____

Reading Selection

1. "the *parched* deserts" _____
2. "Many scientists *wince*" _____
3. "a rash *condemnation*" _____
4. "even *imbecilic* [*people*]" _____
5. "it is *dogma*" _____
6. "could *replicate* outer space" _____
7. "for *feasibility* reasons" _____
8. "*elicited* a polite smile" _____
9. "*boondoggle* of the month" _____
10. "a *riveting* speaker" _____

Comprehension Quiz

Reading Technique

Instructions: Write the letter of the correct answer in the blank provided.

1. The "tools" described in Chapter 8 are:
   a) a part of intensive reading
   b) additions to intensive reading
   c) separate and different techniques
   d) a substitute for taking notes (__)

2. The best procedure to use for studying a chapter in your Sociology textbook is:
   a) careful skimming
   b) thoughtful scanning
   c) intensive reading
   d) none of the above (__)

3. At the beginning of the semester, it would be a good idea to:
   a) skim through the entire book
   b) scan the entire book
   c) read through the entire book
   d) outline the book (__)

4. Skimming used for a lengthy research paper might include:
   a) reading the preface
   b) checking tables of contents
   c) reading the first and last chapter
   d) all of the above (__)

5. OARWET requires the use of:
   a) skimming
   b) scanning
   c) reading
   d) all of the above (__)

6. The reader who finishes a 250-page mystery story in two hours is probably:
   a) scanning the book for the plot
   b) reading intensively
   c) evaluating character development
   d) all of the above (__)

7. Skimming through the alternatives in a multiple-choice test can be dangerous because:
   a) you may miss the correct answer
   b) you may misunderstand the question
   c) there may be two correct answers
   d) all of the above (__)

8. Scanning is a fast method of determining:
   a) the details of a book
   b) the author's slant
   c) the author's style
   d) both b) and c) (__)

9. The *A*sk phase of OARWET calls for:
   a) skimming
   b) scanning
   c) reading
   d) all of the above (__)

10. Together, skimming and scanning, used thoroughly, provide an excellent substitute for:
    a) OARWET
    b) careful reading
    c) both a) and b)
    d) neither a) nor b) (__)

8

Reading Technique
—begin timing—

Effective Semi-Reading:
Skimming and Scanning

More than 35,000 new books were published last year in the United States alone. Chemical Abstracts lists over 6,000 new papers published in that field every week! Your library has several dozen reference books dealing with a paper you're writing. We are being flooded with information as never before in history. It is next to impossible for anyone to read all the new material even in highly specialized fields. Frequently, you need not use intensive reading techniques to handle material which merits less time-consuming methods. Two "semi-reading" procedures frequently can supply your needs with a minimum expenditure of hours and effort.

I. TO READ, OR NOT TO READ

Neither "skimming" nor "scanning" can be classified as reading in the ordinary sense. They are not used to delve deeply into a reading selection, idea by idea, paragraph by paragraph. Each has a worthwhile function; each should be used with that function in mind. To be used effectively, both deserve total concentration. If you are looking for a fast answer to a specific question, *skim*; when you want a general impression of written material, *scan*.

II. THE VALUE OF SKIMMING

Skimming is a process of moving your eyes across a page of print as rapidly as possible looking for one answer to one question. The question may be as abstract as "What is the main theme of this section?" or it may be as concrete as "What is the main product of the coastal areas of Peru?" In either case, *you know in advance what you are looking for*, and you orient your thinking—and your eye movements—toward finding a precise answer. Skimming is of great value in research; it can make possible the utilization of a large number of references in a short period of time. You skim in other situations: when you look for a telephone number, a football score, the closing price of a particular stock.

III. POINTERS ON HOW TO SKIM

Successful skimming calls for instant analysis of the given question. Should the problem involve time, dates, or quantity, look for numbers. Numerals stand out in print. If the question calls for the name of an individual, look for successive words starting with capital letters. Be aware of word length and pointer-words—"What is the *most* prominent *characteristic* of . . ?" Long words are easier to spot; qualifying words are a "must"!

Consider how much skimming you do for a long research project. You skim through the card index at the library for your selection of books; you skim through the table of contents, and again through the important chapters. If there are subheads, you skim those, and, finally, you skim the selected pages and paragraphs for the desired answer.

Good skimming calls for concentration and an alert mind. More often than not, the answer will be couched in words different from those used in the question. For example, "Where do we find the largest quantities of iron ore in the United States:" The answer might be in a paragraph which reads ". . . the heaviest concentrations of hematite are located in. . . ."

You may have to make inferences in order to locate a significant fact. Question: "What impact on our economy will be created by increased enrollment at colleges?" The paragraph which contains the answer reads ". . . in recent years, post-high school education in the United States has accounted for nearly one-fourth of the growth in our gross national product."

Effective skimming requires practice. You will find it worth the effort.   c

IV. THE IMPORTANCE OF SCANNING

Scanning is a procedure that you use every day. Consider what happens when you pick up your newspaper. Your eyes flit from one headline to the next, while your brain quickly gauges the interest level of each article. You   c
reject one column, whip through all or part of another, slow down and read a third carefully. You have been scanning the page of newsprint, headline by headline. You probably scanned that article you "sampled" lightly. Scanning,   b
then, is a semi-reading technique that gives you a quick picture of a headline, a "lead" paragraph, an article, a chapter—or a book. It is used to get a cursory overview of the content, a survey of the material included, an indication of the style.

The word "overview" was used advisedly, because scanning is the basis for   b
the first step in OARWET. It is merely an extension of the Overview procedure. (And when you look for answers, you "skim"—Ask.)

You have used scanning in other ways. You stop at the paperback book counter at the drug store looking for an interesting item. Your eye roves over dozens of titles. A few attract your interest, and you leaf through them   d
rapidly, assessing the contents. If one book is of sufficient interest, you buy it. Two scanning activities here: the selection of a limited number of books, and your speedy evaluation of them. Or you may zip through a magazine, choosing certain articles of interest, eliminating others. You scan the crowd at a basketball game looking for friends. (If you are looking specifically for Jo   a
Anne or Bob, you are skimming, not scanning!)

Scanning of book material closely parallels the steps of Overview. Note the title, the author, and—increasingly important in our fast-moving society—the date of publication. You examine the table of contents in its entirety, not searching out a particular subject as you do when skimming. Your aim is to get an over-all picture of the book. Once you have your frame of reference,   c
you leaf through, "tasting" each chapter, perhaps even several paragraphs in areas of special interest to you. You judge the basic ideas, the style, the "slant" of the author, the summary paragraphs. You have not studied the book—but you have gained a general impression of it, a feeling of its worth, and its applicability to your particular need.   d

Skimming and scanning are not reading; they are invaluable tools in the learning process. Tool One, skimming, provides answers to questions in the fastest possible way. Tool Two, scanning, gives you a broad picture of the material, its structure, and an indication of its value. They are useful tools; they are not substitutes for reading. a
Used intelligently, they save time and increase efficiency.

—end timing—   (min___sec___)

d

ACTIVITY 8-1
Applying the Technique

Instructions:

I. Underline the *key words* in each of the five questions below that you would use as a guide when skimming for answers.

  1. What is the key step in the production of high-quality steel?
  2. Who was the commanding officer of the British forces in the Crimean War?
  3. What is the name of the senior officer in the U.S. Embassy at New Delhi?
  4. What was the outstanding contribution of the Hittites?
  5. What was the increase in the Gross National Product in the last decade?

II. Skim for the answers to the following questions covering pages 94 and 95. Try to cover the entire page with one broad sweep of the eyes. *Do not read!*

  6. Find the word "orient" on page 94.
  7. In what paragraph on the same page is the phrase "time-consuming" used?
  8. What clause states the basic theme of skimming? Why was it easy to find?
  9. In what section is an example of skimming for a specific fact given?
  10. In what section would you expect to find aids for efficient skimming?

III. Skim for answers to the questions in italics above each paragraph:

  1. *Why were field guns useless?*
  In Cairo, the authorities promised gold, rifles, mules, more machine-guns and mountain guns; but the last of these, of course, we never got. The gun question was an eternal torment. Because of the hilly, trackless country, field guns were no use to us; and the British Army had no mountain guns except the Indian ten-pounder which was serviceable only against bows and arrows.

  2. *What is the financial return for each year spent in college?*
  For the student, college offers many personal satisfactions and rewards. While students forego income earned while attending school, there is the promise of substantial remuneration later. Earnings of college graduates at present average roughly $140,000 more over a lifetime than the amount earned by persons who only completed high school—the equivalent of about $35,000 in added income for every year that a person attends college!

  3. *What might cause serious economic problems?*
  As a nation we are already so rich that consumers are under no pressure of immediate necessity to purchase a very large share—perhaps as much as 40 percent—of what is produced, and the pressure will get progressively less in the years ahead. But if consumers exercise their options not to buy a large share of what is produced, a great depression is not far behind.

IV. You have already scanned and skimmed this chapter in the *O*verview and *A*sk phases. For the rest of the chapters, make a practice of *underlining key ideas as you use OARWET.*

ACTIVITY 8-2
Outline: Effective Semi-Reading

Main Idea: _____

_____

I. Two semi-reading techniques

* A. _____

* B. _____

II. _____

   A. _____

   B. _____

III. _____

   A. _____

   B. Look for capital letters—easy spotting of names, places

   C. _____

   D. _____

   E. _____

IV. _____

   A. _____

   B. Frequently used with newspapers, magazines

   C. _____

   D. _____

ACTIVITY 8-3
Vocabulary Exercises

Reading Technique

Instructions: Write the letter of the correct answer in the blank provided.

1. To believe something in its *entirety* is to
   a) be skeptical of some of it.   (__)
   b) accept it as a whole.
   c) believe its intent, not its words.
2. If a fact has *applicability* to a certain problem, it
   a) will help solve it.   b) has no suitability.   c) is invalid.   (__)
3. To *assess* your job skills,
   a) measure them.   b) devaluate them.   c) discard them.   (__)
4. A *cursory* reading is effective for
   a) judging the quality of details.   (__)
   b) deciding whether or not to buy a book.
   c) evaluating the author's total point of view.
5. A successful student best *gauges* the value of a course to herself by
   a) asking questions of friends.   (__)
   b) making an educated guess.
   c) studying the description in the catalog.
6. To *orient* oneself in a foreign land, one should
   a) look for its defects.   (__)
   b) study its language and customs.
   c) compare it disparagingly with his own.
7. An insult *couched* in pleasant words is
   a) indirect.   b) false.   c) direct.   (__)
8. *Delving* into a new subject means
   a) discarding it.   b) depleting it.   c) digging into it.   (__)
9. "*Successive* stages of development" indicates
   a) random sampling.   (__)
   b) following in sequence.
   c) successful mastery.
10. Taxpayers are angry at excessive *expenditures*
   a) in government.   b) by children.   c) of musicians.

Reading Selection

Instructions: Write the letter of the matching word in the blank provided.

a) feasibility   1. repeat, duplicate   (__)
b) elicited   2. attracting and holding completely   (__)
c) parched   3. shrink back or away from   (__)
d) boondoggle   4. capability of being done   (__)
e) riveting   5. drew forth, brought out   (__)
f) replicate   6. like a fool   (__)
g) imbecilic   7. a put-down; negative criticism   (__)
h) condemnation   8. useless or wasteful activity   (__)
i) wince   9. definite point of view of authorities   (__)
j) dogma   10. dry   (__)

8

Comprehension Quiz

Reading Selection

Instructions: Write the letter of the correct answer in the blank provided.

1. The primary intent of this article is:
   a) scientists are unrealistic
   b) Senator Proxmire is unfair
   c) "far-out" ideas may work
   d) about a N.Y. to L.A. tunnel
   (___)

2. Coastal Libya could be paved with asphalt to:
   a) provide water to deserts
   b) improve parking
   c) speed transportation
   d) aid unemployment
   (___)

3. A vacuum tunnel from New York to Los Angeles would:
   a) prevent earthquakes
   b) require impossible engineering
   c) involve political problems
   d) eliminate jet lag
   (___)

4. Soviet scientists are considering reversing rivers to:
   a) refill the Caspian Sea
   b) provide irrigation
   c) aid transportation
   d) both (a) and (b)
   (___)

5. Scientists today are reluctant to ridicule "far-out" proposals because:
   a) it violates professional ethics
   b) Senator Proxmire will
   c) they're too expensive
   d) they can work
   (___)

6. An item today which was once considered far-out is:
   a) the transistor
   b) the helicopter
   c) the wrist radio
   d) all of these
   (___)

7. The idea of a solar-energy-collecting satellite is now:
   a) out of the question
   b) too expensive
   c) given serious consideration
   d) laughed at
   (___)

8. The idea for the train tunnel occurred to Salter while working on:
   a) a tank for the RAND Corp.
   b) satellites and ballistics
   c) political problems
   d) funding problems
   (___)

9. The major worries of "fringe thinkers" are:
   a) lack of "breakthroughs"
   b) public short-sightedness
   c) political obstacles
   d) both (b) and (c)
   (___)

10. An example of "basic research" is a:
    a) high-capacity storage battery
    b) new sub-atomic particle
    c) pollution-free engine
    d) laser rifle
    (___)

8

Reading Selection

SCIENCE NO BARRIER TO 'FAR-OUT' IDEAS

by **Joanne Omang**, *The Washington Post*   (from *The Los Angeles Times*, July 19, 1978)

—begin timing—

Here's an idea. Pave part of coastal Libya with asphalt so that air from the sea will be heated as it passes over, rising to dump its moisture on the parched deserts of the Sudan. Every acre of asphalt will result in 30 inches of rain a year for two acres inland.

Here's another idea. Drill a tunnel from New York to Los Angeles and run a train through it at 6,000 miles per hour so that a coast-to-coast trip can be made in about 45 minutes. The train will run in a vacuum and be driven by electromagnetic pulses.

How about this one? Most of the Soviet Union's Siberian rivers flow into the Arctic Ocean, leaving little water for irrigation; so reverse the flow of one of those rivers and refill the dying Caspian Sea.

These ideas and many others that sound just as harebrained were proposed by serious, respected scientists. They have thoughtful defenders and are the subject of careful study by governments and in learned journals.

* * *

Almost no proposal, no matter how wild, is rejected out of hand nowadays. Too many scientists wince to recall the ideas that were ridiculed when first offered but turned into earth satellites, space travel, Mars landing and color television—and nobody wants to be caught with a rash condemnation showing.

Advances in knowledge apparently have made it boring for scientists to do only the difficult, so projects that laymen regard as impossible impractical or even imbecilic are sought. It is at the level of getting the project funded that reality sets in.

"I remember that jet planes, transistors, helicopters and a radio small enough to wear on your wrist were very far-out ideas in the 20s and 30s," said Frank Drake, director of the National Astronautics and Ionosphere Center at the Cornell University Research Institute. "If a thing is physically possible, and if it's cost-effective at some stage, then no matter how lunatic it seems, it often comes to pass."

That sequence has occurred so often in science that it is dogma, offering continual hope and encouragement to the fertile imaginations of the far-out thinkers.

"Yes, I guess I have always been on the fringe," said Robert M. Salter, father of the concept of an underground bullet train and senior physical scientist for advanced programs at the Rand Corp. think tank in Santa Monica.

The idea for the tunnel came to him, he said, during his work on the space program about 20 years ago.

"We were thinking about satellites and ballistic systems and how they could be used for transportation" he said. "It became apparent that if you could just replicate outer space in a tunnel underground, you could have your cake and eat it, too."

The technical difficulties of creating and then maintaining a coast-to-coast vacuum tube, given earthquakes and rivers and a thousand other things, can be met through competent engineering, Salter said. He is more worried about the political problems of hooking up existing urban subway systems and raising the $250 billion he thinks the project will cost.

100

He shares such a worry with most of the fringe thinkers: Their projects involve no scientific breakthroughs but only sophisticated engineering. The obstacles, they say, are political or personal or, in some cases, simple short-sightedness on the part of the public.

"Only a minority of projects make no sense for technical or scientific reason, things like perpetual-motion machines," said Jerome Wiesner, president of the Massachusetts Institute of Technology and onetime science adviser to several U.S. presidents.

* * *

An idea now becoming respectable is the notion of building massive solar energy collectors in outer space and beaming electricity back to earth. Peter Glaser, a consultant with Arthur D. Little, Inc., proposed the solar satellite a decade ago, but that was before the oil embargo when energy was far cheaper. The idea, Glaser recalled recently, "elicited a polite smile and total disbelief." **c**

Then the public interest in funding space projects began to flag after the moon landings and aerospace industry began to get hungry. Energy prices skyrocketed and the long-planned space shuttle needed something further to justify its existence. As is often the case in this process, other scientists joined the fray. **a** **c**

Princeton physicist Gerard K. O'Neill came up with the refinement of having colonies of workers live in space and build the satellites from moon and asteroid materials instead of hauling the parts up from earth. A riveting speaker, O'Neill toured the campuses and helped to popularize the basic idea. Now "Sunsat" has a board of directors that reads like a who's who of the aerospace industry and has won a $25 million study grant from Congress. Glaser estimates the first satellite would cost $60 billion, and many physicists expect it to be in orbit in about 15 years. **d** **d**

* * *

A sure sign that a project has merit, more than one scientist has suggested, is that it wins the Golden Fleece award of Sen. William Proxmire (D-Wis.). The senator's boondoggle-of-the-month trophy recently went to NASA's Jet Propulsion Laboratory in Pasadena for its plan to spend up to $15 million over seven years to try to find intelligent life in outer space. **d**

* * *

The experts draw a careful line between far-out projects and far far-out research. **b**

"Going to the moon was a trivial step from a scientific point of view, although it was significant technically," said National Science Foundation director Richard C. Atkinson. "telling scientists to forget basic research and work on things of practical value is the great danger of our time. . . . If there had been a war on polio in the '20s or '30s, we'd have ended up engineering the most elegant and beautifully running iron lungs one could imagine." **b**

Drake of the Cornell Institute said Proxmire's judgment of the search for life in space was "quite faulty." If the entire project cost up to $20 billion, as was likely, he said, "that would still be the cost of one good movie for every person on earth and certainly a lot more exciting." **d**

(+50)   —end timing—   (min__sec__) **a**

ACTIVITY 8-4
Summarizing

Instructions: Write a one-paragraph summary of the Reading Selection.

_____

_____

_____

_____

_____

_____

_____

_____

ACTIVITY 8-5
Working with Affixes and Roots

Instructions: For each of the prefixes or roots given below, write two words of which they are a part. Then write a short definition of the word. Use a dictionary only when necessary. Two samples have been completed for you.

ab- (from)

1. *abhor*, *shrink from*
2. _____, _____

ad- (to)

1. _____, _____
2. *adhere*, *stick to*

circum- (around)

1. _____, _____
2. _____, _____

com- (with, together)

1. _____, _____
2. _____, _____

de- (from)

1. _____, _____
2. _____, _____

dis- (apart)

1. _____, _____
2. _____, _____

ACTIVITY 8-6
Main Ideas and Sentence Relationships

Instructions: First read the paragraph below and decide which of the sentences states the main idea. Then, examine the other sentences and decide how they relate to the main idea. In each of the four statements below the paragraph, fill in the blanks with MI if it contains the main idea, N if it is too narrow, B if it is too broad, or NS if it is incorrect or not stated. (Note: Any of the abbreviations can be used more than once except MI.)

> This goes to the heart of the problem of what news is. If every editor decided to offer only news that he could prove was true, unslanted, and properly balanced, he could scarcely claim perfection for his daily news report. For one thing, he would have to seriously consider J. Montgomery Curtis's famous unpublished lead: "While 1286 students of Metropolitan High School pursued their studies quietly this morning, another student murdered the principal in his office." For another, he would have to use the sickening practice, found today in television as well as in the press, of finding a favorable quote to balance an unfavorable one in every news account.
>
> —adapted from John Hohenberg,
> *The News Media: A Journalist Looks at His Profession*

1. The best editor could not turn out a paper that was true, unslanted and balanced, and would not want to.   (__)
2. Television and newspapers both try to balance news.   (__)
3. Newspaper editors are and should be prejudiced.   (__)
4. The quotation about the principal states the main idea.   (__)

Follow the same instructions for this paragraph.

> Big business is thus a basic excuse for big unions and big government. It is true that the extent and evils of big business are usually enormously exaggerated, especially with reference to labor and agriculture, and that more often than not these evils are merely a soapbox for shabby policies elsewhere. To this large extent there is need for wide education of the public on how small a part of the economy is controlled by big business. But in the light of the widespread monopolistic practices—our first criticism of bigness—it is impossible to tell the public that its fears of bigness are without basis. We have no right to ask public opinion to steer away from big unions and big government—and toward big business.
>
> —adapted from George J. Stigler, "The Case Against Big Business," *Fortune*

1. Big business is a cause for big unions and big government.   (__)
2. Fear of big business is exaggerated.   (__)
3. People must be made aware of problems of all three "bigs."   (__)
4. The public needs to be educated.   (__)

ACTIVITY 8-7
Guessing Word Meaning From Context

Instructions: The words in italics are words actually used in sentences or paragraphs from current textbooks. Choose the correct definition from the words or phrases listed under each question, guessing when necessary.

1. An American mother who went to live in Paris was very proud of her two *robust* sons. A French neighbor was helpful and friendly, but one day she confided to the American mother that her two sons looked much like peasants. After a term in French schools, however, the American boys were so pale and tired from nightly homework that their mother was anxious. Just at this time the Frenchwoman congratulated her neighbor on the boys' development and stated that they now looked more like scholars.

   —adapted from Edmund J. Kind, *Other Schools and Ours*

   a) quiet   b) unhealthy   c) red-faced   d) healthy   (__)

2. There is much to be learned about the process of economic growth and the obstacles that lie in its path. Growth processes as such should be *amenable* to economic analysis, but many of the factors that hold back economic developments are outside the *province* of economics proper, lying rather in the fields of political science, sociology, and psychology.

   —Richard H. Leftwich, *An Introduction to Economic Thinking*

   amenable: a) thankful   c) capable of being tested   (__)
               b) male-like   d) affected by

   province: a) proper business or scope   c) provable   (__)
              b) geographical area   d) health

3. Out of their concern for Sally, the parents decided to make a *concerted* effort to give her the kind and amount of attention they now felt she needed. They began to be very careful to divide their attention equally between the babies when they both were present. Since Paul went to sleep more readily, after he was asleep they would give Sally a little extra attention and fondling.

   —Leland H. Stott, *Child Development*

   a) singing   c) false
   b) mutually agreed upon   d) casual   (__)

4. In short, a teacher such as Geoffrey, who had produced a workable *equilibrium* with his children, saw this shift in classes as a major frustration. All the efforts to make the group stable must be started again. Further complications exist, for Geoffrey will have a younger group than he has had before, and he will have a split-level group that in itself presents additional problems.

   —L. M. Smith, W. Geoffrey, *The Complexities of an Urban Classroom*

   a) classroom   b) method   c) disgust   d) balance   (__)

ACTIVITY 8-8
Multi-Paragraph Skimming

Instructions: Read the questions below carefully. *Do not read the paragraphs!* Underline the key words in the questions as you read through them. *Then* skim the paragraphs for answers as rapidly as you can. Try to find the answers in less than 30 seconds.

1. Who had had too much to drink? _____

2. Who complained violently? _____

3. What about? _____

4. To whom? _____

5. What seemed to be his job? (from 4) _____

6. Who needed his help? _____

7. In what room? _____

In contrast to his Duchess, the Duke was untidily dressed, in a creased white shirt and the trousers of a tuxedo. Without thinking, Peter McDermott's eyes sought the tell-tale stain where Natchez, in the Duchess's words, had "poured shrimp Creole over my husband." He found it, though it was barely visible—a tiny spot which a valet could have removed instantly. Behind the Duke, in the spacious living room a television set was turned on.

The Duke's face seemed flushed, and more lined than some of his recent photographs showed. He held a glass in his hand and when he spoke his voice was blurry. "Oh, beg pardon." Then, to the Duchess: "I say, old girl. Must have left my cigarettes in the car."

She responded sharply, "I'll bring some." There was a curt dismissal in her voice and with a nod the Duke turned back into the living room. It was a curious, uncomfortable scene and for some reason it had heightened the Duchess's anger.

Turning to Peter, she snapped, "I insist on a full report being made to Mr. Trent, and you may inform him that I expect a personal apology."

Still puzzled, Peter went out as the suite door closed firmly behind him.

But he was allowed no more time for analyzing. In the corridor outside, the bellboy who had accompanied Christine to the fourteenth floor was waiting. "Mr. McDermott," he said urgently, "Miss Francis wants you in 1439, and please hurry!"

—adapted from Arthur Hailey, *Hotel*

9
TAKING TESTS SUCCESSFULLY
Vocabulary Preview

Reading Technique

1. "To *carouse* the night before" _____

2. "is to *court* disaster" _____

3. "that *generates* good grades" _____

4. "A *defeatist* attitude" _____

5. "the *idiosyncrasies* of the instructor" _____

6. "In *essence*" _____

7. "a process of *incorporating* ideas" _____

8. "logical, *sequential* answer" _____

9. "to *transpose* numbers" _____

10. "go back to the *dubious* ones" _____

Reading Selection

1. "[the YWCA] *heeded* any statement" _____

2. "a self-*inflicted* financial problem" _____

3. "should *refrain* from contributing" _____

4. "worthwhile movements *embroil* themselves" _____

5. "had the *temerity* to take a position" _____

6. "effort to *dissuade* workers from contributing" _____

7. "raises a *lament* about" _____

8. "would become strained and *insipid*" _____

9. "our national *discourse*" _____

10. "are *demeaning* their cause" _____

Comprehension Quiz

Reading Technique

Instructions: Write the letter of the correct answer in the blank provided.

1. Good test grades depend solely on:
   a) intelligence   c) good notes   (__)
   b) cramming   d) none of the above

2. OARWET is mentioned in this chapter as:
   a) an instructor check   c) a physiological   (__)
                                         conditioner
   b) an organized review   d) all of the above
      approach

3. Your physical condition is directly related to:
   a) your success in test-taking   c) both (a) and (b)   (__)
   b) your ability to reason   d) neither (a) nor (b)

4. Knowing as much as possible about a forthcoming test will:
   a) minimize surprise effects   c) cancel the need for   (__)
                                         planning
   b) anger the instructor   d) eliminate the need for
                                         study

5. Test scores are frequently low because the student:
   a) failed to read the   c) was overcome by   (__)
      directions   test-tension
   b) was in poor physical   d) all of the above
      shape

6. An instructor grading an essay test ignores:
   a) grammar errors   c) poor handwriting   (__)
   b) spelling errors   d) none of the above

7. In an objective test, graded on a right-minus-wrong basis, your chances of guessing correctly on a true-false question are:
   a) at least one out of four   c) not worth taking   (__)
   b) good, if a curve is used   d) cannot be determined

8. Which is the best answer to this question in a history test? "The Louisiana Purchase was completed":
   a) in 1805   c) in 1809   (__)
   b) early in the 19th century   d) during the presidency of
                                         Madison

9. "Fighting through" to an answer to a tough multiple-choice question may result in:
   a) an increase of tension   c) a misconception of   (__)
                                         the question
   b) a dangerous loss of time   d) all of the above

10. A good objective test:
    a) is concerned only with   c) requires less preparation   (__)
       factual information   than an essay-type test
    b) can include questions   d) all of the above
       calling for inferences

9

Reading Technique
—begin timing—

Taking Tests Successfully

As long as grade averages are a major consideration in the educational process, successful test-taking deserves consideration. When it comes to examinations, there is little doubt that some students fare much better than others. There are a number of factors which contribute to this: psychological, physiological, and, sometimes, just plain logical!

I. GET THAT OARWET AGAIN

The logical way to prepare for an examination is to use an organized approach; here, again, we call on OARWET. Because OARWET is pointed toward mastery of factual material, it establishes a basis for review: *A*sk critical quesitons; *W*rite, review notes; *O*verview and *E*valuate, a guide to the review of main and secondary ideas. The class examination, then, becomes a reinforcement of the *T*est step. An organized approach is the solution.

II. CONDITIONING: PHYSIOLOGICAL AND PSYCHOLOGICAL

To carouse the night before an important test is to court disaster, nor will you be at your best on Monday after a weekend on the ski trails. What is equally significant and more frequently overlooked is the fact that cramming until two in the morning before facing a final exam (with burning eyes and exhausted body) can be fatal. Your physical condition affects your test-taking ability.

For psychological reasons, know beforehand as much as possible about the test. Have no hesitation in asking the instructor about the kind of examination he or she plans to give. Do everything you can to minimize surprise aspects. (If you have a history of extraordinary test-tension, a few minutes spent with your doctor might be of value. The tranquilizer he or she might prescribe could be the answer. Don't experiment with pills on your own: they might put you to sleep!)

Your psychological attitude is critical when you walk into the examination room. Confidence in your knowledge of the material establishes a "plus-factor" that generates good grades. A defeatist attitude has the opposite effect.

When the exam begins, the most important first step is to *read the instructions*! If they are complicated, outline each specific step on a piece of scrap paper so that you are sure you know exactly how to proceed. More good grades are lost by failure to follow directions than by lack of information. How many times have you heard, post-exam, "Oh, *that* was what he wanted!"

Don't be thrown by "blanking out" on one particular question. Frequently, just the activity of dealing with other questions whose answers you do know will give you the clue to handling the "unanswerable" ones.

In general, getting set for an exam includes more than study. Aim for sound physical and mental conditioning before you step into the classroom.

III. EVALUATING THE COURSE: GOALS, CONTENTS (AND THE INSTRUCTOR)

Preparation for final exams should start the first day of the course, and should be kept current throughout the semester. You must be continually conscious of three all-important factors: the goals of the course; the content, and its application to those goals; the idiosyncrasies of the instructor (his or her particular interests and slants used to arrive at the desired conclusions). An American History course, for example, might include as one major aim "An understanding of the atmosphere and events which led to the Civil War." Content items contributing to this understanding might be: "The economics of slavery" or "Conflicts between state and federal control" or "Agriculture versus industry." Your instructor might have emphasized one of these.

In essence, you have the outline of the material you should know, and have determined relationships and provided structure. Reviewing then becomes a process of incorporating basic ideas into main themes through the use of your notes and questions.

d

Add to this structure the attitudes and interests emphasized by the instructor. Evaluate her testing methods: does she favor questions on broad principles or does she expect knowledge of fine details? Are his questions straightforward or must you look for undercurrents of secondary meanings?

b

IV. THE ESSAY TEST: HOW TO PLAN IT

c

An essay test demands planning. Divide the time for the exam by the number of questions to be answered—set up a schedule and stick to it! In order to arrive at logical, sequential answers, it is highly advisable to outline them in advance. It is even more important to provide time after the paper has been completed to review what you have written. It is only too easy, for example, to transpose numbers—1864, a correct date, may become 1846: two points off! You may catch innumerable spelling and grammar errors—and even find that you cannot read your own writing!

a

Set aside about 25 percent of your allotted time to plan, outline, and review. The result should help to make your paper logical, readable, and grammatical.

d

V. THE OBJECTIVE TEST: HOW TO MAKE THE MOST OF IT

d

If the exam is of the objective type, start by carefully scanning the entire test, noting any differences in point value of questions. Look carefully for directions such as "Do not guess" (don't!) and for the number of questions to be completed. Read true-false and multiple-choice questions carefully, first answering those you know as rapidly as possible and circling the numbers of those which require second thought. Read every alternative in the multiple-choices; the second may be right; the fourth "righter." Question 26 may clarify Question 12. Don't read too much *into* a question.

c

After you have completed all the "sure" questions, go back to the ones you're dubious about. Usually, your first reaction to the possible answer is the better one. Don't change it unless you have a solid reason for doing so. Cross out answers chosen in "matching" questions so that you will not re-read them for the remaining selections.

b

Doing well on exams is the result of organization, and of being physically and psychologically prepared. Be well rested. Know as much as possible about the test in advance in order to minimize tension. Use OARWET as a guide to preparation; evaluate the course goals and contents with special attention to the instructor's emphasis. In essay tests, plan time for outlining and reviewing your answers, in objective tests for intensive reading of the questions, all answers. Above all, READ THE INSTRUCTIONS!

d

b

—end timing—   (min___sec___)

ACTIVITY 9-1
Applying the Technique

Plan for final examinations in the subjects you are taking at the present time. Apply the survey which follows to each of your courses. You can really make a procedure like this work for you. It will eliminate worries about unknown factors, dispose of unpleasant surprises, minimize the need for last-minute cramming and, in many cases, do away with examination "jitters." Select one class and complete this form.

Subject_____ Instructor _____ Sem. hrs. _____

   I. Course analysis:

      A. Major goals: *Text Chapters*   *Notebook Pages*

          1. _____   _____   _____

          2. _____   _____   _____

          3. _____   _____   _____

          4. _____   _____   _____

          5. _____   _____   _____

      B. Additional content analysis: This should include any special projects, field trips, film analyses, research papers, book reviews, and so forth. *Apply these to the specific goals listed above.*

  II. Analysis of instructor:

      A. Have his or her exams been based on major themes _____? or specific details _____?

      B. Can his questions be taken at face value _____? or do you have to look deeper _____?

      C. Has the instructor spent extended lengths of time on any special period or personality _____? You must weigh your study time accordingly.

 III. Nature of final examination:

      A. *Essay:* Number of questions _____? Time allotted _____? All questions of equal value _____?

      B. *Objective:* Number of true-false questions _____? Multiple-choice _____? Matching _____? Completion _____? Right-minus-wrong _____? Equal point values _____?
From your experience with this instructor, will the questions be straight fact _____? or inference _____? or both _____?

      C. Any special preparation needed?

 IV. On the basis of the above analyses, how many hours do you think should be allocated to a thorough review, including the use of OARWET questions and notes _____? How many weeks left in the term _____? How many hours would you spend per week *now* in addition to your regular assignments for this subject _____?

ACTIVITY 9-2
Outline: Taking Tests Successfully

Main Idea: _____

_____

I. Making OARWET pay off
   A. _____
   B. _____
   C. _____

II. _____
   A. _____
   B. _____
   C. Minimize tension.
   D. Really READ THE INSTRUCTIONS.
   E. _____

III. _____

   _____

   _____
   C. _____

IV. _____
   A. _____

   _____
   C. Allow 25% of time for planning and reviewing answers.

V. _____
   A. _____
      1. _____
      2. *watch for special instructions!* _____
   B. _____
   C. _____
   D. _____
   E. _____

ACTIVITY 9-3
Vocabulary Exercises

Reading Technique

Instructions: Write the letter of the matching word in the blank provided.

a) defeatist	1. drinks and parties freely	(__)
b) idiosyncrasies	2. causes to be	(__)
c) generates	3. personal oddities	(__)
d) carouses	4. to tempt or invite	(__)
e) sequential	5. interchange	(__)
f) transpose	6. questionable	(__)
g) court (disaster)	7. following in order of time	(__)
h) essence	8. real nature of thing	(__)
i) dubious	9. accepts failure as inevitable	(__)
j) incorporates	10. merges	(__)

Reading Selection

Instructions: Substitute for the italicized words and phrases the correct word from the list below. (The form of the word as used in the sentence may not be the same as the one in the list.) Write the letter of the correct word in the blank provided.

a) insipid	f) inflicted
b) dissuade	g) refrain
c) heeded	h) temerity
d) lament	i) embroil
e) demeaning	j) discourse

1. The boring guest made many *dull, uninteresting* remarks. (__)
2. The unhappy couple often stated their *expressed sorrow* about marriage. (__)
3. "I don't want to get *involved!*" is heard too often. (__)
4. *Curb* yourself from eating unhealthy food. (__)
5. We *pay attention to* an expert's advice. (__)
6. *To impose* suffering seems to make criminals happy. (__)
7. *Lowering the dignity* of an employee is not a good company policy. (__)
8. The stateman's *speech* was wise but lengthy. (__)
9. Some shy people at times express unexpected *boldness*. (__)
10. Swatting at an angry bee will not help to *stop* it from stinging. (__)

Comprehension Quiz

Reading Selection

Instructions: Write the letter of the correct answer in the blank provided.

1. The main point either suggested or discussed in these articles is:
   a) all guns should be registered
   b) outlawing handguns
   c) *The American Rifleman* vs. the YWCA
   d) blackmail by editorials   (__)

2. *The American Rifleman* editorial argues that the YWCA:
   a) was prejudiced on the gun-control issue
   b) was not informed about gun owners' views
   c) did not properly inform its members before voting
   d) squeezed through a vote opposing the position of the NRA   (__)

3. Because of the YWCA vote, the NRA magazine states that members should:
   a) boycott the YWCA
   b) resign from the YWCA
   c) view the YWCA as un-American
   d) boycott community fund drives   (__)

4. The National Rifle Association position on "debatable causes" is:
   a) organizations should avoid them
   b) opposition to the NRA position is risky
   c) NRA groups should act together
   d) all of the above   (__)

5. *The Washington Post* opposes the NRA editorial because the *Post*:
   a) opposes gun control
   b) agrees with the YWCA
   c) favors gun control
   d) none of the above   (__)

6. The *Post* editorial points out that the YWCA position:
   a) favors banning all handguns
   b) shouldn't have been made public
   c) accepts handguns for worthy purposes
   d) is outside of its field   (__)

7. The *Post* notes that in the past, the YWCA has helped effectively in:
   a) desegregation
   b) dubious causes
   c) public health issues
   d) un-American activities   (__)

8. "Worthwhile movements," says the *Post*, should:
   a) avoid debatable issues
   b) participate in national questions
   c) remain neutral publicly
   d) limit their opinions   (__)

9. The NRA position, says the *Post*:
   a) is justified
   b) is logical in today's society
   c) smacks of blackmail and thought control
   d) all of the above   (__)

10. A member of NRA or its associated groups should:
    a) evaluate the YWCA position
    b) withdraw support from the YWCA
    c) follow the NRA's suggestion
    d) reject the United Way appeal   (__)

9

Reading Selection

—begin timing—

SAY GOODBYE TO THE "Y"?

(from *The American Rifleman*, June, 1973)

Sadly we must report that the national YWCA has thrown its full feminine weight behind the movement to register firearms and even ammunition, license all gun owners and buyers, and ban privately-owned handguns. The YWCA's National Delegate Assembly approved those steps in March at San Diego, California, by what a spokesman described as an "overwhelming" vote.

Gun owners may feel overwhelmed in another sense. When any large national organization of high stated purpose takes a stand on a controversial issue such as this, it would appear that they would first hear and consider both sides of the question. There is nothing to indicate that the YWCA sought or heeded any statement of the gun owners' views. How and why, then, did the YWCA act as it did?

Mrs. Peter Flemming, of Brooklyn, New York, chairman of the YWCA Public Policy Committee, explained to *The American Rifleman* that the resolution was drafted in response to numerous inquiries from across the country on whether the YWCA had adopted a position on gun control. It had not. So Mrs. Flemming drafted the resolution. The National Board of the YWCA, according to YWCA National Executive Director Edith Lerrigo, sent copies of the resolution and a background position paper to all YWCA chapters two months before the San Diego meeting. At the meeting, the resolution was passed substantially as it was drafted.

So the anti-gun forces now have another large national organization that they can quote as being "strongly opposed" to existing firearms ownership. What the YWCA has is another question. It may turn out to be a self-inflicted financial problem. The Sportsmen's Alliance of Michigan, a highly active and vocal organization of gun owners, has already expressed the view that its members should refrain from contributing to community drives whose proceeds go in part to support the YWCA. Others may follow suit.

This is not the first time that a national organization supposedly dedicated to some high, clear purpose has taken a sudden hard poke at gun ownership. It is time that all such organizations realize that while they are unquestionably free to express themselves as they please, so are the targets of their political action.

It is unfortunate to see worthwhile movements embroil themselves in debatable causes that can only cost them their friends.

GUNS AND BLACKMAIL

(from *The Washington Post*, July 6, 1973)

Some of the nation's riflemen are up in arms, so to speak, over something that the Young Women's Christian Association, of all organizations, has done. It seems that at its national convention in San Diego this year, the YWCA had the temerity to take a position regarding the control of the flow of firearms in this society. As a result, the National Rifle Association, through its journal, *The Americal Rifleman*, the Sportsmen's Alliance of Michigan and other gun-loving groups around the country have come out swinging.

Now, what the YWCA did in this instance is not the main point, although this newspaper happens to agree generally with the stand the organization took. Their resolution supports federal legislation licensing all gun purchasers, users and owners, the registration of all firearms—including ammunition—and "the banning of all handguns not used for such purposes as law enforcement, military and licensed guard use, sporting shooting and hunting." That is very close to the position we have long urged upon the Congress and we are pleased to see this major national organization join in the effort to check the unsafe flow of guns through America.

But a more significant point about all of this is that the organizations of sportsmen seem to have forgotten how to play fair, at least in the arena of **d** public debate on major issues in this country. The Sportsmen's Alliance of Michigan has urged its members to withhold financial support from United Way organizations which support, among other organizations, their local YWCAs. There has also been such a strong effort to dissuade industrial workers in large plants from contributing to united community fund-raising **b** efforts which support the YWCA that the AFL-CIO has been moved to issue a biting counterattack against "the gun lobby." Other sporting groups around the nation have followed the lead of their Michigan brethren.

Then, in its June issue, *The American Rifleman* ran an editorial attacking the YWCA. In the course of the editorial, the magazine made it appear that the YWCA position would bar the use of handguns even for sport shooting and **d** hunting—a position the organization clearly did not take. There follows a description of the Michigan tactic and a suggestion that "others may follow suit." Finally the editorial raises a lament about "worthwhile movements" embroiling themselves in "debatable causes."

Somehow, all of that just doesn't strike us as very sporting or very smart. If "worthwhile movements" refrained from expressing views on issues of great **d** national importance, the quality of public debate in the United States would become strained and insipid and the character of our national life would be substantially altered. Over the past 60 years, for example, the YWCA has contributed significantly to our national discourse. It was one of the first major national organizations to speak out for desegregation and moved to implement the policy in its own house. At that time, that surely was a "debatable," **d** though quite healthy, proposition.

But the real point is that the sportsmen's attack is not simply unfair, it's un-American. It is one thing for the sportsmen to debate vigorously the YWCA's **c** views and quite another to exert muscle on united fund operations for helping to finance groups which merely express views which they don't like. The tactic smacks of thought control and blackmail. It seems to us that sportsmen who follow this course are demeaning their cause and detracting from values far more important than the specific issues of any particular debate about gun **a** control.

(+100)   —end timing—   (min___sec___)

b

c

a

115

ACTIVITY 9-4
Summarizing

Instructions: Write a one-paragraph summary of the Reading Selection.

_____

_____

_____

_____

_____

_____

_____

_____

ACTIVITY 9-5
Affixes and Roots

Instructions: Write two words for each of the affixes or roots listed below. Then write a short definition of the word.

ex- (out)

1. _____, _____

2. _____, _____

inter- (between)

1. _____, _____

2. _____, _____

trans- (across)

1. _____, _____

2. _____, _____

in- (into)

1. _____, _____

2. _____, _____

sub- (under)

1. _____, _____

2. _____, _____

retro- (backward)

1. _____, _____

2. _____, _____

ACTIVITY 9-6
Skimming Exercises

Instructions: Read only each numbered question printed in italics. Then sweep your eyes over the paragraphs to find answers to the questions. *SKIM*; do not read the paragraphs. Remember to examine the questions closely for key pointer-words that will help you find the answers as quickly as possible.

1. *Where did the term "Folsom Man" come from?*
In 1926, scientists found stone weapons mingled with animal bones that showed the possibility that America had inhabitants between 10,000 ad 25,000 years ago. No evidence of human bone structure was present, but the weapons were obviously made by men. Since the chipped stone heads were found along with bones from an extinct bison, most anthropologists believe they belong to the same era as the animal bones. The relics were found near Folsom, New Mexico, and, as a result, the weapons are attributed to Folsom Man.

2. *What was the name of the treaty signed to end the Franco-Prussian War?*
In 1870, the Prussian army under the leadership of General Helmuth von Moltke defeated the French in a number of battles in the early part of a war entered into enthusiastically by both countries. When, late in the year, the French, under Marshalls MacMahon and Bazaine, lost the fortresses of Sedan and Metz, the remaining French soldiers fell back to defend Paris. That capital city fell to the Prussians early in 1871. The war ended with the Treaty of Frankfort, signed on May 10th of that year. The treaty was very harsh, and antagonized the French people, who had to pay huge sums to their conquerors. Historians feel that this treaty contributed to the bitterness that caused World War I.

3. *Who invented the first steering bicycle?*
The earliest bicycles were without pedals, the rider "walking along" while seated. Today's kiddie car is similar in its operation. In 1816, Baron Karl Drais invented a steering device which connected to the front wheel. These "swift-walkers," as they were called, were introduced into England in 1818. In 1855, Earnest Michaux, a French locksmith, invented a bicycle with pedals attached to the front wheels.

4. *When was the Rosetta Stone translated?*
After over 3500 years, the use of Egyptian hieroglyphics was forgotten about 500 A.D. In 1799, French soldiers discovered a stone tablet near the Rosetta mouth of the Nile. The stone contained a priestly decree in honor of Ptolemy V in three languages, Egyptian hieroglyphics, Egyptian demotic, and Greek. Scholars worked at translating the Egyptian scripts in the same way a code is broken today. About 23 years later, François Champollion succeeded in interpreting the entire hieroglyphic text.

ACTIVITY 9-7
No-Message Words

Instructions: Every possible no-message word has been omitted from the following paragraphs. Read carefully—but quickly—and see if you can answer the five-question quiz below.

Overfeeding   children   infancy   preadolescent years builds
fat cells   remain   lifetime. Dr. Jules Hirsch, professor
senior physician   Rockefeller University, New York, says studies
show once   cells   laid down,   never disappear.
When weight   lost,   cells shrink but   continue   function.
may send   metabolic signals, demanding   refilled.
demand may account   fact   many   find it difficult
keep   weight down   dieting,   Hirsch says.   constant
craving   food may not be wholly psychological, as many   thought.
may   partly caused   deprived fat cells.
lean person   27 trillion fat cells in   body.
Heavy persons   77 trillion.   means
fat people   have fatter cells,   also three times   many, says
Hirsch.

1. When does dangerous overfeeding occur? _____
2. What is the name and position of the doctor who developed this idea?

   _____

3. Why may dieting to lose weight be a failure? _____

4. How many cells do thin people have? Obese people? _____

5. Craving for food may be not only psychological but also _____?

Now, read the paragraphs as they were printed. Do you feel you missed anything? See if the questions are easier to answer.

Overfeeding of children in infancy and preadolescent years builds up fat cells that remain with them a lifetime. Dr. Jules Hirsch, professor and senior physician at Rockefeller University, New York, says that studies show once these cells are laid down, they never disappear.

When weight is lost, the cells shrink but they continue to function. At times they may send out metabolic signals, demanding to be refilled This demand may account for the act that so many people find it difficult to keep their weight down after dieting, Dr. Hirsch says. The constant craving for food may not be wholly psychological, as many have thought. It may be partly caused by the deprived fat cells.

A lean person has about 27 trillion fat cells in his body. Obese persons, on the other hand, have about 77 trillion. This means that fat people not only have fatter cells, but also three times as many, says Dr. Hirsch.

—"Obesity Starts in Childhood," *Science Digest*, May 1969

ACTIVITY 9-8
Planning for an Examination

Instructions: Spending a few minutes on each course right now to plan for final examinations may save a great deal of agony as the end of the semester approaches. Use a form like this one to analyze each of your standard *lecture* courses, and set up a plan of operations on the basis of what you already know about the course and the instructor.

Subject _____ Instructor _____

I. Course Analysis:

Major Goals	Text Chapters	Lecture Notebook Pages
A. _____	_____	_____
B. _____	_____	_____
C. _____	_____	_____
D. _____	_____	_____
E. _____	_____	_____
F. _____	_____	_____

II. Additional course content: Include research papers, films, etc. _____

_____

III. Analysis of instructor:
   A. Are the exams on major themes? _____ Specific details? _____

   B. Are the exams straightforward? _____ Or complex? _____

   C. Was one area emphasized? _____ An individual? _____

IV. Nature of final examination:
   A. *Essay:* No. of questions? _____ Time? _____ Weighted? _____

   B. *Objective:* No. of questions? _____ What kind (T-F, Matching,

   etc.)? _____ Grading based on no. right? _____ Right-

   minus-wrong? _____ Curve? _____ (Based on your experience)

   Fact quesitons? _____ Inference? _____

V. Advance preparations:

   No. weeks left? _____ Hours required to review this course? _____

   Hours needed per week *now* to prepare? _____

10
ARE YOU A PHILISTINE?
Reading To Expand Your World

Vocabulary Preview

Reading Technique

1. "who lack *sophistication*" _____
2. "no sharp line of *demarcation*" _____
3. "replacing their human *counterparts*" _____
4. "our main *preoccupation* up to this point" _____
5. "an '*Affluent* Society'" _____
6. "will already be *obsolete*" _____
7. "the *dissemination* of information" _____
8. "to faceless *automatons*" _____
9. "a *lethargic* society invites disaster" _____
10. "to establish *rapport* with someone" _____

Reading Selection

1. "to *commandeer* supplies" _____
2. "Latin verb *conjugation*" _____
3. "a vast *array*" _____
4. "*enhance* and simplify" _____
5. "undreamed of by the *utopians*" _____
6. "the *inspiriting* quality" _____
7. "an Oxford *tutorial*" _____
8. "the device's *ubiquitous* eye" _____
9. "mass-produced *homogeneity*" _____
10. "will *accrue* to the young" _____

10

Comprehension Quiz

Reading Technique

Instructions: Write the letter of the correct word in the blank provided.

1. A "Philistine," in the modern meaning of the word, is one who:
   a) is associated with the military
   b) is a resident of Philistia
   c) professes little use for knowledge
   d) is an art lover (___)

2. This chapter emphasizes the need for intellectual:
   a) curiosity
   b) specialization
   c) lethargy
   d) none of the above (___)

3. Reading for "pleasure" should:
   a) be permitted only rarely
   b) provide vicarious experiences
   c) minimize the need for other reading
   d) be restricted to magazine articles (___)

4. Reading for intellectual growth:
   a) provides no pleasure
   b) usually is informative
   c) should be restricted to leisure
   d) none of the above (___)

5. Our expanding technology will:
   a) guarantee human freedom
   b) require a new definition of leisure
   c) make men automatons
   d) lengthen the work week (___)

6. We can better understand others:
   a) through the study of psychology
   b) by understanding ourselves
   c) by becoming aware of human problems
   d) all of the above (___)

7. Anti-intellectualism:
   a) remains a steady movement
   b) changes from time to time
   c) does not exist in colleges
   d) is caused by superiority complexes (___)

8. The most important reason for reading is:
   a) varied with the individual
   b) relaxation
   c) personal growth
   d) escape (___)

9. If "leisure time" becomes more common than "productive time" we may have to change:
   a) our rules for sports
   b) our living standards
   c) our standards of ethics
   d) all of the above (___)

10. Our big corporations are becoming increasingly interested in:
    a) problems of education
    b) community cultural activities
    c) internationalism
    d) all of the above (___)

10

Reading Technique
—begin timing—

Are You a Philistine?
Reading To Expand Your World

The origin of the word "Philistine" as it is used today is most interesting. In Biblical times, Philistia, a small region southwest of Palestine, was peopled by a race of warriors. Their cultural contributions were so few that the word philistine, in the late nineteenth century, was used to describe a "narrow-minded person, devoid of culture and indifferent to art." And in the twentieth century, in every area of the world and at every economic level, we still find philistines—individuals who not only lack sophistication (ideas derived from education and culture), but are inclined to sneer at those who seek knowledge, probably because of feelings of inferiority.

I.   WHAT IS YOUR SOPHISTICATION INDEX?

Where do *you* stand? How wide is *your* world? How active is your sense of curiosity? Are you an excellent mathematics student with no interest in history? Or a dedicated physics major ignorant of philosophy?

If our "cybernetic revolution" continues to explode at the rate anticipated by today's researchers, enormous changes will affect every aspect of living, especially the availability of leisure time. If you are *curious*, if you are unafraid to give your imagination free rein, if you are eager to expand your level of sophistication, you may find these next decades the most exciting that people have ever experienced.

II.   READING FOR PLEASURE, RELAXATION, ESCAPE

"Reading to learn" has been our main preoccupation up to this point. In Chapter 3, a second area was briefly explored: "relaxation reading." There is no sharp line of demarcation, except in purpose. Almost any reading makes some contribution to knowledge, but the chief aim of this second kind is, without apology, pleasure. Reading a book—almost any book—can stimulate an imagination frequently drugged by an overdose of television. In addition to books, hundreds of magazines provide short stories and articles of every conceivable nature.

Weary of nothing but school assignments? Conquer the world with Cyrus the Great; foil an international conspiracy with a cloak-and-dagger hero; solve a five-centuries-old mystery with hospitalized detective Alan Grant (in *The Daughter of Time*, by Josephine Tey). Slip into the twenty-second century in a science fiction novel, taste the triumphs and tragedies of our Civil War. Explore the vast deserts of Australia, the fearsome cold of Alaska, the soft winds and fragrances of the South Seas. If your everyday surroundings press too hard—or become too boring—leave all behind temporarily and enjoy your escape into the limitless universe of books.

III.   READING TO GROW BY

This second half of the twentieth century is a fabulous age. In a review of a new edition of the *Encyclopaedia Britannica*, the point was made that if all the new information pouring out of research laboratories was immediately set into print, it would require 186 volumes *per day*! The rate at which mechanical hands and muscles are replacing their human counterparts is skyrocketing. We are already an "Affluent Society." We are on the verge of becoming a *leisure society*, and many of the greatest minds are coming to grips with a definition of that term. Will you be prepared to enjoy a world which aims at the ultimate in human growth and dignity? Your participation will depend on understanding, understanding will call for knowledge, and knowledge, in large part, will be based on your ablity to read successfully.

You dare not stop growing when school doors close behind you. The chances are great that by the end of your formal education, much of what you have learned will already be obsolete. Government-sponsored research projects in the United States alone have resulted in the annual publication of about 100,000 technical reports; worldwide, the total is close to 900,000. Completely new methods have had to be developed for the dissemination of information; more new methods are being utilized to make use of it. If you are to enjoy the fantastic promise of things to come, you must be able to stay informed through mass communications.

It is equally important to evaluate these changes in terms of human freedom and values. Uncontrolled technology could only too easily reduce men to the faceless automatons of Aldous Huxley's *Brave New World* or to the numbed non-thinkers whom George Orwell describes so frighteningly in *1984*. An informed public can insure the growth of each individual to his ultimate potential; a lethargic society invites disaster.

IV. READING TO UNDERSTAND YOURSELF

From his earliest beginnings, man has asked, "Who am I?", "Who are you?", and "What are we doing here?" In your own way, you too have looked for answers to questions that center on your own actions, those of your friends and family. Perhaps one of the greatest contributions of reading to your own fulfillment is that it can, to some extent at least, make you aware of the fact that the ideas which trouble you have concerned others, both in the past and today. Too frequently you have a tendency to hide your own fears, dislikes, even affections, because you feel that there is something odd or peculiar about them Or perhaps you are afraid that others will consider them odd or peculiar, and you shrink from their "dislike of the unlike." The result is the growth of a protective shell around the "real" you.

If you are lucky, you are able to establish rapport with someone who is empathic enough to allow free inter-communication of "inner selves." Most are not that fortunate. Through books you discover that your questions are the questions that others have asked of themselves and of the world; you are no longer alone. Solutions? Perhaps. But better self-understanding, certainly—and the better you understand yourself, the easier it is for you to understand others.

We desperately need informed human beings, not philistines. We need curious sophisticates, in the best sense of that word. And we need individuals who can stretch the boundaries of their own worlds through the vicarious pleasure of reading. Are you willing to grow in understanding yourself, in understanding others?

—end timing—   (min___sec___)

c

a

b

b

b

d

b

c

c

d

ACTIVITY 10-1
Applying the Technique

Check your own sophistication level. The people listed below have made important contributions to society, past or present. How many can you identify? Two or three words will do.

1. Norman Cousins

2. Leonard Bernstein

3. Ayn Rand

4. Arthur C. Clarke

5. Diego Rivera

6. R. Buckminster Fuller

7. B. F. Skinner

8. John Kenneth Galbraith

9. Martha Graham

10. Arthur Miller

11. Beverly Sills

12. Margaret Mead

13. Louis Leakey

14. William James

15. Robert Hutchins

16. Benjamin Cardozo

17. Andrew Young

18. Niccolo Machiavelli

19. T. S. Eliot

20. John Von Neumann

21. Alexander Calder

22. Virginia Woolf

23. Frank Lloyd Wright

24. Zubin Mehta

ACTIVITY 10-2
Outline: Are You a Philistine?

Main Idea: _____
_____

I.

II.

III.

       D.

IV.

ACTIVITY 10-3
Vocabulary Exercises

Reading Technique

Instructions: From the list of words below, select the letter of the correct word and write it in the blank at the right.

a) sophistication
b) demarcation
c) counterpart
d) preoccupation
e) affluent

f) obsolete
g) dissemination
h) automatons
i) lethargic
j) rapport

1. In the spring a young man's fancy may turn to love, but often it also makes him _____.   (__)
2. Good friends who share unspoken understanding have _____ between them.   (__)
3. The wire services provide _____ of news and information.   (__)
4. Slang expressions often become _____ a short time after they're born.   (__)
5. A truly _____ society should have a healthy economy.   (__)
6. A race car driver's total _____ with his or her motor before a race is understandable.   (__)
7. In military zones, _____ lines are extremely vital.   (__)
8. People who travel a good deal often have an air of _____ about them.   (__)
9. In a foreign exchange program a college student's _____ will come here while he or she will live in another country.   (__)
10. They danced with such rigid motions that it was like watching two _____ moving.   (__)

Reading Selection

Instructions: From the list of words below, select the letter of the correct word and write it in the blank at the right.

a) conjugations
b) accrue
c) commandeer
d) array
e) enhance

f) inspiriting
g) utopians
h) homogeneity
i) ubiquitous
j) tutorial

1. Most people feel that kindness and cheerfulness are _____.   (__)
2. For children, parents seem to have _____ power.   (__)
3. A vast _____ of merchandise is offered on television.   (__)
4. Disliking crowds, some college students signed up for _____;   (__)
5. "People are mostly rotten. I won't join your group of _____."   (__)
6. Verb _____ in languages differ greatly from each other.   (__)
7. Everyone can _____ her or his personality with a pleasing voice.   (__)
8. The soldier could _____ the civilian's car for military reasons.   (__)
9. You can _____ college credits by attending summer school.   (__)
10. _____ is interesting if you like similarity better than variety.   (__)

Comprehension Quiz

Reading Selection

Instructions: Write the letter of the correct answer in the blank provided.

1. According to this article, computers will:
   a) liberate us
   b) eliminate human nature
   c) make life boring
   d) be restricted to the rich   (__)

2. Mr. A's wake-up computer cannot:
   a) raise the heat
   b) give rundowns on world events
   c) dress him
   d) let out the dog   (__)

3. Alice A's morning in the article includes:
   a) easier shopping and homemaking
   b) a sexist assumption she won't be employed
   c) televised art classes
   d) all of these   (__)

4. The technology used in the A household:
   a) is available now
   b) eliminates headaches
   c) makes life complex
   d) becomes possible by 2100 A.D.   (__)

5. The technology revolution is the result of:
   a) new sources of energy
   b) the increase in leisure time
   c) inexpensive micro-computers
   d) psychological break-throughs   (__)

6. Other benefits of the microcomputer may be:
   a) fewer lost letters
   b) safer streets
   c) better education
   d) all of these   (__)

7. According to this article, computers will:
   a) dehumanize us
   b) be difficult to repair
   c) increase custom-made objects
   d) be very expensive   (__)

8. The greatest benefits of the electronic revolution will be for:
   a) the old
   b) farmers
   c) the young
   d) computer salesmen   (__)

9. The use of computers in schools will:
   a) improve the learning experience
   b) improve sporting events
   c) eliminate the three "R's"
   d) control delinquents   (__)

10. The "ultimate applications" of computers will:
    a) be almost limitless
    b) stimulate intellects
    c) make homes a society center
    d) all of these   (__)

10

Reading Selection

LIVING: PUSHBUTTON POWER

(from *Time*, February 20, 1978)

—begin timing—

It is 7:30 a.m. As the alarm clock burrs, the bedroom curtains swing silently apart, the Venetian blinds snap up and the thermostat boosts the heat to a cozy 70°. The percolator in the kitchen starts burbling; the back door opens to let out the dog. The TV set blinks on with the day's first newscast: not your Today *show humph-humph, but a selective rundown (ordered up the night before) of all the latest worldwide events affecting the economy–legislative, political, monetary. After the news on TV comes the morning mail, from correspondents who have dictated their messages into the computer network. The latter-day Aladdin, still snugly abed, then presses a button on a bedside box and issues a string of business and personal memos, which appear instantly on the genie screen. After his shower, which has turned itself on at exactly the right temperature at the right minute, Mr. A. is alerted by a buzzer and a blue light on the screen. His boss, the company president, is on his way to the office. A. dresses and saunters [strolls] out to the car. The engine, of course, is running . . .*

After her husband has kissed her goodbye, Alice A. concentrates on the screen for a read-out of comparative prices at the local merchants' and markets. Following eyeball-to-eyeball consultations with the butcher and the baker and the grocer on the tube, she hits a button to commandeer supplies for tonight's dinner party. Pressing a couple of keys on the kitchen terminal, she orders from the bank her favorite recipes for oysters Rockefeller, boeuf à la bourguignonne *and chocolate* soufflé, *tells the machine to compute the ingredients for six servings, and directs the ovens to reach the correct temperature for each dish according to the recipe, starting at 7:15 p.m. Alice then joins a televised discussion of Byzantine art (which she has studied by computer). Later she wanders into the computer room where Al ("Laddy") Jr. has just learned from his headset that his drill in Latin verb conjugation was "groovy."*

Wellsian fantasy? Verne-Vonnegut put-on? Maybe. But while this matutinal [morning] scenario may still be years away, the basic technology is in existence. Such painless, productive awakenings will in time be as familiar as Dagwood Bumstead's pajamaed panics. And, barring headaches, tummy aches and heartaches, the American day should proceed as smoothly as it begins. All thanks to the miracle of the microcomputer, the supercheap chip that can electronically shoulder a vast array of boring, time-consuming tasks.

The microelectronic revolution promises to ease, enhance and simplify life in ways undreamed of even by the utopians. At home or office, routine chores will be performed with astonishing efficiency and speed. Leisure time, greatly increased, will be greatly enriched. Public education, so often a dreary and capricious [changeable] process in the U.S., may be invested with the inspiriting quality of an Oxford tutorial—from preschool on. Medical care will be delivered with greater precision.

Letters will not so easily go astray. It will be safer to walk the streets because people will not need to carry large amounts of cash; virtually all financial transactions will be conducted by computer. In the microelectronic global village, the home will again be the center of society, as it was before the Industrial Revolution.

Mass production of the miracle chip has already made possible home computer systems that sell for less than $800—and prices will continue to fall.

Many domestic devices that use electric power may be computerized. Eventually, the household computer will be as much a part of the home as the kitchen sink; it will program washing machines, burglar and fire alarms, sewing machines, a robot vacuum cleaner and a machine that will rinse and stack dirty dishes. When something goes wrong with an appliance, a question to the computer will elicit repair instructions—in future generations, repairs will be made automatically. Energy costs will be cut by a computerized device that will direct heat to living areas where it is needed, and turn it down where it is not; the device's ubiquitous eye, sensing where people are at all times, will similarly turn the lights on and off as needed.

The computer might appear to be a dehumanizing factor, but the opposite **a** is in fact true. It is already leading the consumer society away from the mass-produced homogeneity of the assembly line. The chip will make it possible some day to have shoes and clothes made to order—the production commanded and directed by computer—within minutes. The custom-made object, now restricted to the rich, will be within everyone's reach. **c**

* * *

The widest benefits of the electronic revolution (unlike those of most revolutions) will accrue to the young. Seymour Papert, professor of mathematics **d** and education at M.I.T., estimates that there will be 5 million private computers in people's homes and available to students within two years; by 1982, he predicts, 80% of upper-middle-class families will have computers "capable of playing important roles in the intellectual development of their children." Says California Author Robert Albrecht, a pioneer of electronic education: **a** "In schools, computers will be more common than carousel slide projectors, movie projectors and tape recorders. They'll be used from the moment school opens, through recess, through lunch period, and on as far into the day as the principal will keep the school open."

* * * **c**

U.C.L.A. Professor of Computer Science Gerald Estrin, who helped to develop the computer at the Institute for Advanced Study in Princeton in the 1940s, says: "The computers provide an intensely visual, multisensory learning experience that can take a youngster in a matter of a few months to a level he might never reach without it, and certainly would not reach in less than **d** many, many years of study by conventional methods."

* * *

For the mighty army of consumers, the ultimate applications of the computer revolution are still around the bend of a silicon circuit. It is estimated **c** that there are at least 25,000 applications of the computer awaiting discovery. Notes *The Economist*: "To ask what the applications are is like asking what are the applications of electricity." Certainly, the miracle chip will affect American life in ways both benign and productive. Far from George Orwell's gloomy **c** vision of *Nineteen Eighty-Four*, the computer revolution is stimulating intellects, liberating limbs and propelling mankind to a higher order of existence.

(+150)   —end timing—   (min___sec___) **a**

d

ACTIVITY 10-4
Summarizing

Instructions: Write a one-paragraph summary of the Reading Selection.

_____

_____

_____

_____

_____

_____

_____

_____

ACTIVITY 10-5
Affixes and Roots

Instructions: Write two words for each of the affixes and roots listed below. Then write a short definition of the word.

<table>
<tr><td align="center">uni- (one)</td><td align="center">mono- (one)</td></tr>
<tr><td>1. _____, _____</td><td>1. _____, _____</td></tr>
<tr><td>2. _____, _____</td><td>2. _____, _____</td></tr>
<tr><td align="center">duo- (two)</td><td align="center">bi- (two)</td></tr>
<tr><td>1. _____, _____</td><td>1. _____, _____</td></tr>
<tr><td>2. _____, _____</td><td>2. _____, _____</td></tr>
<tr><td align="center">multi- (many, several)</td><td align="center">poly- (several)</td></tr>
<tr><td>1. _____, _____</td><td>1. _____, _____</td></tr>
<tr><td>2. _____, _____</td><td>2. _____, _____</td></tr>
</table>

ACTIVITY 10-6
Scanning Exercise

Instructions: Allow yourself no more than 30 seconds to scan the portion of a newspaper article printed below. See how many of the questions that follow you can answer.

'60s Movement Seeps Into U.S. Life-Style

WASHINGTON—The "Movement" of the 1960s, that passionate crusade to stop the Vietnam war and radically reshape the nation's political and economic system, is long dead. Its leaders are scattered, its slogans blown away in the wind.

Yet the once-reviled counterculture that the Movement spawned, with its long-haired defiance of traditional behavior and its sometimes shocking insistence on alternative life styles, has imprinted lasting marks on American society in ways both frivolous and profound.

Indeed, some aspects of the counterculture are alive and well and living in the suburbs—an outcome fraught with irony, because in many cases what has survived is what was first most vehemently condemned.

Fifteen years ago or so, the counterculture burst upon the nation like the trumpets of the Vandals at the gates of Rome. Self-styled "hippie freaks" proclaimed the joys of psychedelic music, incense, nature vans, guitars and drugs. Radical students advocated Marxism, shouted four-letter words in the name of free speech and challenged the established views of deans, parents and Presidents alike.

Girls went braless and slept where they pleased. Boys slept with them, declined to apoloize for doing so and jeered at the work ethic their parents revered as the cornerstone of the nation. Traditional Western religions, with their emphasis on "doing," were out and Eastern religions, with their mystical emphasis on "being," were in.

Even the humorists of the counterculture, instead of supporting customary values by poking gentle fun at them as most comedians do, satirized and ridiculed much of what Americans held dear.

The reaction was swift, indignant and not a little fearful.

Yet today much of the counterculture has been assimilated and accepted by society as a whole. More important, some of its most controversial underlying values—including its open distrust of official leaders and its conviction . . .

—Robert C. Toth, *The Los Angeles Times*

1. In which city was the article written? _____
2. Where was it published? _____
3. What period was it talking about? _____
4. What war was mentioned? _____
5. What effect does the "counterculture" have today? _____
6. Whom did the counterculture challenge? _____
7. What did boys jeer at? _____
8. "Today, much of the counterculture has . . ." _____

And that is the way that most of us read a newspaper. If the article—especially its headline—attracts us, we read it through. If not, we further scan the page, selecting what is of interest, rejecting what is not.

11
EYES OPEN, MINDS OPEN

Vocabulary Preview

Reading Technique

1. "*retrieve* them at the touch of a button" _____

2. "noted *semanticist*" _____

3. "cannot be the *ultimate*" _____

4. "contain no *overt* indication" _____

5. "A *partisan* newspaper" _____

6. "state, without *equivocation*" _____

7. "classify yourself as a *liberal*" _____

8. "or as a *conservative*" _____

9. "to *espouse* a position" _____

10. "which provide new *insights*" _____

Reading Selection

1. "has *insinuated* itself" _____

2. "to *dominate* their debates" _____

3. "*reinstating* the death penalty" _____

4. "a *vindictive* jury" _____

5. "to *justify* rationally" _____

6. "most *humane* persons" _____

7. "that would urge *clemency*" _____

8. "an *effectual* consensus" _____

9. "Gilmore *parlayed* his death" _____

10. "Death is *definitive*" _____

Comprehension Quiz

Reading Technique

Instructions: Write the letter of the correct answer in the blank provided.

1. Creative reading requires:
   a) an active mind
   b) an open mind
   c) both (a) and (b)
   d) neither (a) nor (b)
   (__)

2. The key to awareness of the use of propaganda involves:
   a) knowing the source
   b) avoiding the newspaper editorials
   c) reading factual information only
   d) reading "journals of opinion"
   (__)

3. A typical "snarl" word of today, according to Hayakawa, is:
   a) masterful
   b) empathy
   c) radical
   d) gentle
   (__)

4. Many people make value judgments on the basis of:
   a) information and evaluation
   b) environmental influences
   c) considered decisions
   d) disliked associates
   (__)

5. Creative reading demands:
   a) emotional reactions
   b) mastery of facts
   c) that you understand the significance of the material
   d) all of the above
   (__)

6. In a newspaper, expressions of opinion may be found:
   a) in editorials
   b) in a columnist's comments
   c) in comic strips
   d) all of the above
   (__)

7. A "Great Book" is one which:
   a) has sold 100,000 copies
   b) was written at least three centuries ago
   c) deserves creative reading
   d) is nonfiction
   (__)

8. All propaganda is:
   a) false
   b) dangerous
   c) illegal
   d) a "sales" effort
   (__)

9. The creative reader approaches new material:
   a) with no prejudices
   b) knowing his or her prejudices
   c) willing to accept it as valid
   d) with suspicion
   (__)

10. Truly creative reading provides:
    a) enjoyment
    b) information
    c) the basis for growth
    d) all of the above
    (__)

11

Reading Technique
—begin timing—

Eyes Open, Minds Open

Reading that contributes to your growth as an individual is more demanding than reading for information. (A computer can be fed facts perhaps more efficiently than can the human brain–and retrieve them at the touch of a button!) To read critically and creatively requires that your approach be an active one, that your mind be open as well as your eyes.

I. WHICH SIDE ARE YOU ON? RECOGNIZING PROPAGANDA, SPOTTING "EMOTION WORDS"

You are faced with propaganda from the time you awake in the morning until you close your eyes at the end of the day. Newspaper, radio, and television advertising, many books (certainly this one) are trying to sell you a specific idea, program, or item. There is nothing wrong with the propaganda in itself, but it is important that you recognize and evaluate it.

In some instances, propaganda is so obvious that you spot it immediately. Every advertised brand of detergent cannot make your wash "the whitest," every sports car cannot be "the ultimate," and every watch is not "the finest." On the basis of your own experience, you make value judgments on propaganda of this nature. Similarly, you accept or reject a variety of claims ranging from impassioned political pleas to the crying-towel claims of football coaches before a big game.

Other propaganda techniques, however, are more subtle, and you must be on the alert for slanted approaches that contain no overt indication of their true purpose. Slanting news, for example, is an only too common practice. No one objects to the fact of an editorial slant; that is the privilege of a publisher. The news column is another matter. A partisan newspaper can proclaim in four-inch headlines, "Mayor Accused of Theft," but you may find that the charge is simply one of a local homeowner who considers an increase of two cents in the tax rate as "outright robbery."

Your first step toward the recognition of propaganda—toward critical reading—is to determine the character and purpose of its source. Several reputable magazines state, without equivocation, that they are "journals of fact and opinion": typical among these are *The New Republic* and *The National Review*. Many other publications are not that frank. You must consider the source!

S. I. Hayakawa, semanticist, politician, points out that the use of certain words colors your reaction to statements or situations. He calls them "purr words" or "snarl words." Contrast, for example, "a hard, steely glance" with "a firm, determined look." An author's selection of words which have these characteristics can make a great deal of difference in your reaction to them. You must be on the alert for the "connotations"—the significant meanings—of words as well as for their "denotations," or dictionary definitions. Note also that the slant of a word changes with time and that words which were merely descriptive in the recent past today may bring other things to mind. Consider *opportunist*, for example, or *promoter* or *politician*.

All of these factors contribute to your value judgments and to your determination of "which side you are on."

II. WHERE DID YOU GET YOUR "PRE-JUDGMENTS"?

How did you develop your prejudices? Do you classify yourself as a "liberal" or as a "conservative"? Do you favor states' rights, or do you feel the need of a strong federal government? And where do you think is the woman's place? More important, what was the background of these value judgments? To espouse a position, you must first be prepared to assemble information, evaluate it, weigh your conclusions, and make decisions.

III. SEPARATING FACTS FROM FEELINGS

Reading just a single source for information may not be enough. Examine the differences in these statements:

> 1. An unruly, highly emotional group of students was curtly dismissed by President Jones today when presenting a petition at a Board of Regents meeting demanding the immediate reinstatement of Dr. Smith. The president refused to commit himself to any positive action.
> 2. President Jones interrupted a Board of Regents meeting today to receive a student petition containing 8000 signatures and asking for the reinstatement of Dr. Smith. Before returning to the Board meeting, the president told student leaders that the question would be given further consideration at the earliest opportunity.

Note how certain words or phrases are "loaded" because they present opinion rather than fact. In the first paragraph, you read "unruly," "highly emotional," "curtly," "demanding," "immediate reinstatement," "would not commit himself." The second paragraph is far more factual, and reports news rather than the feelings of the writer. Critical readers distinguish between *facts* and *opinions*.

IV. CREATIVE READING

Recognition of propaganda, of your own prejudices, of a writer's slant, of the necessity of thoughtful evaluation—all contribute to your ability to read critically. And once you have become able to apply an open mind to written material, you are prepared for creative reading. Creative reading takes you beyond your emotional involvement; it transcends, moreover, mastery of an assortment of facts. It means you are ready to recognize the *significance* of the ideas expressed, and can add to this recognition your own deliberate evaluation. Your imagination, experience, and considered thought may create a totality of ideas which exceeds the author's thinking. In other words, the book has provided a "mental springboard." Not all books merit this full application; an oversimplified definition of "Great Books" might simply be those that deserve creative reading. The definition might be expanded to include those books which provide new insights each time they are read, and which invite you to re-read them often. They are the books you wish to own rather than borrow.

Reading, then, may be assigned three levels. The simplest is reading for relaxation or enjoyment, responded to mostly by emotional reactions. On a higher plane is reading for information, a process calling for logical thinking and critical reactions. For the top level, your response includes enjoyment and learning which is colored by critical analysis—plus the creative contributions that you can make to the significant ideas expressed by the author. All three levels are essential.

—end timing—   (min___sec___)

ACTIVITY 11-1
Applying the Technique

1. List ten words which Hayakawa would consider to be "purr" words, or words which have a pleasant connotation:

   a)   f)
   b)   g)
   c)   h)
   d)   i)
   e)   j)

2. List ten "snarl" words:

   a)   f)
   b)   g)
   c)   h)
   d)   i)
   e)   j)

3. List five sources of propaganda to which you are exposed daily:

   a)
   b)
   c)
   d)
   e)

4. Evaluate your local newspaper. Do you consider its *news* columns to be prejudiced or objective? Bring in at least one example to prove your position.

5. Evaluate the position of at least two newspaper columnists in the same paper. Are columnists expected to have their own points of view? Can you anticipate the stands that their authors would take on a local issue?

ACTIVITY 11-2
Outline: Eyes Open, Minds Open

Main Idea: _____

_____

_____

I.

II.

    B.

III.

IV.

    D.

ACTIVITY 11-3
Vocabulary Exercises

Reading Technique

Instructions: Write the letter of the correct answer in the blank provided.

1. Penetrating understanding of self:
   a) insight   b) hindsight   c) foresight   (__)
2. To recall information to mind:
   a) retain   b) retrieve   c) relieve   (__)
3. Beyond which there is no other:
   a) rationale   b) crucial   c) ultimate   (__)
4. Open to view:
   a) culvert   b) overt   c) covert   (__)
5. Takes a definite stand:
   a) defector   b) partisan   c) nonconformist   (__)
6. Using ambiguous language:
   a) equivocating   b) equalizing   c) extrapolating   (__)
7. Favoring change or progress:
   a) reactionary   b) conservative   c) liberal   (__)
8. Opposed to change, cautious:
   a) radical   b) conservative   c) liberal   (__)
9. Support:
   a) expose   b) espouse   c) eschew   (__)
10. A specialist in words:
    a) philosopher   b) gynecologist   c) semanticist   (__)

Reading Selection

Instructions: Substitute for the italicized words and phrases the correct word from the list below. (The form of the word as used in the sentence may not be the same as the one in the list.) Write the letter of the correct word in the blank provided.

a) dominate   f) reinstating
b) insinuated   g) humane
c) vindictive   h) clemency
d) justify   i) effectual
e) parlayed   j) definitive

1. Dogmatists feel *their* ideas on a subject are _____.   (__)
2. Kim _____ extra reports into a top grade.   (__)
3. A slick salesperson can "_____" any statement made for a sale.   (__)
4. "I didn't *say* you lied; I just _____ it."   (__)
5. Trying to _____ the party, they did silly tricks.   (__)
6. The _____ driver stopped to help the wounded animal.   (__)
7. _____ an old habit, they began to smoke again.   (__)
8. After asking for _____ for his client, the lawyer then sat down.   (__)
9. Not being _____, the neighbors renewed their friendship after the quarrel.   (__)
10. The _____ magician produced wonders on stage.   (__)

Comprehension Quiz

Reading Selection

Instructions: Write the letter of the correct answer in the blank provided.

1. The main theme of this article is that Americans are:
   a) against the death penalty more than ever
   b) thinking objectively about death sentences
   c) highly emotional about capital punishment
   d) not concerned enough about murderers (__)

2. In regard to the death sentence, the Supreme Court has:
   a) softened its opposition   c) declared it useful   (__)
   b) outlawed it altogether   d) both (a) and (c)

3. According to this author, the death penalty today is:
   a) a political football   c) being reinstated in many   (__)
                                          states
   b) more strongly favored   d) all of these

4. One possible legitimate argument against, says Tucker, is:
   a) it does not cut crime   c) it is barbarous and cruel   (__)
   b) it costs too much   d) many innocents will die

5. Capital punishment is an emotional issue because it is:
   a) an unnerving life and   c) a financial concern   (__)
      death issue
   b) popular among politicians   d) none of these

6. In an era of national unanimity the issue of capital punishment:
   a) would provoke more   c) would be unimportant   (__)
      anxiety
   b) would provoke less   d) could not occur
      anxiety

7. Ours is not a time of unanimity because:
   a) of communism   c) the Kennedys are dead   (__)
   b) of anti-communism   d) none of these

8. Lacking an exterior evil to mobilize against, Americans are:
   a) happy-go-lucky and   c) certain of right and   (__)
      unconcerned   wrong
   b) introspective and   d) eager to kill
      questioning

9. The author senses that sane and sensitive people may feel:
   a) death penalties debase   c) confused   (__)
      respect for life
   b) lack of death penalties   d) all of these
      debases life's value

10. Tucker feels America is returning to capital punishment because:
    a) of frustration with   c) it's God's will   (__)
       liberalism, crime, courts
    b) it solves our problems   d) we have cooly decided it
                                          is for the best

Reading Selection

THE BACK DOOR: Death on the Comeback Trail

by **Carll Tucker**   (*from* Saturday Review, April 29, 1978)

—begin timing—

The question in the following article is one which must be decided by the electorate, the registered voters of the states of this nation through their elected representatives. And by voters is meant all of us. It is issues such as this one which demand an informed public.

The most skillful television anchor man or woman cannot possibly cover the many sides of this social problem in the three minutes available for it on the six o'clock news. Articles such as this in journals of the quality of the Saturday Review *can help you arrive at your opinion.*

Like a dogged [stubborn] politician, capital punishment is on the comeback trail. Since the Supreme Court softened its opposition by ruling that the death penalty was not invariably [always] unconstitutional, capital punishment has insinuated itself into headlines and election campaigns, where it often has no practical excuse for being. Despite their awareness that capital punishment would have little effect on New York City's grievous [serious] problems, last fall's mayoral candidates allowed the issue to dominate their debates and divide the electorate. A recent nationwide poll of high school seniors showed that 60 percent favor capital punishment today, as compared with 30 percent in 1971. Last month, the New York State Assembly approved a capital punishment bill by a few votes less than the two thirds necessary to override the governor's veto. Other states are moving, more or less slowly, toward reinstating the death penalty.

Why now? one can't help wondering. What in our national character is prompting us to return to capital punishment after our long abstention [staying away] from it?

Viewed coolly, our opinions, whether they be for or against capital punishment, are emotional, not rational. Neither criminologists nor enlightened law enforcers can agree that the existence of capital punishment discourages capital crimes. Similarly, the economic justification for capital punishment—that by snuffing out capital criminals we save tax dollars, which we can then spend more productively—is deceptive, as the cost of maintaining capital criminals represents a negligible fraction of any community's budget. Finally, the facts do not support the familiar argument that an unlucky innocent may fall victim to trumped-up evidence or to a vindictive jury. If a man today is executed for a crime by the state, the likelihood is as close to a certainty as possible that the man committed the crime.

Pro and con arguments such as these attempt to justify rationally an emotional inclination. Capital punishment is our only purely, unmistakably life-and-death political question, and it unnerves us. Most humane persons would prefer to take their stand on the basis of facts rather than feelings.

In an era of national unanimity [agreement], the issue of capital punishment would provoke less anxiety. When a nation is wholeheartedly committing young lives to a cause, for instance, one finds less disagreement about how to treat traitors to that cause. If one soldier's betrayal results in the unnecessary massacre of a battalion, even voices that would urge clemency tend not to speak up lest they be suspected of traitorous sympathies.

Ours is not an era of unanimity. Since 1945, Americans have lacked a unifying cause. There have been causes—anticommunism, civil rights, the Asian wars, and Watergate—but they united one segment of the population against another. For a brief, exhilarating moment, we felt unified in our race to the moon. But except for that and for a few eruptions of national grief, at the deaths of the Kennedy brothers, for example, we have felt almost no national unanimity about anything.   c

Lacking an exterior evil to mobilize against, we became introspective. The closer we looked, the more the certainties of an earlier generation shrank into questionable propositions in the postwar years. The prosperity, military power, and technological prowess [ability] in which we had once taken pride   a
came to seem mixed blessings, at best. We began to notice the inequities [injustices] and limitations of our style of governing and to feel more curious about and sympathetic toward alternative goals and styles. For the first time in   d
American history, we began to sympathize with the impulses that turned men to crime, and to question the punishments meted out for those crimes. The deaths of Julius and Ethel Rosenberg in particular undermined our confidence in our system of justice and in the propriety [acceptability] of the death penalty. As Mme. de Staël wrote, "To understand all is to pardon all." The   c
more we understood about ourselves, the more urgently we asked were we certain enough about what was right and wrong to end a life on the basis of those convictions.   a

Those who were uncertain joined with those who held a different certainty—that the taking of a life by the state, under any circumstances, is wrong—to create an effectual consensus. For seven years, until the gruesome Gary Gilmore parlayed his death throes [struggles] into a million dollar legacy and lasting fame, there were no legal executions in America. If the present   b
trends continue, executions by the state will become less uncommon occurrences.

One can debate forever the morality of the death penalty. There are sane, sensitive persons who argue that the death penalty is a barbarous instrument and that its use indicates a lack of respect for life. There are others, no less sane or sensitive, who argue that not having a death penalty debases [lowers]   d
the value of life (for, after all, what greater price can one assess for a life than a life?). Because I cannot conceive of a legal system that would not permit an Adolf Hitler to be put to death, I favor the latter argument.   b

But the sad fact is that the issue will not be decided on the basis of moral or logical arguments. The nation is returning to capital punishment because it is fed up with the complexities of liberalism, fed up with rising crime rates and an ineffective judicial system. Even though capital punishment does nothing to solve these problems, supporting capital punishment is a way of stomping one's foot on the ground and saying, "Enough! I will not tolerate any more."   d

Death is definitive.

(+200)   —end timing—   (min___sec___)

a

ACTIVITY 11-4
Summarizing

Instructions: Write a one-paragraph summary of the Reading Selection.

_____

_____

_____

_____

_____

_____

_____

ACTIVITY 11-5
Affixes and Roots

Instructions: Write two words using each of the affixes and roots listed below. Then write a short definition of the word.

ex- (out)	in- (into)
1. _____, _____	1. _____, _____
2. _____, _____	2. _____, _____
inter- (between)	sub- (under)
1. _____, _____	1. _____, _____
2. _____, _____	2. _____, _____
trans- (across)	retro- (backward)
1. _____, _____	1. _____, _____
2. _____, _____	2. _____, _____

ACTIVITY 11-6
Fact or Opinion?

Instructions: In the blank following each sentence in these paragraphs, write an F in the sentence states a fact, an O if it's an opinion. If it is a combination of the two, write Both.

To cure the country's nutritional ailments, Ralph Nader prescribed a heightened sense of responsibility for the food industry and stepped-up Government inspection. _____ The latter is likelier than the former. _____ Congress has already responded to Nader's campaign against unsafe automobiles by legislating strict safety requirements for new cars. _____ It reacted to his testimony on the quality of meat products by passing the Wholesome Meat Act of 1967, and to his disclosures on poultry with the Wholesome Poultry Act of 1968. _____ Unless his latest charges prove to be exaggerated, Congress will probably again be responsive to his warnings. _____ All Americans may not drive cars, but all of them do eat. _____

—adapted from *Time*, July 25, 1969

The first thing that anyone says about John Marchi is that he's a nice guy. _____ Usually they have trouble thinking of a second thing. _____ He's not tall, he's not short. _____ He's not young, he's not old. _____ He's not handsome, he's not ugly. _____ There are a multitude of things that Marchi is not. _____ He's not witty, forceful, passionate; often he is not articulate; he is not truly ambitious. _____ Naturally, he is not recognized; he walks along Broadway on a sunny May day, slightly stooped under the shadows of a dark coat and brown fedora, talking quietly of destroying the political career of John V. Lindsay. _____

—adapted from Richard Reeves, "Lindsay Tries To Stay in There," *The New York Times Magazine*, June 15, 1969

NOTHING NEW IN STUDY OF POLICE: Book Review
Cop by L. H. Whittemore

Cop is nothing more than a long newspaper story, and after you've read it you wonder why you did. _____

There's nothing new in this book. _____ Nothing, unless it's been forgotten that people can't be put into molds; everyone is different, and no two cops are the same. _____

Whittemore is a good, young reporter with a great gift for interviewing. _____ The book is an interview with four cops. _____

Radio-car officer Joe Minelli in New York's Harlem, detective Ernie Cox in Chicago's South side and patrolmen Colin Barker and Gary Cummings in the Haight-Ashbury district of San Francisco. _____

Several writers could have done *Cop* better, but Whittemore was the first to do the blue jacket side from their own mouths—therefore *Cop* is going to climb on the best seller lists and stay there. _____

And, anyway, even if someone else had done it, Whittemore convinces you that the result would be the same—a "cop" is a human being. _____

—adapted from Logan McKechnie, *The Arizona Republic*, August 3, 1969

ACTIVITY 11-7
Using the Dictionary

Instructions: To answer the following questions, use one of the accepted *college* dictionaries. If you have trouble with any question, refer to the guide chapters usually found at the beginning of the dictionary. (Few, if any, pocket or paperback dictionaries can handle college needs. Get to know how to use a college dictionary quickly and easily.)

1. Name of the dictionary you are using: _____

   Publisher: _____ Latest copyright date: _____

2. Locate the following: Complete guide(s) to pronunciation: _____

   _____ Partial guides: _____

3. In the pages before the regular entries, does your dictionary contain

   any special information besides pronunciation symbols? _____ What

   are they? _____

   On what pages are the abbreviations used with the entries listed? _____
   What section tells you exactly how to use all the dictionary information?

   _____

4. What special information sections are found at the end of the entry

   portion of the book? List five of them: _____

   _____

5. What does a small 1 in front of a word entry mean? _____

6. Show how your dictionary syllabicates *calendar*: _____

7. About how many column inches does your dictionary take up for the

   word "run"? _____

8. From what language did we get the word *calico*? _____

9. What part of speech is *calisthenic*? _____ *calisthenics*? _____

10. What is the population of *Abilene*? _____ Where is the *Ain*? _____

11. In what state is *Clarinda Community College*? _____ *Co-ed*? _____

12. What do the letters *lc* in the margin mean to a proofreader? _____

ACTIVITY 11-8
Getting to Know Your Library

Instructions: To answer the questions below, you must visit your school library. If you have difficulty answering any of the questions, ask one of your librarians for help. This activity is meant to give you as complete a picture of your school library as is possible in a short time. There are dozens, perhaps hundreds, of details that a short activity like this cannot cover, but you should find these items very useful.

1. What card catalog system is used? _____

2. About how many volumes are shelved in your library? _____

3. To how many periodicals does the library subscribe?_____ Where

   are they kept? _____ Can you take out magazines? _____

4. Does your library use a call-desk system or an open-stack system? _____

5. How many different *general* encyclopedias do you have? _____ Which

   one is the latest? _____ What is the copyright date? _____

6. Does the library have *Who's Who* (British)? _____ *A Dictionary

   of American Biography?* _____ *The Oxford English Dictionary*

   (sometimes called the *New English*, or *Murray*)? _____ *Who's

   Who in America?* _____ *World Almanac?* _____ *American

   Yearbook?* _____ *Book Review Digest?* _____ *New York

   Times Index?* _____ Bartlett's *Familiar Quotations?* _____

7. List three books written by Aldous Huxley: _____

   _____, _____ When was *Brave

   New World* published *originally?* _____ How many pages? _____

8. Who is Morris West? _____ How old is he? _____ For what

   book did he win an award? _____

9. Where would you find the *latest* information on solar energy? _____

10. List three magazines which regularly include book review columns:

    _____, _____, _____

12

A SUCCESSFUL
READING PROGRAM

Vocabulary Preview

Reading Technique

1. "The *paradox* of today's world" _____

2. "earn the *wherewithal*" _____

3. "Be *ruthless* with what you do read" _____

4. "knowledge *obliterates* that fear" _____

5. "are *inexorably* moving toward a credit-card system" _____

6. "machines have ended untold *drudgery*" _____

7. "To keep our system *viable*" _____

8. "between the lines of political *dialogue*" _____

9. "in this changing *ethos*" _____

10. "there are great dangers *inherent* in" _____

Reading Selection

1. "*dabbling* in possibilities" _____

2. "according to the *futurephiles*" _____

3. "wrote a *prospectus*" _____

4. "a *galaxy* of minority interests" _____

5. "dark side to the *millenium*" _____

6. "a multiplicity of *mediocrities*" _____

7. "various commercial *formats*" _____

8. "our *perceptions* of one another" _____

9. "the new *aristocracy*" _____

10. "*ominous* alien presence" _____

12

Comprehension Quiz

Reading Technique

Instructions: Write the letter of the correct answer in the blank provided.

1. A leisure-oriented society will occur first in:
   a) the western hemisphere
   b) the eastern hemisphere
   c) highly industrialized nations
   d) all of the above   (__)

2. The solution suggested for finding time for reading is to:
   a) eliminate relaxation
   b) minimize social activities
   c) program time for reading
   d) all of the above   (__)

3. The most important criterion in evaluating time spent on your various activities:
   a) personal growth
   b) reading for knowledge
   c) keeping abreast of business trends
   d) your physical condition   (__)

4. The best example of a magazine helpful in keeping up to date with news is:
   a) *Redbook*
   b) *Playboy*
   c) *Newsweek*
   d) *Sports Illustrated*   (__)

5. Automation is contributing to:
   a) audio-visual aids
   b) new production methods
   c) new inventions
   d) all of the above   (__)

6. With the acceleration of the computer revolution, we face major readjustments in many areas. These include:
   a) economics
   b) politics
   c) ethics and morality
   d) all of the above   (__)

7. To retain a truly democratic society, regardless of economic changes:
   a) is probably impossible
   b) is constitutionally guaranteed
   c) demands well-informed voters
   d) all of the above   (__)

8. A leisure-oriented society will be welcomed by:
   a) all people
   b) flexible, curious people
   c) conservative people
   d) all of the above   (__)

9. It is important that education provide students with:
   a) greater self-understanding
   b) a new meaning for "leisure"
   c) both (a) and (b)
   d) neither (a) nor (b)   (__)

10. A successful reader has the capacity to:
    a) raise his sophistication level
    b) better understand this society
    c) retain her individual freedom
    d) all of the above   (__)

12

Reading Technique
—begin timing—

A Successful Reading Program

The paradox of today's busy world is that our accelerating technical growth may be rapidly pointing us toward an affluent, "leisure-oriented" society–or toward disaster. Despite the unlimited potential of new sources of power, we face worldwide shortages: fuel for factories, generators, the family car. Which crisis will be next: sufficient food, pure water, breathable air? Have we exhausted our resources or have we, uninformed or uncaring, simply failed to do the planning and research *that could have averted these problems?*

We must adjust to new moralities, new income-distribution methods, earlier retirement, new concepts about women and minority groups, new life-styles. We are "threatened" with free time. . . .

To cope with these issues, you must be informed–and to be informed, you must read!

I. "I HAVE NO TIME!"

You have demands on your time from a dozen directions. You must eat and be housed—and frequently earn the wherewithal to do so. You have responsibilities at home, at school, at business, and time is consumed in traveling from one of these activities to another. To exist as a human being, your life must contain social activities, recreational periods, and, just as important, a chance simply to sit back and relax. Where does the time for reading come from?

The basic answer to this question is a philosophical one, a deliberate decision on your part, a determination of values. Can you afford *not* to read?

What did you do with your day today—or yesterday or the day before? How many 15-minute coffee breaks turned into an hour of discussion (forgotten almost immediately)? How many times last week did you relax on the sofa after dinner to watch a television show which was worthwhile—only to find yourself still sitting there when the late news came on? Time is one of your most valuable commodities. It must be used with discretion.

If reading is important to you, budget time for it. Be ruthless with what you do read. There is nothing wrong with putting aside a best-seller half-finished if you find it of little interest. If your reading is for information, deliberately apply every reading technique you have at your command. Make your reading time pay.

Above all, weigh your activities in terms of personal development. It will be the individual of many interests who will shape the new society. The time of the philistine is drawing to an end.

II. KEEP UP WITH WHAT'S HAPPENING

This is a world that is really moving! Every month, every day, new discoveries, decisions, and events have a tremendous effect on the lives of each of us. To stay abreast of changes is a major task in itself.

You may find that the late news on television is much more important than the late, late movie; you may find that several articles in the newspaper are more important than either. And you may also discover that to be conscious of the changes that are the real "happenings" in today's world, a weekly news magazine is a must. *Time, Newsweek, U.S. News and World Report* can bring you information that could change your total direction of living. Sharp, hard-hitting, brief articles covering a broad spectrum of world affairs from art to zoology are yours for a few cents and a few hours. Many of the keenest intellects in the mass communications industry contribute columns in the fields of politics, art, religion, business, medicine, the creative world, law, people—and books.

You have a choice to make. Cut yourself off from the mainstream of the currents that sweep us into a fascinating future—or become a part of that mainstream. Know the individuals who contribute to it; be able to face with confidence the endless challenge of change.   c

III. STAY AHEAD ON THE JOB

Business has been a vital contributor to our dynamic society. *Almost half of*   c
the products being marketed today did not exist 20 years ago. Accounting methods have been revolutionized by new machines; sales techniques include use of audio-visual machinery unknown to merchandisers until long after World War II. The credit and collection functions of business are inexorably moving toward a credit-card banking system. Copying or duplicating machines have   a
ended untold drudgery at the secretary's desk. The businessman who remains blissfully unaware of procedural advances will not be blissful very long. New materials have replaced old—from synthetic fabrics to newly created metals. New production methods have made it possible to produce vast quantities of goods automatically, but, at the same time, have raised the specter of unac-   c
ceptable unemployment figures. Every level of business enterprise has been affected. Tomorrow's production worker will find even less need for his muscle; an electronic box may even minimize the need for his brain. For you to stay ahead—even to keep up—successful reading must be included in your   b
collection of tools.

IV. A DYNAMIC SOCIETY DEMANDS READERS
                                                                              d
There are great dangers inherent in a dynamism as fast-moving as ours. If each person is to retain his or her individuality, then he or she must be informed about the questions our elected officials must consider and the deci-   c
sion they must render. If your vote is to be meaningful at all, it must be cast on the basis of understood issues and a careful weighing of parties, planks, and politics. To keep our system viable and flourishing, you must be able to read between the lines of political dialogue so that you can determine the true issues.

If you are truly to be a success in this changing ethos, you must make time for   b
reading; you must keep up with what's happening; you must stay on top of the changes taking place daily in industry, technology, society. If you don't know or, even worse, don't care, you have nothing to look forward to but confusion—political, economic,   c
social. The choice is yours. Our physical world shrinks in terms of distances; our universe expands in terms of ideas. Become a successful reader and participate in a dynamic society!

—end timing—   (min___sec___)

                                                                              d

ACTIVITY 12-1
Applying the Technique

1. The "T" of OARWET stands for "*Test*," of course. . . . Perhaps, in this last application activity, you might test your ability to summarize the goals of this book. Chapter 1 discussed the various elements that underlie successful reading. Can you name four? Can you name three negative factors detracting from it?

2. Chapter 2 stressed the need for an organized approach when reading for information. Can you list the significance of each letter of OARWET? Have you applied OARWET to other nonfiction reading?

3. Do you deliberately vary speed depending on your *purpose* and the *difficulty* of the material?

4. Do you: minimize no-message words? attempt to follow the author's thinking by reading in *idea-phrases*? exercise those little-used eye muscles—and rest them when doing a lot of reading?

5. Have you made *purpose* a starting-point when beginning a learning-understanding-remembering unit? Are you now watching for clues from *typography, pointer-words, punctuation, graphics*? Do you *screen* factual information and dispose of the unimportant details?

6. Have you become more aware of *main ideas, topic sentences*, and their relationships? How are your note-taking techniques now, particularly your outlining?

7. Have you sharpened your ability to determine the meaning of words from *context*? And do you find that *affixes* and *roots* can be helpful with a new word?

8. Do you practice *skimming* when it is called for, *scanning* when it is a time-saver?

9. Are you conscious of the necessity for getting into test-taking condition, physiologically and psychologically? Are you aware of the special demands of the essay test, the peculiarities of the objective test? Have you "analyzed" *your* instructors?

10. How is your "sophistication index"? Are you more aware of *why* you read for pleasure or growth? Are you making progress in understanding yourself?

11. Do you recognize *propaganda, news-slanting, prejudice*? And for serious reading, are your *critical* and *creative responses* adding to the material?

12. Have you developed a reading program for yourself? Can you use the suggestions offered for making reading selection easier? Are you taking full advantage of your library?

History has given us an unlimited bequest in the printed word. Enjoy it!

ACTIVITY 12-2
Outline: A Successful Reading Program

ACTIVITY 12-3
Vocabulary Exercises

Reading Technique

Instructions: Write the letter of the matching phrase in the blank provided.

a) unyielding, relentless	1. inherent	(___)
b) workable, practicable	2. wherewithal	(___)
c) seemingly self-contradictory	3. paradox	(___)
d) necessary means or resources	4. dialogue	(___)
e) conversation of two or more	5. ethos	(___)
f) without mercy	6. ruthless	(___)
g) blot or wipe out	7. obliterate	(___)
h) character of culture or group	8. inexorable	(___)
i) dull, wearisome work	9. drudgery	(___)
j) inborn, essential quality	10. viable	(___)

Reading Selection

Instructions: Write the letter of the matching word in the blank provided.

a) ominous	1. unexceptional people	(___)
b) dabbling	2. those who study possibilities ahead	(___)
c) aristocracy	3. members of class with money or power	(___)
d) futurephiles	4. preliminary printed statement	(___)
e) perceptions	5. concepts, ideas, notions, understanding	(___)
f) formats	6. foreshadowing evil, fateful, dangerous	(___)
g) prospectus	7. great period of time	(___)
h) galaxy	8. playing around	(___)
i) millenium	9. general plans of organization or arrangement	(___)
j) mediocrities	10. an assemblage	(___)

Comprehension Quiz

Reading Selection

Instructions: Write the letter of the correct answer in the blank provided.

1. The intent of this article is to indicate:
   a) television is dying
   b) television causes cancer
   c) new possibilities in TV
   d) a coming all-sports channel   (___)

2. New developments in TV may include:
   a) multiple-screen homes
   b) two-way cable channels
   c) giant-screen receivers
   d) all of these   (___)

3. Through television, Shale thinks, we will be able to:
   a) watch Congress
   b) voice opinions at the U.N.
   c) re-write the 1934 Communications Act
   d) forecast weather   (___)

4. By 1981, cable TV will:
   a) reach 30% of U.S. homes
   b) eliminate set breakdowns
   c) have national impact
   d) both (a) and (c)   (___)

5. Satellites are important to TV's future because:
   a) telephone "long-lines" are too short
   b) they're easier to use
   c) they're cheaper
   d) long lines don't work on cassettes   (___)

6. TV's advancement today is hampered by:
   a) the "mob-rule of ratings"
   b) low-flying planes
   c) a shortage of technicians
   d) the death of "Free TV"   (___)

7. "Plain, old, dull TV" will someday be:
   a) extinct
   b) hurt by "static-cling"
   c) abandoned by advertisers
   d) improved by competition   (___)

8. NBC's predictions for the next 10 years do *not* include:
   a) a drop in advertising
   b) advances in micro-processors
   c) long-form programs
   d) the end of broadcast seasons   (___)

9. The "dark side" of the new TV era may involve:
   a) cable channels representing only commercial formats
   b) giving a machine more control of our perceptions
   c) technicians' triumph of form over context
   d) all of these   (___)

10. The author's attitude toward the future of TV is:
    a) excited but cautious
    b) angry and unhappy
    c) depressed
    d) dubious   (___)

12

Reading Selection

TUNING IN ON TOMORROW

by **Tom Shales,** *The Washington Post* (*from* The Los Angeles Times, July 10, 1978)

—begin timing—

Television will be born again.

* * *

The Hope of All Humanity!—again.

America has always been in love with the future. The national mood toward television as it is may be one of resigned disenchantment, at best, but the prospects for what is still to come are potentially exhilarating [refreshing].

Multiple-screen homes will be the rule, not the exception, in the oncoming media renaissance [re-birth]. It will involve such earthly wonders as cable television, pay-cable channels, two-way-cable channels, fiber optics (a kind of super-cable), station interconnections via satellite, direct satellite-to-home transmission, over-the-air subscription ("pay") television, video cassette players and recorders, video disc players, giant-screen receivers and so on.

What all this means, basically, is that the number of program sources will greatly multiply and so will the uses to which the television screen is put. We will look at television in a new way, as not only a source of news and diversion but as an aid in learning, shipping, banking, and citizenship.

Through television, we may be able to attend meetings of the board of education, the city council, the state legislature, Congress or the United Nations General Assembly.

But dabbling in possibilities is really too easy, and it can raise silly hopes. By now, according to the futurephiles of the past, we were already supposed to be a "wired nation" (through cable) and TV sets were supposed to be flat giant murals. What really happens will depend on the health of the economy and the degree to which the broadcasting industry allows change to occur. Right now, Congress is waiting to see what the industry will permit in the rewrite of the 1934 Communications Act.

Even the forecasts of the decidedly pragmatic sound promising, however. William J. Donnelly, vice president for new electronic media at the Young and Rubicam ad agency, wrote a prospectus on TV's '80s called "The Emerging Video Environment" and among his predictions is that cable TV will reach a 30% penetration of American television homes by 1981. Donnelly considers 30% the magic snowball number (as it was with TV and then color TV), the point at which a new medium truly makes a national impact.

There are 12 million cable subscribers in the U.S.; Donnelly predicts between 20 and 26 million by the end of 1981. He also thinks there will be a million video cassette units at work in American homes the same year, and 1,000 satellite earth stations for video signals. Satellites are important to the future of television because they provide transmission of signals at a much lower cost than the current telephone long-line method. By satellite, Donnelly writes, "it costs the same to send a signal from New York to Philadelphia as it does from New York to Los Angeles," and it's cheap.

What largely hampers [curbs] television now is the sophisticated mob rule of ratings and the desirability of drawing as many hundreds of millions to advertisers at a low cost-per-thousand rate. What cable and satellite interconnection of cable systems promises is at long last liberation from this mentality. Television will be able to serve a galaxy of minority interests.

What will happen to plain old, dull TEE Vee? Donnelly thinks it will hardly disappear: "We believe that there will always be advertiser-supported television designed to reach large market segments [portions] and significant blocks of consumers."

If anything, the increased competition should make commercial and public television better, and yet the broadcasting industry can be counted on to stub- **c** bornly discourage advances. "We should be extremely wary of dismantling or curtailing [cutting short] a system that functions as well as our present one before we have a very clear idea of the social, political, economic and human consequences of whatever we choose to replace it," bleats Leonard H. Golden- **d** son, board chairman of ABC.

What broadcasters will try to make the public believe is that cable or pay TV will of necessity "replace" free TV—which is not true—and that people will have to pay for what they now see free. Of course, anybody who'd pay to see **a** "The Love Boat" deserves it.

Meanwhile, NBC's corporate planning department has taken a nonhysterical look at TV's future in an in-house report called "Broadcasting: The Next 10 Years." Among its predictions:

—By 1985, when the U.S. population has reached 234 million and the me- **d** dian age advanced from the present 28.8 to 31.1, television advertising revenues will reach $14.1 billion a year.

—Advances in "microprocessors" (tiny transmission units) and minicams **c** will make possible not only expanded live news coverage from remote locations, but also "instant commercials" with which local stations will lure still more advertising money away from print media.

—"Fully half" of the entertainment programming in prime time of the '80s will consist of "long-form programs, miniseries, special events and specials" and "the notion of broadcast seasons will have faded away," with new pro- **a** grams introduced year-round.

There is naturally a dark side to the millennium. The expansion of choices offered by cable TV may just turn out to mean a multiplicity of mediocrities; **d** we may have all-news and all-sports TV stations as there are now such radio stations, and cable channels may end up representing various commercial formats rather than public interests.

Beyond that, there is the fact that more, not less, of our daily lives will in **a** some way involve the television screen. We will be surrendering more waking hours to its vicarious experience and giving a machine greater control over our perceptions of one another and of the world. Technicians will be the new aristocracy of this megamedia age that could see the triumph of form over **d** content.

One can anticipate problems and still be excited by prospects. The first house on the block to be hooked up to cable and whatever refinements and attachments come with it will be like the first house on the block to get a TV set in the late '40s and early '50s. There will be an ominous alien [strange] presence in the living room again. It will be something new and, in time, **a** something new to kick around.

Television is dead.

Long live whatever comes next.

(+200)   —end timing—   (min___sec___)

ACTIVITY 12-4
Summarizing

Instructions: Write a one-paragraph summary of the Reading Selection.

_____

_____

_____

_____

_____

_____

_____

_____

_____

_____

What were your reactions?

_____

_____

_____

_____

_____

_____

_____

_____

_____

_____

_____

_____

_____

ACTIVITY 12-5
Affixes and Roots

Instructions: Write two words using each of the roots listed below. Define each word.

fact (do, make)

1. ————————, ————————————
2. ————————, ————————————

aud, audit (hear)

1. ————————, ————————————
2. ————————, ————————————

demos (people)

1. ————————, ————————————
2. ————————, ————————————

dic, dit (speak)

1. ————————, ————————————
2. ————————, ————————————

port (carry)

1. ————————, ————————————
2. ————————, ————————————

mit, mis (send)

1. ————————, ————————————
2. ————————, ————————————

spec (see)

1. ————————, ————————————
2. ————————, ————————————

voc (call)

1. ————————, ————————————
2. ————————, ————————————

pathy (feeling)

1. ————————, ————————————
2. ————————, ————————————

logy (knowledge)

1. ————————, ————————————
2. ————————, ————————————

gynos (woman)

1. ————————, ————————————
2. ————————, ————————————

anthropo (man, mankind)

1. ————————, ————————————
2. ————————, ————————————

cred, credit (believe)

1. ————————, ————————————
2. ————————, ————————————

phob (fear)

1. ————————, ————————————
2. ————————, ————————————

graphy (writing)

1. ————————, ————————————
2. ————————, ————————————

ced, cess (go, give up)

1. ————————, ————————————
2. ————————, ————————————

APPENDIX

The 12 selections that follow have been selected to provide a wide range of subject matter. Each has been abridged to 1500 words and requires the use of the 1500-word Time-Rate Conversion on the lower half of page 232.

As usual, each article is preceded by a vocabulary preview. These should be completed before starting the unit.

OARWET should be used as before, and the comprehension quizzes are again placed before the reading. There are no answers given with the questions.

The last page of each unit provides space for two activities. Complete the section headed "Summary" with a concise paragraph covering the main ideas of the article. Try to do this without referring back to the selection. Use the lower half of the page ("Comment") to Evaluate the material in terms of your own background and tastes. Be completely frank and wholly critical. You may find it interesting to compare your comments with those of the other students.

A 1

Comprehension Quiz

To Build a Fire

Instructions: Write the letter of the correct answer in the blank provided.

1. The action of this story takes place in:
   a) the Arctic   c) the Yukon Territory   (__)
   b) the Antarctic   d) Labrador

2. The protagonist, or main character of the story, was a part of a group which was:
   a) searching for gold   c) fishing   (__)
   b) hunting   d) looking for timber

3. The man was described as:
   a) tall and husky   c) bearded   (__)
   b) in his late thirties   d) all of the above

4. He was surprised when the spittle crackled sharply because:
   a) it froze in midair   c) it was stained brown from   (__)
                    tobacco
   b) it froze when it hit   d) none of the above

5. The actual temperature was:
   a) 50 degrees below zero   c) 75 degrees below zero   (__)
   b) 60 degrees below zero   d) 85 degrees below zero

6. The man expected to reach his goal:
   a) before sundown   c) by six o'clock that evening   (__)
   b) after sundown   d) both (b) and (c)

7. The author has given the dog:
   a) almost human characteristics   c) the knowledge of fire   (__)
   b) the instinct of a wolf   d) all of the above

8. From the description of the protagonist, the reader infers that the man is:
   a) a veteran of the cold country   c) in excellent health   (__)
   b) a comparative newcomer   d) cannot be determined

9. These early paragraphs of London's short story manage to present:
   a) an undercurrent of doom   c) both a) and b)   (__)
   b) a threat of nature   d) neither a) nor b)

10. From what you have read, what do you think will be the critical threat?
    a) the wildness of the dog   c) the danger of frostbite   (__)
    b) the need for a fire   d) the threat of a blizzard

A 1

Vocabulary Preview

1. "his *spittle* crackled" _____

2. "the *protruding* bundle" _____

3. "without *temperamental* difference from the wolf" _____

4. "thrust *aggressively* into the air" _____

5. "a vague *apprehension*" _____

6. "*subdued* the dog" _____

7. "question every *unwonted* movement" _____

8. "continued *monotonously* to chew" _____

9. "the thought *reiterated* itself" _____

10. "he *shied* abruptly, like a startled horse" _____

11. "*floundered* to one side" _____

12. "from the deep *crypts* of its being" _____

13. "numbness that *smote* his fingers" _____

Exercises

Instructions: Write the letter of the correct answer in the blank provided.

14. Antonym of *monotonous*:
    a) dull   b) varied   c) monotone   (__)

15. *To flounder* means:
    a) to struggle awkwardly   b) to fish   c) to flounce   (__)

16. Something that *protrudes* is a:
    a) profusion   b) protrusive   c) protuberance   (__)

17. The present tense of *smote* is:
    a) smight   b) smitten   c) smite   (__)

18. *Crypt* is usually associated with:
    a) a place of burial   b) puzzles   c) a secret   (__)

19. *Apprehension* is usually caused by:
    a) understanding   b) fear of the future   c) dislike   (__)

20. *One who begins a quarrel* is called
    a) an arbitrator   b) an aggressor   c) an aggressive   (__)

TO BUILD A FIRE

by Jack London   (from *Collected Short Stories of Jack London*)

—begin timing—

As he turned to go on, he spat speculatively. There was a sharp, explosive crackle that startled him. He spat again. And again, in the air, before it could fall to the snow, the spittle crackled. He knew that at fifty below spittle crackled on the snow, but this spittle had crackled in the air. Undoubtedly it was colder than fifty below—how much colder he did not know. But the temperature did not matter. He was bound for the old claim on the left fork of Henderson Creek, where the boys were already. They had come over across the divide from the Indian Creek country, while he had come the roundabout way to take a look at the possibilities of getting out logs in the spring from the islands in the Yukon. He would be into camp by six o'clock; a bit after dark, it was true, but the boys would be there, a fire would be going, and a hot supper would be ready. As for lunch, he pressed his hand against the protruding bundle under his jacket. It was also under his shirt, wrapped up in a handkerchief and lying against the naked skin. It was the only way to keep the biscuits from freezing. He smiled agreeably to himself as he thought of those biscuits, each cut open and sopped in bacon grease, and each enclosing a generous slice of fried bacon.

He plunged in among the big spruce trees. The trail was faint. A foot of snow had fallen since the last sled had passed over, and he was glad he was without a sled, traveling light. In fact, he carried nothing but the lunch wrapped in the handkerchief. He was surprised, however, at the cold. It certainly was cold, he concluded, as he rubbed his numb nose and cheekbones with his mittened hand. He was a warm-whiskered man, but the hair on his face did not protect the high cheekbones and the eager nose that thrust itself aggressively into the frosty air.

At the man's heels trotted a dog, a big native husky, the proper wolf dog, gray-coated and without any visible or temperamental difference from its brother the wild wolf. The animal was depressed by the tremendous cold. It knew that it was no time for traveling. Its instinct told it a truer tale than was told to the man by the man's judgment. In reality, it was not merely colder than fifty below zero; it was colder than sixty below, than seventy below. It was seventy-five below zero. Since the freezing point is thirty-two above zero, it meant that one hundred and seven degrees of frost obtained. The dog did not know anything about thermometers. Possibly in its brain there was no sharp consciousness of a condition of very cold such as was in the man's brain. But the brute had its instinct. It experienced a vague but menacing apprehension that subdued it and made it slink along at the man's heels, and that made it question eagerly every unwonted movement of the man as if expecting him to go into camp or to seek shelter somewhere and build a fire. The dog had learned fire, and it wanted fire, or else to burrow under the snow and cuddle its warmth away from the air.

The frozen moisture of its breathing had settled on its fur in a fine powder of frost, and especially were its jowls, muzzle, and eyelashes whitened by its crystalled breath. The man's red beard and mustache were likewise frosted, but more solidly, the deposit taking the form of ice and increasing with every warm, moist breath he exhaled. Also, the man was chewing tobacco, and the muzzle of ice held his lips so rigidly that he was unable to clear his chin when he expelled the juice. The result was that a crystal beard of the color and solidity of amber was increasing its length on his chin. If he fell down it would shatter itself, like glass, into brittle fragments.

It was the penalty all tobacco chewers paid in that country, and he had been out before in two cold snaps. They had not been so cold as this, he knew, but by the spirit thermometer at Sixty Mile he knew they had been registered at fifty below and at fifty-five.

The dog dropped in again at his heels, with a tail drooping discouragement, as the man swung along the creek bed. In a month no man had come up or down that silent creek. The man held steadily on. He was not much given to thinking, and just then particularly he had nothing to think about save that he would eat lunch at the forks and that at six o'clock he would be in camp with the boys. There was nobody to talk to; and, had there been, speech would have been impossible because of the ice muzzle on his mouth. So he continued monotonously to chew tobacco and to increase the length of his amber beard.

Once in a while the thought reiterated itself that it was very cold and that he had never experienced such cold. As he walked along he rubbed his cheek-bones and nose with the back of his mittened hand. He did this automatically, now and again changing hands. But, rub as he would, the instant he stopped his cheekbones went numb, and the following instant the end of his nose went numb. He was sure to frost his cheeks; he knew that. But it didn't matter much, after all. What were frosted cheeks? A bit painful, that was all; they were never serious.

Empty as the man's mind was of thoughts, he was keenly observant, and he noticed the changes in the creek, the curves and bends and timber jams, and always he sharply noted where he placed his feet. Once, coming around a bend, he shied abruptly, like a startled horse, curved away from the place where he had been walking, and retreated several paces back along the trail. The creek he knew was frozen clear to the bottom—no creek could contain water in that arctic winter—but he knew also that there were springs that bubbled out from the hillsides and ran along under the snow and on top the ice of the creek. He knew that the coldest snaps never froze these springs, and he knew likewise their danger. They were traps. They hid pools of water under the snow that might be three inches deep, or three feet. Sometimes a skim of ice half an inch thick covered them, and in turn was covered by the snow. Sometimes there were alternate layers of water and ice skin, so that when one broke through he kept on breaking through for a while, sometimes wetting himself to the waist.

That was why he had shied in such panic. He had felt the give under his feet and heard the crackle of a snow-hidden ice skin. And to get his feet wet in such a temperature meant trouble and danger. At the very least it meant delay, for he would be forced to stop and build a fire, and under its protection to bare his feet while he dried his socks and moccasins. He stood and studied the creek bed and its banks, and decided that the flow of water came from the right.

The dog did not want to go. It hung back until the man shoved it forward, and then it went quickly across the white, unbroken surface. Suddenly it broke through, floundered to one side, and got away to firmer footing. It had wet its forefeet and legs, and almost immediately the water that clung to it turned to ice. It made quick efforts to lick the ice off its legs, then dropped down in the snow and began to bite out the ice that had formed between the toes. This was a matter of instinct. To permit the ice to remain would mean sore feet. It did not know this. It merely obeyed the mysterious prompting that arose from the deep crypts of its being. But the man knew, having achieved a judgment on the subject, and he removed the mitten from his right hand and helped tear out the ice particles. He did not expose his fingers more than a minute, and was astonished at the swift numbness that smote them. It certainly was cold. He pulled on the mitten hastily, and beat the hand savagely across his chest.

At twelve o'clock the day was at its brightest. He unbuttoned his jacket and shirt and drew forth his lunch. The action consumed no more than a quarter of a minute, yet in that brief moment the numbness laid hold of his exposed finger. He did not put the mitten on, but, instead, struck the fingers a dozen sharp smashes against his leg. Then he sat down on a snow-covered log to eat. The sting that followed upon the striking of his fingers against his leg ceased so quickly that he was startled. He had had no chance to take a bite of biscuit. . . .

(—0—)   —end timing—   (min__sec__)

A 1

To Build a Fire—Jack London

SUMMARY:

COMMENT:

A 2

Comprehension Quiz

Camping Is for the Birds

Instructions: Write the letter of the correct answer in the blank provided.

1. John Steinbeck's essay on camping:
   a) was written tongue-in-cheek
   b) should be considered seriously
   c) is a helpful satire
   d) both (a) and (c)
   (⎯)

2. Our nationwide camping activities, says Steinbeck, result in:
   a) relaxed nerves
   b) divorce and bankruptcy
   c) a true return to nature
   d) all of the above
   (⎯)

3. For millions of years all mankind "camped" because:
   a) of the lure of open spaces
   b) city living was too crowded
   c) the whole family enjoyed it
   d) it had to
   (⎯)

4. The author himself has camped:
   a) to follow the crops as a worker
   b) to gather material for a book
   c) both (a) and (b)
   d) neither (a) nor (b)
   (⎯)

5. Because of his experiences, he is sure all readers of his article will:
   a) take him seriously
   b) give up the camping idea
   c) laugh, and plan the next trip
   d) all of the above
   (⎯)

6. Advertisements for camping equipment, says Steinbeck:
   a) eliminate the human factor
   b) glorify the weather
   c) picture children as angels
   d) all of the above
   (⎯)

7. According to the article, the center of the American home is:
   a) the family room
   b) the bathroom
   c) the living room
   d) the hearth
   (⎯)

8. The ideal number of participants in a camping trip, according to Steinbeck, is:
   a) one
   b) two
   c) four
   d) six
   (⎯)

9. The American dream exists behind:
   a) the Iron Curtain
   b) the Bamboo Curtain
   c) the Kleenex Curtain
   d) none of the above
   (⎯)

10. Steinbeck's statement "... find people from your own ... state and be protected from anything new and strange" is:
    a) meant seriously
    b) satirical
    c) good advice
    d) all of the above
    (⎯)

165

A 2

Vocabulary Preview

1. "an *ethnic* development" _____
2. "the *relentless* nervous drive" _____
3. "all the *frantic* effort" _____
4. "every last *raddled* one of us" _____
5. "lives of quiet *desperation*" _____
6. "*domesticate* food animals" _____
7. "a *hamlet* and city" _____
8. "any *novice* nature lover" _____
9. "an *abysmal* liar" _____
10. "age *impaired* my judgment" _____
11. "a *pride* of horrible children" _____
12. "too grisly to *contemplate*" _____
13. "less than *civil*" _____
14. "the lovely *sylvan* turnouts" _____
15. "*roust* you out of bed" _____
16. "tiny flowers bloom in *microscopia*" _____
17. "is a definite *soporific*" _____

Exercises

Instructions: Write the letter of the correct answer in the blank provided.

18. *Frantic* people are:
    a) frank   b) frenzied   c) frolicsome   (__)

19. A *novice* player would be apt to:
    a) play as well as others   b) win   c) make mistakes   (__)

20. *Sylvan* does not mean:
    a) of the woods   b) of the forest   c) of the city   (__)

CAMPING IS FOR THE BIRDS

by John Steinbeck   (from *Popular Science*, May, 1967)

—begin timing—

When the editors of *Popular Science* asked me to set down some observations on camping, I felt a certain reluctance, the same kind of hesitance I have for stepping on a butterfly I know is going to lay the eggs that make the worms that eat up my cabbages.

The present American passion for moving about in motorized caravans is surely interesting as an ethnic development, and to the gadget manufacturers highly profitable, and as far as I can see results in little permanent damage beyond divorce and bankruptcy.

It is presumed that because I have done some camping and have written about it that I must approve of it. This is not necessarily so, though I do understand the universal urge. Polluted air, hysterical traffic, the pressures of crowding and competition, the fears of age and failure under stress, the relentless nervous drive to get ahead or just stay even, and on top of these the demands, the confusion, the noise, and, finally, the gray disappointment in the rewards after all the frantic effort—all these are bound to raise in weary souls a dream of simplicity and peace, a folk memory of man close to nature and of a nature dear and kindly toward man.

The dream is inevitable. Thoreau said it and did it, and every last raddled one of us wants it. If Thoreau found that in his time "The mass of men lead lives of quiet desperation," what would he have said of our time, when Pandora and Pandemonium are going steady? But so strong and sweet is the dream of escape to our personal Walden Pond that we are reluctant to inspect the dream for fear that it may turn out to be a dream.

For X millions of years our species camped because we had no choice. We followed the food supply, living in caves, brush piles, hollow trees, or under the dried skins of animals. Only when we learned to plant and store crops, and to control and domesticate food animals, had we need or reason to build a house, and then a hamlet, and then a city; and that great advance happened very recently in our history. Meanwhile we have a built-in memory of the good, old, simple millions of years of our prehistory and no conception of the misery, the discomfort, and the danger that were man's constant neighbors. It is true, however, that one night in the open, in rain or snow, with no hot-dog stand in sight, nor any of the other modern conveniences we take for granted, will revive that old and terrible memory in any novice nature lover.

Camping is, and should be, a way of doing something you couldn't do in any other way. Anyone who doesn't prefer a good bed in a warm room to lumpy pine boughs and a sleeping bag that feels like a plaster cast is either insane or an abysmal liar. And so we try vainly for the best of both worlds—the so-called simplicity of nature plus the comfort of a modern apartment—hence the great and increasing interest in the caravan, the mobile home, the camper top, and the wheelborne penthouse.

I've done it all ways. Once, following the crops, I had an old bakery truck with a mattress on the floor. It was pretty nice in there when it rained, sitting on the bedding, heating a can of beans over a Sterno flame. Much later, when age had further impaired my judgment, I toured the country with Charley. But then I had as much comfort as I could pack into a small space, and I did the camping routine because it was the only way I could see and hear what I wanted to. In the process, I guess I made nearly every mistake possible. This gives me the right to offer advice to the new camper, and I don't for a moment believe that he will any more listen to my words of wisdom than I would have.

The dream. Everyone has seen the slick advertising of beautiful new camping equipment. "Sleeps four," the copy says, or "sleeps six."

Six people in one outfit no matter how shiny and new is too grisly to contemplate. The picture shows a sunny meadow littered with buttercups across which a lovely little stream rushes to find its home in a deep blue lake. A glowing wife is cooking something delicious just as the father brings a two-pound rainbow trout to the net. The children, little angels, wait patiently for their dinners after which they go immediately to serene beddy-bye dreams.

The actuality. Don't believe it. It rains. The kids get to fighting. You are trapped in a small, smelly, miserable box, with a pride of horrible children and a husband-eating wife. The land beside the road is posted, the game warden is watching. You have looked for hours for some place where you are allowed to pull off the road and you finally settle for a camp city with an entrance fee of five dollars which has all the natural simplicity of a city slum. Right away your dog tangles with the dog next door, and next door is so next that you can't get out of your car.

By the time you've settled the quarrel with the neighbors, your kids are making a sound like whooping cough. The beds are wet and there isn't any television. Your lovely wife, trying to heat three cans of corned beef hash, has spilled the alcohol and the truck is on fire.

Togetherness. Sleeps six, my eye! No marriage, no family can survive three rainy days cooped up in a camper. Your teenage daughter is in deep mourning for the steady she had to leave behind, which makes her less than civil. Your older son has his transistor radio turned on full to drown out the 300 other transistors howling on all sides, no two on the same station. Togetherness gets to be a pretty crummy institution with murder stalking the edges.

But suppose you have taken only your beloved out in your camper. She is a good little scout who loves to feel the rain on her face, who adores the wind in her hair in a convertible. She will peel to the bone with sunburn and laugh gallantly.

In this romantic situation you will soon learn some basic truths: The center of the American home is not the hearth. It is the bathroom. Take a dame out of reach of facilities and you are in trouble. I have seen many campers and, with one exception, the sanitary facilities wouldn't keep a romance going for a weekend.

You will learn further that the good little scout is afraid of nothing in the world except getting her hair blown or wet, that for women, the peace and inner security once found in church are now sought out and found under the dryer, and the confessor is a creamy-voiced character whose upper register edges into the soprano. Mark Twain once described women as "lovely creatures with a backache." Well, nothing can bring out the backache like a camping trip.

The Kleenex Curtain. You will find to your surprise that every night finds your expensive rig parked at a motel with twin beds, hot water, and a flush toilet. No matter how you may lust for simplicity, just try running out of Kleenex. The Russians have the Iron Curtain, the Chinese the Bamboo Curtain, but we surely have the Kleenex Curtain.

The lovely sylvan turnouts with barbecue pits and picnic tables maintained by the states for rest and quiet are not for you at night. A state trooper will roust you out before you can make up a bed.

The state and national parks have nice places to camp, with toilets and showers for a small fee. There you may find people from your own state or your own town, and thus be protected from anything new and strange.

If, however, you are bruised and a little raw from the discotheque tempo of our enlightened culture—go camping, but go alone. Find a pleasant place and then find the owner and get his permission to stop there, even if you have to pay him. And, finally, stay there. Don't try to find a better place. You may get to read some of the books you hadn't time for. When it rains, it is lovely—if you are alone. And when the sun comes out, it is pleasant to lie on your belly in the meadow, to refresh your memory of grass and of the tiny flowers that bloom in microscopia. Then you may discover that ants have to work hard for a living, too, and before long that chlorophyl is a definite soporific.

A week or so of this may mend your defenses and send you back into the fight refreshed and rearmed—or it may bore the hell out of you. But don't believe in ads. Find out for yourself.

(+25)   —end timing—   (min___sec___)

A 2

Camping Is for the Birds—John Steinbeck

SUMMARY:

COMMENT:

A 3

Comprehension Quiz

Jesus Lopez, 42

1. A key indicator of the "angle" of this descriptive selection is:
   - a) Lopez is a steel worker
   - b) he earns $10,000 a year
   - c) he is highly skilled
   - d) the subject's name is Lopez

   (__)

2. The basic problem faced by Lopez is:
   - a) he was born in South Chicago
   - b) he is a Chicano
   - c) he is unintelligent
   - d) he didn't go to college

   (__)

3. The reason Lopez says he stopped going to the bar was that he:
   - a) was overcharged
   - b) didn't like the other patrons
   - c) would have to fight
   - d) has become a moral coward

   (__)

4. Which of the following is *not* a clue to his inner feelings?
   - a) the wrecked cars
   - b) his high school record
   - c) the death of his daughter
   - d) the neighborhood of his home

   (__)

5. As a young man, Lopez reacted to insulting remarks by:
   - a) fighting back
   - b) picking on other minorities
   - c) laughing them off
   - d) keeping quiet

   (__)

6. At age 42, his reaction to blacks is:
   - a) one of active dislike
   - b) very friendly
   - c) almost sympathetic
   - d) not mentioned

   (__)

7. The author's description of the nature of Lopez's work indicates it is:
   - a) unskilled
   - b) semi-skilled
   - c) skilled
   - d) tricky and dangerous

   (__)

8. The language used by Lopez is:
   - a) rough and slang-laden
   - b) a mixture of slang and quality
   - c) that of an educated man
   - d) typical of a Chicano

   (__)

9. In view of the incidents described by Lopez:
   - a) he can do nothing about things
   - b) he is proud of his adopted country
   - c) he hopes for a better society
   - d) both (a) and (b)

   (__)

10. An article like this one:
    - a) "tells it like it is"
    - b) is an exaggerated picture
    - c) harms minority groups
    - d) is un-American

    (__)

A 3

Vocabulary Preview

1. "on *excursions*, visited relatives" _____

2. "unbelievable *squalor*" _____

3. "child died . . . was *malpractice*" _____

4. "these *principles* . . . I let them slide" _____

5. "paid a *substantial* down payment" _____

6. "*Ostensibly* I'm the boss" _____

7. "you have to *interpret* [what's happening]" _____

8. "test the *carbon* content" _____

9. "everybody's scared . . . about this *automation*" _____

10. "I'm not a *metallurgist*" _____

11. "might have *identical* thoughts" _____

12. "I was an *idealist*" _____

Exercises

Instructions: Write the letter of the correct answer in the blank provided.

13. An *idealist* is one who has high-minded:
    a) friends   b) principles   c) national origins   (__)

14. Which way would you prefer to be boss?
    a) ostensibly   b) in reality   c) theoretically   (__)

15. To live in *squalor* is to live in a:
    a) castle   b) ranch house   c) shack   (__)

16. The best practice for a doctor is *not*:
    a) general practice   b) surgery   c) malpractice   (__)

17. A *metallurgist* would know most about:
    a) steel   b) farms   c) forests   (__)

18. To be able to pay a *substantial* sum for something you must be:
    a) reasonably well off   b) on welfare   c) just getting along   (__)

19. Children enjoy being taken on an:
    a) exposition   b) impression   c) excursion   (__)

20. If we have *identical* opinions, our ideas are:
    a) the same   b) opposite   c) disagreeing   (__)

JESUS LOPEZ, 42

by Studs Terkel   (from *Division Street: America*)

—begin timing—

He is a first helper at the open hearth, U. S. Steel Company. His work is highly skilled. He earns about $10,000 a year and is due for a thirteen-week vacation. On past excursions, he had visited relatives in Mexico, as well as his town of birth. "As I remember it, it was a big town; but when I went back a couple of years ago, it was just a tiny, little thing. It's nothing there, little shacks. It made me sick. Squalor, unbelievable, really unbelievable that people could live like that. You see rows of kids standing like that with their hands out."

His American boyhood was in Joliet and South Chicago, among "Polacks, Hunkies," and other Mexicans. "It was called the bush then. Oh, we had some grand old fights." He was a brilliant student at school, without too much effort, but he bypassed a chance at college to make some money fast.

He was once an outgoing person, with many friends and many curiosities: literature, politics. Today, he lives with his Anglo wife in a modest-income suburb, to the city's southwest. Their only child, a girl, died during one of their trips to Mexico. He is convinced it was malpractice.

He has had a few drinks:

I smash cars up left and right. I have a Corvair out there, you see it? It's all smashed up, not fixed. I got a Hudson sitting in a garage, one of these Green Hornets. It's green, too. And it's a Hornet. (Laughs.) And something's wrong with the transmission or something. . . . I got a '64 Le Mans in the garage that's gettin' fixed. That's one I'm gonna pick up Saturday.

It's mixed around here. Polacks next door. Over here's a German, I think. And next to that there, that's another Polack. And there's a Filipino.

I noticed a bar over here where other people were paying thirty cents a bottle and I was paying thirty-five cents a bottle of beer. I stopped goin'. I wouldn't bother to ask. I know. A lot of things that I would fight at the drop of a hat years ago, I just let go and think about it maybe. Like that business about the five cents. You may get sore inside, but you no longer make an issue of it, even though I feel sick inside most of the time. No, I've become a moral coward.

What do I mean by that? Let's say these principles and all that, I let them slide under to keep things at an even keel and all that. In other words, I've fallen into that pattern that everybody's crying' about. That security. I'm forty-two years of age now. If I get fired from my job, what am I gonna do? How many first helpers do they want there in the back yard?

Like I happen to ride in Oklahoma City last summer and there was a motel, very fancy motel. They got those big neon signs and flashy lighted things around. And it was late, about 12:30 A.M. Drove in. I was with my mother. I was taking her down to Nogales. My sister's graduating from school down there. And there was nobody in there but one man. I asked for a room and I got it. I went and took my mother and got her settled and all that.

And there was some guy that looked like a salesman. Oh, when I walked in, I knew what he was talking about. About those people and all that business. When I walked in, he said the Negroes, you know. And the man who was behind the desk, he said, "We have to take them." I almost started to make an issue right then and there. Because I saw this guy looking at me and you sort of sense these things. I mean you get a feeling when you've lived with it. And I asked him "How about let's say a Mexican citizen or something like that?"

He didn't know that the papers in my pocket says that I'm a citizen of the United States by Act of Congress. I put that in when I was sold this house. The real-estate agent . . . I paid a substantial down payment and all that business. Went to the loan outfit for the balance. The minute we get back in the real-estate agent's office, after the thing was to be all settled, phone call. Real-estate agent answered the phone, he talks, then he asks me, "Are you a citizen?" (Laughs.) I told him "By Act of Congress. Who wants to know? Tell him by Act of Congress." And how many people can say that? By Act of Congress. In other words, I was made a citizen of the United States of America through service in World War Two. And I gotta put that in. When somebody asks me: Are you a citizen? I tell 'im by Act of Congress.

The guy next door, he mentioned to me that somebody came to visit him one time, and I was out mowing the lawn and he asked since when were niggers living around here? So he said, "He's not a nigger." (Laughs.) Sometimes in the summertime . . .

. . . One winter I had my car blocked, all four wheels, you know. I was standing on the corner, 95th and Central, waiting for a bus, and cars, kids: "Hi, Nigger," and all that. All I can do is forget it. A moral coward. Oh, well, I could carry a gun. Shoot somebody. I could carry a six-inch blade and kill somebody. Oh yeah, I used to fight at the drop of a hat. I used to be called the cock o' the walk. Yeah, I quit that long ago.

I run the furnace. Ostensibly I'm the boss of my second helper and the third helper. I say ostensibly because a lot of third helpers try to tell us how to run furnaces and things like that.

It's skilled, if skill is something you learn through practice. Half the moves we make are just an educated guess. We have seven doors and you have to be able to see in your mind what's happening in there and to interpret. We also take the temperature and test the carbon content. We're supposed to know exactly what moves to make. Intuition plays a great part. There's the son of a smelter foreman that's working there, he tells me it's an art. Well, it used to be an art before we had all these oxygen analyzers that will regulate your fuel. But they go on the blink a lot of times.

. . . Oh, everybody's scared. Especially about this automation. You ought to hear it on the job. With these oxygen furnaces you know, they're gonna knock out all the open hearths. Well, it might. But I understand there will have to be some open hearths, because I don't believe oxygen furnaces can make all that steel, like some of the alloys we make, and things like that. But then I'm not a metallurgist. I'm just what is called an overpaid laborer. (Laughs.) That's exactly what they call us, overpaid laborers and like that. Actually we don't notice this fear among the furnace workers. It's the machine operators like the charging-car operators, the crane operators, and things like that there. They seem more worried about it, I don't know why.

So . . . at work and all that, what do we talk about and have a few beers? Work. Problems we've had there and what somebody should have done and didn't do. Oh, once in a while you hear them about—what? . . . Actually I've come to the conclusion that people are more indrawn toward themselves and all that business.

So I stick to myself and I'm sort of a loner. Once in a while I'll get with a couple of guys and we might have identical thoughts and ideas and something like that. But the majority of the time, I keep to myself. Everybody's concerned more about themselves and why that is I don't know. . . .

Have you found any hope, some other kind of people?

Hardly, hardly. When it comes to Negroes, I'm a little more than halfway neutral. (Laughs.) I can put myself in their shoes, because of things that happened to me. I did tell one, though: "You're not gonna get anywhere by wearing a chip on your shoulder." Any word that anybody says, you might say in a kidding way, they take it serious. I found too many people like that. . . .

Is it true you don't care?

No, it's not really true. It's a world I have to live in, how can I not care? But the thing is *what can I do about it?* There we go. The Bomb. Nobody ever talks about it, nobody ever says boo about it. There's no such thing.

I was an idealist, I, oh boy! Now I feel we should all be happy as monkeys. No problems, just eat, sleep and—what's after that? It hurts me to think. For the last three years I just about given up thinking. I'm just going along day to day and day to day, like that.

What do you do in your leisure time?

I drink. (Laughs.) and read—*Playboy.* Look at the nude girls. I stopped being disturbed when I got over age for the draft. (Laughs.) Yeah.

You think the world's going to hell?

(Astonished.) Why, don't you think so?

I have a sense of humor. In this day and age, how could you survive without a sense of humor? Ask my wife if I have a sense of humor. She complains I sit here like a bump on a log, hours and hours. I'm doing nothing but thinking. What am I thinking? I better not be thinking. I hate myself. I'm weak. I'm too weak. (Takes a long swig out of the beer can.)

(+25)   —end timing—   (min___sec___)

A 3

Jesus Lopez, 42—Studs Terkel

SUMMARY:

COMMENT:

A 4

Comprehension Quiz

Whatever Happened to Leisure Education?

Instructions: Write the letter of the correct answer in the blank provided.

1. The theme of this article is that Americans:
    a) are easily bored
    b) must work harder
    c) must be educated for leisure
    d) are unhappy people   (___)

2. The Institute of the Future's predictions for 2000 A.D. include:
    a) tri-dimensional TV
    b) plentiful picturephones
    c) longer vacations, more holidays
    d) all of these   (___)

3. At present, Americans:
    a) deal well with leisure
    b) have trouble with leisure
    c) love to relax
    d) have too little leisure   (___)

4. Americans also:
    a) distrust unoccupied time
    b) enjoy the "great emptiness" of free time
    c) feel guilty when working
    d) both (a) and (b)   (___)

5. According to the article, Americans:
    a) worked 60 hours weekly in 1900
    b) worked 40 hours weekly in 1950
    c) have 3700 hours off yearly
    d) all of these   (___)

6. If leisure time increases as expected, we should have:
    a) truly satisfied people
    b) greater beer sales
    c) fewer nervous break-downs
    d) fewer auto accidents   (___)

7. The boredom that is a by-product of abundant time could:
    a) create great art and music
    b) cause antisocial behavior
    c) cure cancer
    d) all of these   (___)

8. According to the article, the need for leisure education has been:
    a) recognized, but no action taken
    b) greatly exaggerated
    c) unrecognized
    d) declared unnecessary   (___)

9. We are advised that in order to cope with leisure, we must learn:
    a) basic trade skills
    b) new attitudes and behavior
    c) to avoid free time
    d) to become "random warriors"   (___)

10. With proper education, Americans may someday find leisure:
    a) destroying free enterprise
    b) destructively self-indulgent
    c) a blessing
    d) a terrifying ordeal   (___)

Vocabulary Preview

1. "has projected a *scenario*" _____

2. "*tridimensional* color TV" _____

3. "*optional* retirement" _____

4. "shifts from a work *orientation*" _____

5. "free-time *phobia*" _____

6. "people *afflicted* with TGIM" _____

7. "with occupational *therapy*" _____

8. "*vaunted* jet-set values" _____

9. "increasing *mobility*" _____

10. "*pell-mell* pursuit" _____

11. "failed to *dislodge*" _____

12. "*jeopardize* our enjoyment" _____

13. "its *corrosive* effects" _____

14. "*suave* man-of-the world" _____

15. "slaughters *sadistically*" _____

16. "every fad and *frivolity*" _____

17. "modern *hucksters*" _____

18. "*indulging* in activities" _____

19. "*infinitesimal* fraction" _____

20. "fraction of this *freneticism*" _____

21. "*cardinal* principles" _____

22. "paid to its *implementation*" _____

23. "faculty for using . . . became *atrophied*" _____

24. "Toynbee is no *Cassandra*" _____

25. "human *solidarity* prevails" _____

A 4

WHATEVER HAPPENED TO LEISURE EDUCATION?

by Edward R. Walsh   (from *The Plain Truth*, July-August, 1978)

—begin timing—

What kind of world will our children inherit? What new challenges will they face? Abundant leisure time is sure to be one. Some sociologists are forecasting a workweek of between 20 and 24 hours by the turn of the century, and the IBM Corporation has identified leisure developments as a major clue to future life-styles.

If we could peek into the future, what might we find? The Institute for the Future, a think-tank operation based in Menlo Park, California, has projected a scenario of American society for the year 2000. Here's what you have to look forward to. Most homes will be equipped with tridimensional color TV sets mounted on wall screens, with a third of them wired for pay TV. Nearby holiday travel centers will provide you with instantaneous [immediate] fare information and ticket reservations on a global basis. Push a button and you'll learn in an instant about forthcoming leisure events throughout the world. TV sets will be toted about much like transistor radios are today. The Picturephone will be commonplace. Units will record messages automatically, even provide you with photographic reproductions if you need them. Remember those old movies you never could get enough of? Well, your local library will lend them to you for home viewing on video cassettes. Even current films and plays can be yours for a fee. You'll have more free time to enjoy these technological marvels because of more flexible work schedules, longer vacations, additional holidays, optional retirement, and a life expectancy of 75 years. "Leisure time pursuits will become an increasingly important basis for differences between people, as society itself shifts from a work orientation toward greater involvement in leisure," predicts Alvin Toffler in his book *Future Shock*. But will Americans have developed the ability to handle the new leisure life-style thrust upon them by changing times?

There's reason to believe they won't, since we seem to be having difficulty dealing with even currently available leisure. Many of us go to pieces when faced with unoccupied hours, judging from the increase in free-time phobia. Dr. William Flynn, a Georgetown University psychiatrist, sees such symptoms in some of his patients. He calls it the "Thank-God-it's-Monday" sickness. Many people afflicted with TGIM become more depressed on weekends and can't wait for Monday to roll around. Some TGIMers know they're supposed to be having fun, so they overdo it by playing too hard. They' e unable to relax, and soon their recreation becomes just another weekend job.

LEISURE TIME PROBLEM

Why can't people enjoy their leisure without suffering such psychological hang-ups? Max Gunther, author of *The Weekenders*, explains why: "Nearly all people in our society need work to hang their lives upon. Some need it so badly that when work is snatched away their lives start to disintegrate."

Leisure time is already such a problem, adds sociologist Lorenz Stucki, that whole organizations concern themselves with occupational therapy to fill in such freedom. Expressed more brutally, leisure time must somehow—anyhow—be killed.

Despite its vaunted jet-set values our modern age betrays a lack of sophistication when it comes to handling leisure creatively. Though increasing affluence, mobility, and a pell-mell pursuit of "the good life" have provided us with an array of options, we have failed to dislodge a deep-rooted distrust of unoccupied time.

"A guilt complex will inevitably [without doubt] cramp our style for enjoying leisure," writes Leslie Dowling, "if we have a feeling we are wasting our time, if not actually committing a sin by not being gainfully and seriously occupied."

Thus, "the great emptiness," as one sociologist characterizes this fear of free time, threatens to deplete our energies and jeopardize our enjoyment of leisure. Because more leisure looms on the horizon, the crisis is bound to intensify. Look at what's happened to our work week, for example. In 1850, when America was still an agrarian [farming] society, people worked about 70 hours a week; by 1900 they were working 60 hours. Forty years later the workweek was trimmed to 44 hours, and by 1950 the 40-hour, five-day schedule was standard. Today, Americans work a 35- to 38-hour workweek, but that's only part of the picture.

Bold new experiments with the four-day week, the three-day week, and flexitime schedules (flexible working hours) have increased available leisure for workers. A few years ago one sociologist estimated that Americans enjoyed some 3,700 hours off the job each year. That comes to over 230 full days of 16 hours each. What's more, the trend toward more free time will continue. Max Kaplan, a member of the UNESCO Commission on Leisure and Education, predicts that our children will be working half-days or half-weeks for only half of their lives.

PSYCHOLOGICAL CONSEQUENCES

What further dislocations might this create? Dr. Lawrence C. Hartlage, a faculty member of the Georgia Medical School, expresses alarm. "The implications of increasing leisure time in a country still strongly rooted in a work ethic can be of serious psychological consequence for such variables as self-concept, self-esteem and related measures of worth which people have traditionally derived from their work."

Boredom is one by-product of abundant free time. Boredom, in turn, can breed antisocial behavior—crime, drug abuse, sexual excesses and other social ills. Not even the famous escape its corrosive effects. When suave, man-of-the-world screen idol George Sanders took his life in 1971, he left this note: "I commit suicide because I am bored and because I have already lived enough." Sanders, 65 and in good health, still had a promising movie career going for him.

A classic case of boredom-induced violence can be seen in Stanley Kubrick's film *A Clockwork Orange*. Through his pointless viciousness Alex displays what Kansas psychologist Maynard Shelly calls "random warrior" behavior. Kubrick's anti-hero slaughters his victims sadistically as he seeks escape from boredom. Most of us, horrified at such a solution for releasing pent-up [confined] emotions, don't kill people but do kill plenty of time. In so doing, our ability to use leisure in fulfilling ways declines, leaving us at the mercy of every fad and frivolity modern hucksters toss our way.

"The American, like nature, abhors [hates] a vacuum," writes Norman Lobsenz in *Is Anybody Happy?* "As a result, he is increasingly engaged in an heroic effort to fill it. And filling it he is. More people are indulging in more activities, going more places, and spending more money buying things than ever before. The trouble is that only an infinitesimal fraction of this freneticism equals fun. Behind the masks of gaiety hides a growing incapacity for true pleasure."

EDUCATION FOR LEISURE

Warnings about the dangers of misused leisure time are hardly new. "The possession of surplus free time, in the use of which one has not been trained, is more dangerous than surplus money under the same circumstances," wrote George Cullen over 50 years ago.

One reason why leisure has become such a problem is that people have never been taught how to use it in meaningful ways. Schools have prepared students for the world of work but not for the world of leisure. This oversight was not deliberate. In 1918 the National Education Association declared "the worthy use of leisure" to be one of the seven cardinal principles of education. In following years the Educational Policies Commission reaffirmed this objective, even though nothing more than lip service has been paid to its implementation.

Those who favor the concept consider it to be more than just fun and games. Education for leisure is seen as a total developmental process through which a person grows into a better understanding of himself, leisure, and the relationship of leisure to the rest of life.

* * *

Dr. Richard Kraus, author of *Recreation and the Schools*, sees four major purposes of leisure education: namely, the development of attitudes, knowledge, skills, and appropriate behaviors. Schools should create activities or instructional units, he says, which contribute to growth in these areas, with carry-over into program participation.

* * *

Professor Tony Mobley of Indiana State University endorses an approach which links leisure education to classroom subjects. The effort "must be interdisciplinary in nature and embrace science, art, music, literature, history, geography, mathematics, human ecology, physical education, dramatic arts and all other studies," he contends.

* * *

QUEST FOR QUALITY LIFE

But man's inability to deal with his own fears about free time has caused the quest for the good life to falter. Society has contributed to the confusion by failing to provide resources for using leisure in life-enhancing ways.

Will fear of leisure be our downfall? What psychiatrist William Flynn reports about his patients, historian Arnold Toynbee observes on a cosmic scale. "In industrialized man the faculty for using leisure has become atrophied and the traditional community life has disintegrated," writes the late great British historian in his book *Surviving the Future*. "Modern man positively dreads leisure because it confronts him with his own self, isolated, terrifyingly in the 'lonely crowd.'"

But Toynbee is no Cassandra contemplating the certain destruction of the human race. He goes on to suggest that universal leisure education may provide the answer to man's age-old quest for quality of life. "The faculty for using leisure positively in intellectual, artistic, and above all, religious activities is the essence of being human."

What kind of world will our children inherit?

God's gift of abundant leisure, meant to be a blessing, not a burden, can provide us with a future in which freedom, happiness, and human solidarity prevail.

(+200)   —end timing—   (min__sec__)

A 4

Whatever Happened to Leisure Education?—
Edward R. Walsh

SUMMARY:

COMMENT:

A 5

Comprehension Quiz

It's Been Done

Instructions: Write the letter of the correct answer in the blank provided.

1. Another title for this article might be:
   a) The Story Behind Those   c) The Fastest Bird   (__)
   Facts
   b) The Memory Twins   d) The Value of Pen Pals

2. Norris McWhirter, Rusty Shuse, and Nruturam are all:
   a) record holders   c) stout drinkers   (__)
   b) freaks   d) none of these

3. The *Guiness Book of World Records* is:
   a) limited to record-holders   c) includes trivia, records,   (__)
   nature facts
   b) exclusively trivia   d) all of the above

4. The editor of the book:
   a) actually has a poor   c) has a good memory   (__)
   memory
   b) has a fair memory   d) lost his memory when his
   brother died

5. The authentication of facts is:
   a) approximated   c) done by the editor   (__)
   b) all from newspapers   d) checked out carefully

6. The McWhirter twins were originally:
   a) Siamese   c) press researchers   (__)
   b) members of the IRA   d) birdlovers

7. The idea for the records book started with:
   a) a missed shot at a plover   c) a bar-room brawl   (__)
   b) a senseless shooting   d) a lack of encyclopedias

8. The McWhirters were hired:
   a) after a demanding   c) because of their skill in   (__)
   interview   Turkish
   b) by their reputations   d) because they didn't drink

9. The first edition was completed:
   a) in two years   c) after years of research   (__)
   b) in six weeks   d) during World War II

10. The most important source for new items is:
    a) agents in the field   c) newspapers and   (__)
    magazines
    b) Guiness drinkers   d) the Guiness World
    Record Exhibit Hall

A 5

Vocabulary Preview

1. "*aptly* nicknamed" _____

2. "*authenticated* records" _____

3. "*intricately* carved" _____

4. "'*Sadist* Factory'" _____

5. "all possible *permutations*" _____

6. "not all is *trivia*" _____

7. "details on space *probes*" _____

8. "year of *compiling* facts" _____

9. "final *galley* proofs" _____

10. "are *irretrievably* at the printers" _____

11. "*verifying* and codifying them" _____

12. "verifying and *codifying*" _____

13. "annual *compendium*" _____

14. "a *lucrative* profession" _____

15. "*allegedly* 150-year-old Russians" _____

16. "local *commissars*" _____

17. "*Devastated* by his loss" _____

18. "*magpies* for facts" _____

19. "*eked* out a living" _____

20. "a golden *plover*" _____

21. "Irish *grouse* moor" _____

22. "The *errant* shot" _____

23. "widely consumed *stout*" _____

24. "his winged *quarry*" _____

25. "the *duo* . . . in their 20's" _____

IT'S BEEN DONE

by Arturo F. Gonzalez   (from *The Rotarian*, July, 1978)

—begin timing—

What can Rusty Skuse of England, Roy Sullivan of West Virginia, U.S.A., Paul Wilson of New Zealand, and Nruturam of India possibly have in common? Rusty Skuse (neé Field), who lives in Aldershot, England, is the most completely tattooed woman. In 12 years her tattoo artist-husband's needle has covered 85 percent of her body. Roy Sullivan, aptly nicknamed "Dooms" by his fellow forest rangers, has been hit by lightning in the West Virginia woods seven times, surviving every bolt although they've melted the rubber soles on his shoes.

Paul Wilson has notched a new record, unbroken since it was set 70 years ago by dancer Bill "Bojangles" Robinson, for running backwards. Wilson did the 100-yard dash (91.44 metres) in full reverse in 13.3 seconds. And 49-year-old Nruturam, of Naydwar, India, checks in as the world's smallest living dwarf, just 71 centimetres high (or more correctly, low).

Their common denominator? All are unusual champions with their feats listed in the "Guinness Book of World Records," produced by 52-year-old Norris McWhirter and his staff of 20—the world's biggest collection of know-it-alls.

The records Norris McWhirter details concern the fastest, biggest, longest, shortest, smallest. The latest Guinness volume contains authenticated records concerning everything from the world's most expensive pipe (an intricately carved Meerschaum, which sells in New York for $8,000) to the longest musical composition (Philip Crevier's "Sadist Factory," the printout of which fills 16 volumes because it consists of all 40,320 possible permutations of the C major scale, required nine musicians 100 hours to reach the best part—the end).

Not that all the book is trivia. Among the offbeat records are included serious highlights of man's and nature's accomplishments: details on space probes, heights of mountains, and depths of seas. The expanding scope of the Olympics now requires a completely separate book for Olympic records.

* * *

Once he has finished a year of compiling facts and figures like these, and the final galley proofs of the year's 704-page book are irretrievably at the printers, Norris sets out on the road, doing as many as 50 radio and TV shows a week, dazzling listeners, viewers, readers, and his interviewers with his seemingly infinite ability to remember every imaginable fact from the longest human walk on hands instead of feet ("1,402 kilometres from Vienna to Paris in 1900") to the most common name in the world ("Chang. There are about 75 million of them.")

Tracking down superlatives, verifying and codifying them, and then putting them between the covers of what is arguably the most fascinating and fact-filled annual compendium in world publishing has become a life's work and a lucrative profession for this Englishman.

* * *

The ubiquitous Norris McWhirter is to fact-fanciers today what Bob "Believe It or Not" Ripley was to the generations growing up in the 1930's. "That Ripley," sighs Norris. "Used the greatest title in the world. His facts didn't have to be correct, just interesting. We authenticate everything. We believe nothing unless we can verify it in some way. All those allegedly 150-year-old and 160-year-old Russians? They're all from the Georgian section of Russia. Stalin was a Georgian. Liked to boast his people were a super-race. So the local commissars started adding on years to the elders' lives at census times to build up Stalin's legend. We can't *prove* anyone has ever lived for more than 113 years, 124 days and so that's the record."

Originally, there were two McWhirters, Norris and his younger (by 20 minutes) twin, Ross. The pair were virtually inseparable until late 1975 when Ross, a vocal critic of terrorism in Britain, was cruelly murdered on his front doorstep by IRA gunmen. Devastated by his personal loss, Norris has carried on the book's authorship alone, knowing that his twin would have wanted their life's work to continue and that its success represents the best hope for long-range financial security for Ross's widow and family.

The senseless shooting closed the book on a joint authorship which was as fascinating as it was intimate and interchangeable. Journalists who interviewed both McWhirters never failed to comment on how totally alike the two Scots were. "They had linked minds like transistorized calculators," one recalls, "and talked to each other in a code that only they fully comprehended. One would start a sentence and the other would finish it up. When you called them on the phone you never could really be sure which one you were talking to. When I met them, I used to fasten on an identifying item during the interview—Ross wearing a red tie, for instance—it was the only way I could keep straight who was giving me which quote."

* * *

Graduating from Oxford in 1951, the twins, who had been magpies for facts since their youth, became professional press researchers, setting up business in a London garret. For three years they eked out a precarious [insecure] living. And then a missed gunshot, aimed at a golden plover on an Irish grouse moor, started a chain of events that made their book the world's most widely-published annual.

The errant shot was fired by Sir Hugh Beaver, then managing director of Guinness, the makers of the most widely consumed stout in the world. After missing his winged quarry, Beaver grumbled about it being "the fastest game bird there is in the world." "Not so sure about that old chap," another hunter murmured. By the time the frustrated Beaver got back to the hunting lodge he was intent on proving his point and found there wasn't a book available which contained all the necessary facts.

Slowly, an idea hardened in the stubborn brewer's mind. All over the world, Guinness, coal-black and delicious, is served in pubs and bars, where men of strong opinions argue about everything from the fastest heavy-weight KO on record, to the number of troops that went ashore on D-day. Often the arguments were being settled violently with fists or the sawed-off end of a billiard cue. What about a book—a Guinness book—that a barkeep could use peacefully to determine for sure which gamebird in the world flies fastest?

When he strode into work on Monday, Sir Hugh summoned a junior executive and ordered him to report back with a researcher to produce a book of records. The young management man was Chris Chataway, a college chum of the McWhirters, whom he eventually presented to Sir Hugh.

"We were interviewed in their London boardroom," Norris recalls. "All the directors were there." They could say anything they liked, be as caustic as they wanted to be in their grilling of us. The duo, still in their 20's, won every round. A director asked piercingly if the two could tell them the broadest river in the world that freezes? "The Ob, of course," Ross answered casually and correctly. Sir Hugh mentioned that he was on his way to Turkey shortly. "Interesting language, Turkish," Norris murmered. "Only one irregular verb," he added, giving it in its correct tenses and accents. Finally, the duo broke it to Sir Hugh. "Sorry, sir, but the golden plover—the *Charadrius Apicarius*, to label it correctly—probably went over your gun butt at no more than 96 kilometres an hour, if that. The spur-wing goose—or *Plectroplorus Gambiensis*—has been clocked at 141 kilometres-an-hour in level flight."

The board caved in, agreed with Sir Hugh's plan to hire the twins, and left the luncheon thinking that the hare-brained project would probably take a couple of years—if ever—to move from drawing board to printed book. Instead, the twins went into overdrive, working night and day in an intensive 16-week spurt and came out with a book that was printed in time for the 1955 Christmas sales season.

To this day, Guinness still purchases 15,000 copies for the firm's key clients and friends, but the enterprise has long since outgrown being a brewer's promotion giveaway and is now a publishing empire in its own right, owned in large part by Norris.

"Newspapers and magazines are probably my most important early-warning system," Norris explains. "They tell me where and when records might have been set. But then we authenticate the marks ourselves. We have a pen pal relationship with libraries, museums, record-keepers of all sorts in about 150 countries. And we keep a man or two in the field going to things like the recent California Record Olympics."

* * *

During a recent trip to the U.S.A., Norris presided over the opening of the new Guinness World Record Exhibit Hall, down below ground in Manhattan's Empire State Building.

(+100)   —end timing—   (min___sec___)

A 5

It's Been Done—Arturo F. Gonzalez

SUMMARY:

COMMENT:

A 6

Comprehension Quiz

The Two Cultures

Instructions: Write the letter of the correct answer in the blank provided.

1. C. P. Snow feels that there are three great threats which block human progress. The major one he discusses in this excerpt is:
   a) technological unemployment
   b) pollution of natural resources
   c) gap between rich and poor nations
   d) over-population   (__)

2. He states positively that the problem:
   a) can be solved
   b) will be solved
   c) both (a) and (b)
   d) cannot be solved   (__)

3. The "have-not" nations cannot provide capital because of:
   a) limited education
   b) shortage of trained engineers
   c) over-population
   d) all of the above   (__)

4. Snow feels that the most ideal source of the tremendous capital investment needed might come from:
   a) Western governments
   b) private Western industry
   c) an East-West combination
   d) the U.S.S.R.   (__)

5. The second vital requirement for an uplift program is:
   a) paternalistic advisers
   b) non-patronizing engineers
   c) dedicated missionaries
   d) expert politicians   (__)

6. At the present time, this requirement can best be met by:
   a) the U.S.S.R.
   b) the British
   c) the U.S.
   d) Communist China   (__)

7. A third demand for a successful program would call for:
   a) English teachers
   b) scientific educators
   c) both a) and b)
   d) population control   (__)

8. Opponents of the author's thinking argue it's impossible to get:
   a) the necessary capital
   b) the number of engineers
   c) the quality of men needed
   d) all of the above   (__)

9. In the years that have passed since the article was written, Americans can point to the breed of men Snow says is necessary in our:
   a) Peace Corps
   b) State Department
   c) CIA
   d) FBI   (__)

10. If the West refuses to take positive action in these vast portions of the globe, says the article, Snow foresees that:
    a) the U.S.S.R. will take the initiative
    b) the Western nations will be isolated
    c) starvation and war will endanger mankind
    d) all of the above   (__)

Vocabulary Preview

1. "*confrontation* of two individuals" _____
2. "short-sighted, *inept*, incapable" _____
3. "*adaptable* engineers" _____
4. "remove every trace of *paternalism*" _____
5. "need scientists and *linguists*" _____
6. "with *negligible* rewards" _____
7. "a *palliative* for one's disquiet" _____
8. "the West will have become an *enclave*" _____
9. "necessity in the most *abstract* intellectual sense" _____
10. "living *precariously* rich" _____
11. "it is *obligatory*" _____

Exercises

Instructions: Write the letter of the correct answer in the blank provided.

12. A desirable carpenter would be:
    a) inept   b) competent   c) novice   (__)

13. An antonym of *abstract* is:
    a) random   b) specific   c) raddled   (__)

14. An *obligatory* task is one:
    a) you must do   b) that is forbidden   c) that is optional   (__)

15. *Adaptable* people are:
    a) active   b) rigid   c) flexible   (__)

16. The root of *paternal* refers to:
    a) father   b) parent   c) patriotism   (__)

17. To live *precariously* is to live:
    a) dangerously   b) cautiously   c) moderately   (__)

18. If a dog *confronted* a cat there would probably be:
    a) a fight   b) no action   c) an enclave   (__)

19. *Negligible* receipts makes a businessman:
    a) unhappy   b) delighted   c) obscure   (__)

20. Most *linguists* have a knowledge of:
    a) weapons   b) botany   c) Latin   (__)

A 6

Man of Two Cultures

—begin timing—

In this age of super-specialization, Lord Snow stands out as a most unique contributor. He has had the formal training of a scientist, in physics. As a high-ranking administrator in the British government science program during World War II, he made an admirable record. Finally, he is a most successful author.

Snow's evaluation of the confrontation of the "literary-intellectual" and the "scientist"—the "Two Cultures" that he considers—has been of profound world interest. An excerpt follows from this book of the same title.

THE TWO CULTURES: AND A SECOND LOOK

by C. P. Snow

There is no getting away from it. It is technically possible to carry out the scientific revolution in India, Africa, Southeast Asia, Latin America, the Middle East, within fifty years. There is no excuse for western man not to know this. And not to know that this is the one way out through the three menaces which stand in our way—H-bomb war, over-population, the gap between the rich and the poor. This is one of the situations where the worst crime is innocence.

Since the gap between the rich countries and the poor can be removed, it will be. If we are short-sighted, inept, incapable either of good-will or enlightened self-interest, then it may be removed to the accompaniment of war and starvation: but removed it will be. The questions are, how, and by whom. To those questions, one can only give partial answers: but that may be enough to set us thinking. The scientific revolution on the world-scale needs, first and foremost, capital: capital in all forms, including capital machinery. The poor countries, until they have got beyond a certain point on the industrial curve, cannot accumulate that capital. That is why the gap between rich and poor is widening. The capital must come from outside.

There are only two possible sources. One is the West, which means mainly the U.S., the other is the U.S.S.R. Even the United States hasn't infinite resources of such capital. If they or Russia tried to do it alone, it would mean an effort greater than either had to make industrially in the war. If they both took part, it wouldn't mean that order of sacrifice—though in my view it's optimistic to think, as some wise men do, that it would mean no sacrifice at all. The scale of the operation requires that it would have to be a national one. Private industry, even the biggest private industry, can't touch it, and in no sense is it a fair business risk. It's a bit like asking Duponts back in 1940 to finance the entire development of the atomic bomb.

The second requirement, after capital, as important as capital, is men. That is, trained scientists and engineers adaptable enough to devote themselves to a foreign country's industrialisation for at least ten years out of their lives. Here, unless and until the Americans and we educate ourselves both sensibly and imaginatively, the Russians have a clear edge. This is where their educational policy has already paid big dividends. They have such men to spare if they are needed. We just haven't, and the Americans aren't much better off. Imagine, for example, that the U.S. government and ours had agreed to help the Indians to carry out a major industrialisation, similar in scale to the Chinese. Imagine that the capital could be found. It would then require something like ten thousand to twenty thousand engineers from the U.S. and here [U.K.] to help get the thing going. At present, we couldn't find them.

These men, whom we don't yet possess, need to be trained not only in scientific but in human terms. They could not do their job if they did not shrug off every trace of paternalism. Plenty of Europeans, from St. Francis Xavier to Schweitzer, have devoted their lives to Asians and Africans, nobly but paternally. These are not the Europeans whom Asians and Africans are going to welcome now. They want men who will muck in as colleagues, who will pass on what they know, do an honest technical job, and get out. Fortunately, this is an attitude which comes easily to scientists. They are freer than most people from racial feeling; their own culture is in its human relations a democratic one. In their own internal climate, the breeze of the equality of man hits you in the face, sometimes rather roughly, just as it does in Norway.

That is why scientists would do us good all over Asia and Africa. And they would do their part too in the third essential of the scientific revolution—which, in a country like India, would have to run in parallel with the capital investment and the initial foreign help. That is, an educational programme as complete as the Chinese, who appear in ten years to have transformed their universities and built so many new ones that they are now nearly independent of scientists and engineers from outside. Ten years. With scientific teachers from this country and the U.S., and what is also necessary, with teachers of English, other poor countries could do the same in twenty.

That is the size of the problem. An immense capital outlay, an immense investment in men, both scientists and linguists, most of whom the West does not yet possess. With rewards negligible in the short term, apart from doing the job: and in the long term most uncertain.

People will ask me, in fact in private they have already asked me—"This is all very fine and large. But you are supposed to be a reaslistic man. You are interested in the fine structure of politics; you have spent some time studying how men behave in the pursuit of their own ends. Can you possibly believe that men will behave as you say they ought to? Can you imagine a political technique, in parliamentary societies like the U.S. or our own, by which any such plan could become real? Do you really believe that there is one chance in ten that any of this will happen?"

That is fair comment. I can only reply that I don't know. On the one hand, it is a mistake, and it is a mistake, of course, which anyone who is called realistic is specially liable to fall into, to think that when we have said something about the egotisms, the weaknesses, the vanities, the power-seekings of men that we have said everything. Yes, they are like that. They are the bricks with which we have got to build, and one can judge them through the extent of one's own selfishness. But they are sometimes capable of more, and any "realism" which doesn't admit of that isn't serious.

On the other hand, I confess, and I should be less than honest if I didn't, that I can't see the political techniques through which the good human capabilities of the West can get into action. The best one can do, and it is a poor best, is to nag away. That is perhaps too easy a palliative for one's disquiet. For, though I don't know how we can do what we need to do, or whether we shall do anything at all, I do know this: that, if we don't do it, the Communist countries will in time. They will do it at great cost to themselves and others, but they will do it. If that is how it turns out, we shall have failed, both practically and morally. At best, the West will have become an *enclave* in a different world—and this country will be the *enclave* of an *enclave*. Are we resigning ourselves to that? History is merciless to failure. In any case, if that happens, we shall not be writing the history.

Meanwhile, there are steps to be taken which aren't outside the powers of reflective people. Education isn't the total solution to this problem: but without education the West can't even begin to cope. All the arrows point the same way. Closing the gap between our cultures is a necessity in the most abstract intellectual sense, as well as in the most practical. When those two senses have grown apart, then no society is going to be able to think with wisdom. For the sake of the intellectual life, for the sake of this country's special danger, for the sake of the western society living precariously rich among the poor, for the sake of the poor who needn't be poor if there is intelligence in the world, it is obligatory for us and the Americans and the whole West to look at our education with fresh eyes. This is one of the cases where we and the Americans have the most to learn from each other. We have each a good deal to learn from the Russians, if we are not too proud. Incidentally, the Russians have a good deal to learn from us, too.

Isn't it time we began? The danger is, we have been brought up to think as though we had all the time in the world. We have very little time. So little that I dare not guess at it.

(+100)   —end timing—   (min___sec___)

A 6

The Two Cultures—C. P. Snow

SUMMARY:

COMMENT:

A 7

Comprehension Quiz

"Wasteland" Speech

Instructions: Write the letter of the correct answer in the blank provided.

1. The general attitude of the famous "Wasteland" speech made by the Chairman of the Federal Communications Commission to the National Association of Broadcasters is:
   a) understanding   c) critical   (__)
   b) praiseful   d) none of the above
2. Minow feels that his *primary* duty—and that of the broadcasters—is:
   a) to protect the public   c) to eliminate TV violence   (__)
      interest   shows
   b) to control TV   d) all of the above
      programming
3. He warns that the powerful effects of TV will be judged eventually by:
   a) the public   c) the "rating" companies   (__)
   b) history   d) the FCC
4. Minow specifically describes television's over-all programming as:
   a) a hodgepodge of   c) a vast wasteland   (__)
      commercials
   b) a mixture of sadism and d) serving the nation's needs
      cartoons
5. He is particularly concerned with the fact that children:
   a) watch too much TV   c) are used as judges of   (__)
   b) are exposed to endless   quality
      violence and nonsense d) all of the above
6. The most vital single programming guide, says Minow, should be:
   a) elimination of westerns c) fewer commercials   (__)
   b) fewer cartoons   d) more balanced
                                programming
7. He promises that his administration will make a determined effort to:
   a) establish more   c) control general   (__)
      educational TV   programming
   b) eliminate advertisers' d) all of the above
      influence
8. He feels that television's "finest hours" are those which:
   a) provide entertainment c) are most popular   (__)
   b) keep the public informed d) are good "show business"
9. The FCC now re-licenses television stations every three years. It could control programming with this power. To do so might:
   a) raise the level of programs c) control free speech   (__)
   b) increase stimulating shows d) all of the above
10. Since Minow's retirement several years ago, the general quality of television programming has:
    a) remained the same   c) improved   (__)
    b) gone down   d) cannot be measured

A 7

Vocabulary Preview

1. "to enrich or *debase* them" _____
2. [shows about] "*mayhem*, violence" _____
3. "and *sadism*" _____
4. "screaming, *cajoling* commercials" _____
5. "public's *insatiable* appetite" _____
6. "problems not *susceptible* to answers" _____
7. "your young *beneficiaries*" _____
8. "the *lovelorn* columns" _____
9. "old *coaxial* cable" _____
10. "more *diversity* is needed" _____
11. "don't *cater*" _____
12. "to public *whims*" _____
13. "*exemplify* public service" _____
14. "decency and *decorum*" _____
15. "*propriety* in advertising" _____
16. "*mediocrity* in programming" _____
17. "experimentation, not *conformity*" _____
18. "power of *instantaneous* sight" _____
19. "without *precedent* in our time" _____
20. "carries *awesome* responsibilities" _____

PROGRAM CONTROL

by Newton N. Minow   (from *Vital Speeches of the Day*)

A Speech Delivered to the
National Association of Broadcasters Convention, May 9, 1961

—begin timing—

Your industry possesses the most powerful voice in America. It has an inescapable duty to make that voice ring with intelligence and with leadership. In a few years, this exciting industry has grown from a novelty to an instrument of overwhelming impact on the American people. It should be making ready for the kind of leadership that newspapers and magazines assumed years ago, to make our people aware of their world.

Ours has been called the jet age, the atomic age, the space age. It is also I submit, the television age. And just as history will decide whether the leaders of today's world employed the atom to destroy the world or rebuild it for mankind's benefit, so will history decide whether today's broadcasters employed their powerful voice to enrich the people or debase them.

But when television is bad, nothing is worse. I invite you to sit down in front of your television set when your station goes on the air and stay there without a book, magazine, newspaper, profit and loss sheet or rating book to distract you—and keep your eyes glued to that set until the station signs off. I can assure you that you will observe a vast wasteland.

You will see a procession of game shows, violence, audience participation shows, formula comedies about totally unbelievable families, blood and thunder, mayhem, violence, sadism, murder, western badmen, western good men, private eyes, gangsters, more violence, and cartoons. And, endlessly, commercials—many screaming, cajoling, and offending. And most of all, boredom. True, you will see a few things you will enjoy. But they will be very, very few. And if you think I exaggerate, try it.

Why is so much of television so bad? I have heard many answers: demands of your advertisers; competition for ever higher ratings; the need always to attract a mass audience for the high cost of television programs; the insatiable appetite for programming material—these are some of them. Unquestionably, these are tough problems not susceptible to easy answers.

But I am not convinced that you have tried hard enough to solve them.

I do not accept the idea that the present over-all programming is aimed accurately at the public taste.

Certainly, I hope you will agree that ratings should have little influence where children are concerned. The best estimates indicate that during the hours of 5 to 6 P.M. 60 percent of your audience is composed of children under 12. And most young children today, believe it or not, spend as much time watching television as they do in the schoolroom. It used to be said that there were three great influences on a child: home, school, and church. Today, there is a fourth great influence, and you ladies and gentlemen control it.

If parents, teachers, and ministers conducted their responsibilities by following the ratings, children would have a steady diet of ice cream, school holidays, and no Sunday school. What about your responsibilities? Is there no room on television to teach, to inform, to uplift, to stretch, to enlarge the capacities of our children? Is there no room for programs deepening their understanding of children in other lands? Is there no room for a children's news show explaining something about the world to them at their level of understanding? Is there no room for reading the great literature of the past, teaching them the great traditions of freedom? There are some fine children's shows, but they are drowned out in the massive doses of cartoons, violence, and more violence. Must these be your trademarks? Search your consciences and see if you cannot offer more to your young beneficiaries whose future you guide so many hours each and every day

What about adult programming and ratings. You know, newspaper publishers take popularity ratings too. The answers are pretty clear: it is almost always the comics, followed by the advice to the lovelorn columns. But, ladies and gentlemen, the news is still on the front page of all newspapers, the editorials are not replaced by more comics, the newspapers have not become one long collection of advice to the lovelorn. Yet newspapers do not need a license from the government to be in business—they do not use public property. But in television—where your responsibilities as public trustees are so plain, the moment that the ratings indicate that westerns are popular there are new imitations of westerns on the air faster than the old coaxial cable could take us from Hollywood to New York. Broadcasting cannot continue to live by the numbers. Ratings ought to be the slave of the broadcaster, not his master. And you and I both know that the rating services themselves would agree.

Let me make clear that what I am talking about is balance. I believe that the public interest is made up of many interests. There are many people in this great country and you must serve all of us. You will get no argument from me if you say that, given a choice between a western and a symphony, more people will watch the western. I like westerns and private eyes too—but a steady diet for the whole country is obviously not in the public interest. We all know that people would more often prefer to be entertained than stimulated or informed. But your obligations are not satisfied if you look only to popularity as a test of what to broadcast. You are not only in show business; you are free to communicate ideas as well as relaxation. You must provide a wider range of choices, more diversity, more alternatives. It is not enough to cater to the nation's whims—you must also serve the nation's needs. There are still not enough educational stations, and major centers of the country still lack usable educational channels. If there were a limited number of printing presses in this country, you may be sure that a fair proportion of them would be put to educational use. Educational television has an enormous contribution to make to the future, and I intend to give it a hand along the way.

Tell your sponsors to be less concerned with costs per thousand and more concerned with understanding per millions. And remind your stockholders that an investment in broadcasting is buying a share in public responsibility.

The networks can start this industry on the road to freedom from the dictatorship of numbers.

But there is more to the problem than network influences on stations or advertiser influences on networks. I know the problems networks face in trying to clear some of their best programs—the informational programs that exemplify public service. They are your finest hours—whether sustaining or commercial, whether regularly scheduled or special—these are the signs that broadcasting knows the way to leadership. They make the public's trust in you a wise choice.

They should be seen. As you know, we are readying for use new forms by which broadcast stations will report their programming to the Commission. You probably also know that special attention will be paid in these reports to public service programming. I believe that stations taking network service should also be required to report the extent of the local clearance of network public service programming, and when they fail to clear them, they should explain why. If it is to put on some outstanding local program, this is one reason.

I can suggest some words that should serve to guide you:

"Television and all who participate in it are jointly accountable to the American public for respect for the special needs of children, for community responsibility, for the advancement of education and culture, for the acceptability of the program materials chosen, for decency and decorum in production, and for propriety in advertising. This responsibility cannot be discharged by any given group of programs, but can be discharged only through the highest standards of respect for the American home, applied to every moment of every program presented by television.

"Program materials should enlarge the horizons of the viewer, provide him with wholesome entertainment, afford helpful stimulation, and remind him of the responsibilities which the citizen has towards his society."

We need imagination in programming, not sterility; creativity, not imitation; experimentation, not conformity; excellence, not mediocrity. Television is filled with creative, imaginative people. You must strive to set them free.

What you gentlemen broadcast through the people's air affects the people's taste, their knowledge, their opinions, their understanding of themselves and of their world, and their future.

The power of instantaneous sight and sound is without precedent in mankind's history. This is an awesome power. It has limitless capabilities for good—and for evil. And it carries with it awesome responsibilities, responsibilities which you and I cannot escape.

(+100)   —end timing—   (min__sec__)

A 7

Program Control—Newton N. Minow

SUMMARY:

COMMENT:

Name_____ Class_____

A 8

Comprehension Quiz

Margaret Sanger: Victimized Saint

Instructions: Write the letter of the correct answer in the blank provided.

1. Margaret Sanger was most concerned with:
   a) the danger of overpopulation
   b) the spread of disease
   c) the dignity of each woman
   d) women's right to vote   (___)

2. The only movement that compares in importance to Mrs. Sanger's American Birth Control League, says Manker, was:
   a) freeing the slaves
   b) ending child labor
   c) women's right to vote
   d) the rise of the labor movement   (___)

3. As a public health nurse in New York City, Sanger was angered by:
   a) poverty
   b) the stupidity of doctors
   c) the tragedy of too-large families
   d) all of these   (___)

4. She was first arrested and jailed because of:
   a) her writing in the *New York Call*
   b) her birth control pamphlets
   c) her birth control clinic
   d) her fight against those in power   (___)

5. The changes in the laws that resulted from her jail sentences actually:
   a) did not make birth control devices legal
   b) restored the dignity of women
   c) promoted prostitution
   d) both (a) and (c)   (___)

6. The lawmakers approved contraceptive devices for:
   a) controlling family size
   b) preventing disease
   c) stopping illegal abortions
   d) raising moral standards   (___)

7. As late as 1946, despite changes in the attitude of the general public, Margaret Sanger:
   a) was jailed again
   b) was snubbed by many
   c) was refused permission to visit Japan
   d) both (b) and (c)   (___)

8. Margaret Sanger became the first foreign woman to:
   a) address the upper house of the Japanese Parliament
   b) meet with General MacArthur
   c) practice birth control in Japan
   d) talk with the emperor   (___)

9. Reverend Manker argues that in a prostitution arrest:
   a) the woman should face trial
   b) both should be tried
   c) the man should be tried
   d) neither should be tried   (___)

10. As a result of her determination, today's population explosion problem:
    a) has been solved
    b) is openly discussed
    c) has been kept quiet
    d) all of these   (___)

Vocabulary Preview

1. "*Victimized* Saint" _____
2. "*abolitionist* movement" _____
3. "coercing Abraham Lincoln" _____
4. "signing the *Emancipation* Proclamation" _____
5. "Emancipation *Proclamation*" _____
6. "woman's *suffrage*" _____
7. "the *morass*" _____
8. "needless human *degradation*" _____
9. "*prematurely* aged by childbirth" _____
10. "*forbade* the dispensing" _____
11. "*dispensing* and use" _____
12. "use of *contraceptives*" _____
13. "*barbaric* thinking" _____
14. "*contend* with stupidity" _____
15. "*provoked* a storm of protest" _____
16. "the first *diaphragm* was smuggled in" _____
17. "it was considered *obscene*" _____
18. "to help the *wayward* husband" _____
19. "to have his *illicit* sex" _____
20. "*venereal* disease" _____
21. "is *vindictively* showing" _____
22. "*contempt* of women" _____
23. "women should be *accorded* dignity" _____
24. "Mrs. Sanger was *revered*" _____
25. "seeing the *hypocrisy* of laws" (hypocritical) _____
26. "conscience and sense of *outrage*" _____
27. "openly *flouting* such laws" _____
28. "didn't stop the *crusading* lady" _____
29. "welcomed her and *endorsed* her work" _____
30. "dignity . . . above every *vested* interest" _____

MARGARET SANGER: VICTIMIZED SAINT

by Raymond G. Manker

—begin timing—

Margaret Sanger, truly one of America's Saints, is dead. Not since the abolitionist movement succeeded in coercing Abraham Lincoln into signing the Emancipation Proclamation freeing the slaves in America has there been any movement to compare in importance with the birth control movement started by Margaret Sanger—not child labor, basic and important though that was; not woman's suffrage; possibly not even the rise of the labor union movement, which I consider to be one of history's most important events. Margaret Sanger's American Birth Control League, established in 1921 and which, in 1946, became the Planned Parenthood Federation of America, was far more than merely a birth control league. Basically, it dealt with human dignity—the human dignity of a woman's body, the same human dignity destroyed in slavery and in forced prostitution.

Sometimes I look at humanity and its history, and I see the marvelous steps it has taken down through the centuries, and I am proud to be a human being. But, at other times, I see the morass of needless human degradation from which one portion of humanity makes its living at the expense of the human dignity of other portions and I am sick at heart. Then, like Stringfellow Barr, I want to resign from the human race.

Margaret Sanger was the sixth of the eleven children of Michael and Ann Higgins. Her father was a stonecutter in Corning, N.Y. and could not support his large family adequately. She once said: "I can never look back on my childhood with joy. To me the distinction between happiness and unhappiness in childhood was one of small families and of large families, rather than of wealth and poverty." Her mother died at 48 prematurely aged by childbirth and tuberculosis.

Margaret went on to become a public health nurse in New York City. Here she saw the needless degradation caused by the laws which forbade the dispensing and the use of contraception. She had knowledge of many instances of tragedy, such as that of one young mother whom she nursed back to health after near death from a self-induced abortion. She heard the mother plead with her doctor for protection against another pregnancy and he turned away with a brusque "Tell your husband to sleep on the roof!" Six months later she was dead from another self-induced abortion.

Somewhere, somehow there must be an answer—there must be someone who could help. Margaret Sanger gave up her job determined to do something. The stupidity and barbaric thinking with which she had to contend in the power structure of the United States would be hard to believe were it not all faithfully recorded.

She began by writing articles on birth control for the *New York Call*, but they were declared illegal and never saw print. Then she started a monthly magazine, *The Woman Rebel*, and she edited a birth control pamphlet, "Family Planning," distributing over 100,000 copies before she was indicted and brought to trial. The case was dismissed, however, when it provoked a world-wide storm of protest.

She opened the first birth control clinic in the United States in Brooklyn after a trip to the Netherlands, where she learned the most modern methods of birth control. She had to smuggle into the United States the first diaphragm because it was considered obscene by the law. Her clinic was raided and she spent 30 days in jail. Her jail sentence led to a relaxation in the laws to permit physicians to give contraceptive advice "for the prevention and cure of disease." What stupidity! What a lack of appreciation of human dignity! Forced to do something, the legislators refused to help restore the dignity of a woman and her family. Instead, they legislated to prevent the spread of disease caused by prostitution and loose living! They did nothing, you note, to discourage prostitution or loose living. In fact, they encouraged it! Not only did they give no relief to the wife and her family, forcing her either to continue getting pregnant or to refuse to have intercourse with her husband (thus making loose living and prostitution infinitely more attractive). But they allowed the doctor to help the wayward husband to have his illicit sex without so great a danger of contracting venereal disease! That legislation was actually another slap at the dignity of women. A woman now did have an out. Instead of facing another pregnancy and probably fatal self-abortion, she could now go to her doctor and tell him that she was planning to have an affair with a man who had venereal disease and he could then legally instruct her and prescribe for her contraceptive material.

This legal degradation of women is still, to this very day, a part of the American scene. Perhaps you women do not know, but in at least 50% of the men's restrooms in gasoline service stations, restaurants, road houses and the like, along major highways of America, there is on the wall a self-service machine for dispensing contraceptive devices—always labelled "for prevention of disease only"! There is absolutely no concern for the poor woman who might get pregnant, only a concern that the man be able to have his sex without undue worry about contracting disease!

I was furious with the law and the Scottsdale, Arizona police late last spring when two police officers arrested as prostitutes two women who accepted their proposition. In the possession of these women was a list of clients in the Scottsdale area. The police issued a call through the newspaper to the public asking that any man, figuring he might be on the list, call the police and volunteer to help them in their case against the two women. The men, of course, were to be fully protected. No one would ever learn their identity.

It so seldom occurs to people that prostitution, in the usual manner, is impossible without male participation—active participation. If it were up to me there would never be a charge of prostitution against a woman without charging both the man and the woman, and each should receive the same sentence.

But this is somewhat beside the issue under discussion. While Margaret Sanger, like almost every well-educated, democratically oriented person in the world, was concerned over the spread of venereal disease, war, over-population, and many, many other related problems, her main concern was the dignity of the individual woman. "No woman can call herself free until she can choose consciously whether she will or will not be a mother." In these words, Margaret Sanger pinpointed her cause. Any law, or court, or public official— or church official—who states that a woman must run the risk of pregnancy if she has intercourse, when there are possible means of contraception, is vindictively showing his contempt of women. The individual woman should be accorded *at least* the same dignity of person as is shown the individual man.

While Mrs. Sanger was revered beyond the national boundaries of the United States she was never fully honored within the United States. I guess this is to be expected when a person, no matter in which contry he or she lives, seeing the hypocrisy of the laws, law-givers and law-enforcers of the community, openly applies civil disobedience to those hypocritical or humanly degrading laws. That person often will be applauded everywhere except in his or her own community.

Margaret Sanger's conscience and sense of outrage against laws degrading to women would not allow her to respect those hypocritical laws. She went to jail eight different times for openly and publicly flouting such laws, and each time a small gain was made in human dignity. But she was not openly loved, for all her concern. As late as 1946 when she requested a visa to visit Japan, at the request of the Japanese people, to bolster their much-needed birth control effort, Gen. Douglas MacArthur used his influence to see that it was denied. But that didn't stop the crusading little lady, then 63 years old. She went anyway, and became the first foreign woman to address the upper house of the Japanese Parliament. Seeing the respect and love with which she was received, MacArthur then welcomed her and endorsed her work—in Japan. In America she continued to be snubbed by far too many who should have "called her blessed."

* * *

Lack of world population control is one of the real dangers threatening humankind, and something needs to be done about it, and quick. But this was not Mrs. Sanger's project. Actually, she was rather cynical about birth control as a means of population control. She was concerned about the dignity of each individual woman. . . .

Margaret Sanger's plea may be used to further the cause of population control, but her real message was of human dignity—especially the human dignity of women, and through them, of families. She is a victimized saint whose real message should not be allowed to die with her, for it is the most important message facing humankind—the dignity and worth of every human individual above all law, above all tradition, above every vested interest.

(+150)   —end timing—   (min___sec___)

A 8

Margaret Sanger: Victimized Saint—Raymond G. Manker

SUMMARY:

COMMENT:

A 9

Comprehension Quiz

Deciding When Death Is Better than Life

Instructions: Write the letter of the correct answer in the blank provided.

1. This article might be titled:
   a) When Is the Patient Dead?
   b) The Patient's Right To Die
   c) The Legality of Euthanasia
   d) The Death of Freud
   (__)

2. The most active opponents of "mercy-killing" have been:
   a) clergymen of all faiths
   b) fatally ill patients
   c) psychoanalysts
   d) terminal patients' families
   (__)

3. Giving to a dying patient an overdose of a normally beneficient drug in order to hasten death is called, in Western countries:
   a) active euthanasia
   b) murder
   c) a dilemma
   d) legal
   (__)

4. Concern about euthanasia and the "right to die" has grown because of:
   a) new medical technology
   b) legal definitions of death
   c) cures for formerly fatal illnesses
   d) all of the above
   (__)

5. A harsh factor that affects decisions about a dying patient is the:
   a) patient's wishes
   b) family's desires
   c) staff doctors' scientific needs
   d) family physician's wishes
   (__)

6. For thousands of years, death was defined as taking place when:
   a) the patient's eyes closed
   b) the heart and breathing stopped
   c) the heart-lung machine stopped
   d) brain activity ceased
   (__)

7. Legally, in most cases today, a patient is dead when:
   a) brain activity stops for 24 hours
   b) all machines are removed
   c) heart action ceases
   d) breathing stops
   (__)

8. Areas affected by a new "death definition" include:
   a) transplants
   b) hospital regulations
   c) legal problems
   d) all of the above
   (__)

9. Dr. Max Schur administered a fatal dose of morphine to Freud. He was:
   a) charged with homicide
   b) no longer allowed to practice
   c) condemned by his peers
   d) not discussed in the article
   (__)

10. The problems of euthanasia and the right to die are basically:
    a) humane
    b) legal
    c) medical
    d) political
    (__)

Vocabulary Preview

1. "President's *rhetorical* skills" _____

2. "Lester *complied*—using a shotgun" _____

3. "he was in a *coma*" _____

4. "growing emotional *controversy*" _____

5. "*impulsive* taking of life" _____

6. "a far *subtler* question" _____

7. "most *emphatic* opponents" _____

8. "reminded of their own *mortality*" _____

9. "professor of *geriatric* medicine" _____

10. "a *panoply* of new techniques" _____

11. "ill and cruelly *debilitated*" _____

12. "given *intravenously* to medicate" _____

13. "they are *converging*" _____

14. "*triumphalism* in the profession" _____

15. "*precludes* a search for knowledge" _____

16. "search for *existential* knowledge" _____

17. "search for *symbolic* knowledge" _____

18. "all-too-*tangible* present crisis" _____

19. "the physician's *prognosis*" _____

20. "*humane* rather than legal" _____

DECIDING WHEN DEATH IS BETTER THAN LIFE

by Gilbert Cant   (from *Time*, July 16, 1973)

—begin timing—

I am a broken piece of machinery. I am ready.
—Last words of Woodrow Wilson, January 31, 1924

George Zygmaniak, 26, lacked the former President's rhetorical skills, but as he lay in a hospital bed last month in Neptune, New Jersey, paralyzed from the neck down because of a motorcycle accident, he felt that he was a broken piece of machinery. He was ready to go. He begged his brother Lester, 23, to kill him. According to police, Lester complied—using a sawed-off shotgun at close range. Lester, who had enjoyed an unusually close relationship with his brother, has been charged with first-degree murder.

Last December Eugene Bauer, 59, was admitted to Nassau County Medical Center on Long Island with cancer of the throat. Five days later he was in a coma and given only two days to live. Then, charges the district attorney, Dr. Vincent A. Montemarano, 33, injected an overdose of potassium chloride into Bauer's veins. Bauer died within five minutes. Montemarano listed the cause of death as cancer, but prosecutors now say that it was a "mercy killing" and have accused the doctor of murder.

The two cases underscore the growing emotional controversy over euthanasia ("mercy killing") and the so-called right to die—that is, the right to slip from life with a minimum of pain for both the patient and his family. No one seriously advocates the impulsive taking of life, as in the Zygmaniak shooting. A person suddenly crippled, no matter how severely, may yet show unpredictable improvement or regain at least a will to live. Whether or not to speed the passage of a fatally ill patient is a far subtler question. The headlong advances of medical science make the issue constantly more complex for patients and their families, for doctors and hospitals, for theologians and lawyers.

* * *

The doctor's dilemma—how long to prolong life after all hope of recovery has gone—has some of its roots in half-legendary events of 2,400 years ago. When Hippocrates, the "Father of Medicine," sat under his giant plane tree on the Aegean island of Kos, euthanasia (from the Greek meaning "a good death") was widely practiced and took many different forms. But from beneath that plane tree came words that have been immortalized in the physician's Hippocratic oath, part of which reads: "I will neither give a deadly drug to anybody, if asked for, nor will I make a suggestion to this effect."

Down the centuries, this has been interpreted by most physicians to mean that they must not give a patient a fatal overdose, no matter how terrible his pain or how hopeless his prospects. Today many scholars contend that the origin of this item in the oath has been misinterpreted. Most likely it was designed to keep the physician from becoming an accomplice of palace poisoners or of a man seeking to get rid of a wife.

The most emphatic opponents of euthanasia have been clergymen, of nearly all denominations. Churchmen protest that if a doctor decides when a patient is to die, he is playing God. Many physicians still share this objection. However much they may enjoy a secret feeling of divinity when dispensing miraculous cures, to play the angel of death is understandably repugnant [offensive]. Moreover, as psychoanalysts point out, they are chillingly reminded of their own mortality.

At a recent conference chaired by the Roman Catholic Archbishop of Westminster, Dr. W. F. Anderson of Glasgow University, a professor of geriatric medicine, called euthanasia "medicated manslaughter." Modern drugs, he argued, can keep a patient sufficiently pain-free to make mercy killing, in effect, obsolete. Perhaps. There is no doubt, however, that a panoply of new techniques and equipment can be and often are used to keep alive people who are both hopelessly ill and cruelly debilitated. Artificial respirators, blood-matching and transfusion systems, a variety of fluids that can safely be given intravenously to medicate, nourish and maintain electrolyte balance—these and many other lifesavers give doctors astonishing powers.

Until about 25 years ago, the alternatives facing a doctor treating a terminally ill patient were relatively clear. He could let nature take its sometimes harsh course, or he could administer a fatal dose of some normally beneficient drug. To resort to the drug would be to commit what is called active euthanasia. In virtually all Western countries, that act is still legally considered homicide (though juries rarely convict in such cases).

On the record, physicians are all but unanimous in insisting that they never perform active euthanasia, for to do so is a crime. Off the record, some will admit that they have sometimes hastened death by giving an overdose of the medicine they had been administering previously. How many such cases there are can never be known.

Now, with wondrous machines for prolonging a sort of life, there is another set of choices. Should the patient's heart or lung function be artificially sustained for weeks or months? Should he be kept technically alive by physico-chemical legerdemain [tricks], even if he has become a mere collection of organs and tissues rather than a whole man? If a decision is made not to attempt extraordinary measures, or if, at some point, the life-preserving machinery is shut off, then a previously unknown act is being committed. It may properly be called passive euthanasia. The patient is allowed to die instead of being maintained as a laboratory specimen.

While legal purists complain that euthanasia and the right to die peacefully are separate issues, the fact is that they are converging. With the increasing use of extraordinary measures, the occasions for passive euthanasia are becoming more frequent. The question of whether terminal suffering can be shortened by active or passive means is often highly technical—depending on the type of ailment. Thus the distinctions are becoming blurred, particularly for laymen.

* * *

"The idea of not prolonging life unnecessarily has always been more widely accepted outside the medical profession than within it," says a leading Protestant (United Church of Christ) theologian, University of Chicago's Dr. James Gustafson. "Now a lot of physicians are rebelling against the triumphalism inherent in the medical profession, against this sustaining of life at all costs. But different doctors bring different considerations to bear. The research-oriented physician is more concerned with developing future treatments, while the patient-oriented physician is more willing to allow patients to make their own choices."

House-staff physicians, says Tufts University's Dr. Melvin J. Krant in *Prism*, an A.M.A. publication, "deal with the fatally ill as if they were entirely divorced from their own human ecology. The search for absolute biological knowledge precludes a search for existential or symbolic knowledge, and the patient is deprived of his own singular humanism." The house staff, Krant says, assumes "that the patient always prefers life over death at any cost, and a patient who balks at a procedure is often viewed as a psychiatric problem."

Technical wizardry has, in fact, necessitated a new definition of death. For thousands of years it had been accepted that death occurred when heart action and breathing ceased. This was essentially true, because the brain died minutes after the heart stopped. But with machines, it is now possible to keep the brain "alive" almost indefinitely. With the machines unplugged, it would soon die. In cases where the brain ceases to function first, heart and lung activity can be artificially maintained. While legal definitions of death lag far behind medical advances, today's criterion is, in most instances, the absence of brain activity for 24 hours.

The question then, in the words of Harvard Neurologist Robert Schwab, is "Who decides to pull the plug, and when?" Cutting off the machines—or avoiding their use at all—is indeed passive euthanasia. But it is an ethical decision—not murder, or any other crime, in any legal code. So stern a guardian of traditional morality as Pope Pius XII declared that life need not be prolonged by extraordinary means.

* * *

Faced with a painful and tenuous future and an all-too-tangible present crisis, how does the doctor decide what to do? Does he make the decision alone? Dr. Malcolm Todd, president-elect of the American Medical Association, wants doctors to have help at least in formulating a general policy. He proposes a commission of laymen, clergy, lawyers and physicians. "Society has changed," says Todd. "It's up to society to decide." The desire to share the responsibility is reasonable, but it is unlikely that any commission could write guidelines to cover adequately all situations. In individual cases, of course, many doctors consult the patient's relatives. But the family is likely to be heavily influenced by the physician's prognosis. More often than not, it must be a lonely decision made by one or two doctors.

* * *

When Sigmund Freud was 83, he had suffered from cancer of the jaw for 16 years and undergone 33 operations. "Now it is nothing but torture," he concluded, "and makes no sense any more." He had a pact with Max Schur, his physician. "When he was again in agony," Schur reported, "I gave him two centigrams of morphine. I repeated this dose after about twelve hours. He lapsed into a coma and did not wake up again." Freud died with dignity at his chosen time.

Dr. Schur's decision was, in the end, relatively easy. More often, there are unavoidable uncertainties in both active and passive euthanasia. Doctors may disagree over a prognosis. A patient may be so depressed by pain that one day he wants out, while the next day, with some surcease, he has a renewed will to live. There is the problem of heirs who may be thinking more of the estate than of the patient when the time to pull the plug is discussed. Doctors will have to live with these gray areas, perhaps indefinitely. Attempts to legalize active euthanasia—under severe restrictions—have failed in the U.S. and Britain but will doubtless be revived. The fundamental question, however, is humane rather than legal. To die as Freud died should be the right of Everyman.

(+200)   —end timing—   (min__sec__)

A 9

Deciding When Death Is Better Than Life—Gilbert Cant

SUMMARY:

COMMENT:

A 10

Comprehension Quiz

Don't Use the Law to Dispose of Used Wives

Instructions: Write the letter of the correct answer in the blank provided.

1. The central theme in this article is that in divorce cases:
   - a) judges must use common sense and decency
   - b) housewives are entitled to annuities
   - c) men exploit women
   - d) women may be used as breeding stock
   (__)

2. In this particular divorce:
   - a) the division of community property was unjust
   - b) child custody was contested
   - c) alimony was contested
   - d) medical opinions were argued
   (__)

3. The wife's employment future was bleak because she was:
   - a) going blind
   - b) arthritic
   - c) uneducated and unskilled
   - d) all of these
   (__)

4. Under the lower court's ruling, the woman would:
   - a) be able to live well
   - b) be provided for during her lifetime
   - c) probably become a charity case
   - d) have immediate financial problems
   (__)

5. The California Family Law Act is sometimes called:
   - a) a Bill of Rights for ex-wives
   - b) a Bill of Rights for ex-husbands
   - c) a child-protection law
   - d) a constitutional amendment
   (__)

6. According to Judge Gardner, a divorced woman should:
   - a) support herself if she can
   - b) always be given a lifetime pension
   - c) be responsible for her children
   - d) get a job immediately
   (__)

7. When a woman has been a homemaker for years, and is unemployable:
   - a) she deserves an ex-husband's support
   - b) her children should support her
   - c) she should become a feminist
   - d) to support her is male chauvinism
   (__)

8. From the details in this decision, we can infer:
   - a) the law on divorce is precise
   - b) ex-husbands are ruthless
   - c) judges are human
   - d) the lower court judge was delighted
   (__)

9. In this particular case, Judge Gardner believes that:
   - a) the lower court was reasonable
   - b) the husband must pay for life
   - c) the woman's situation must be considered
   - d) the wife is permanently unemployable
   (__)

10. The judge ordered:
    - a) the case dismissed
    - b) alimony of $200 per month for life
    - c) both parties to jail
    - d) the case remanded for further consideration
    (__)

Vocabulary Preview

1. "shifts in sexual *mores*" _____
2. *"turbulence* of this period" _____
3. "acquired *community property*" _____
4. "an *equity* in a home" _____
5. "The *meager* balance" _____
6. "balance of community *assets*" _____
7. "in regard to *spousal* support" _____
8. "picture is *bleak*" _____
9. "a mere *pittance*" _____
10. *"discretion* of the court" _____
11. *"heralded* as a Bill of Rights" _____
12. *"harried* former husbands" _____
13. "for the *summary* disposal" _____
14. "years of *fecundity*" _____
15. "male *chauvinism*" _____
16. "there is nothing *talismanic*" _____
17. "an eternal *verity*" _____
18. "an *immutable* principle" _____
19. "a universal *panacea*" _____
20. "an *interlocutory* judgment" _____

DON'T USE THE LAW TO DISPOSE OF USED WIVES

by Justice Robert Gardner   (from *The Los Angeles Times*, May 8, 1977)

—begin timing—

In a dynamic society, almost every area of living is subject to shifts of public attitudes. The period since World War II has included more "pendulum swings" than any other period of similar length in the history of humankind. We have experienced economic upheavals, energy problems, intense surges of nationalistic fervor, extreme minority unrest, major shifts in sexual mores.

The changing roles of women, marriage, the nuclear family are indicative of the turbulence of this period. With huge numbers of married and unmarried women now employed, with more and more individuals, both men and women, choosing independence rather than a spouse, marriage has been subjected to enormous stress. And women who elected the position of homemaker can find themselves in an impossible position.

The two selections that follow describe some of the problems that have resulted. In this first article, Justice Robert Gardner of the Orange County 4th District Court of Appeals reverses the decision of a lower court judge.

The parties had been married for 25 years. They had acquired a modest amount of community property—basically, an equity in a home, some furniture and furnishings and the usual two cars. The proceeds from the sale of the home were divided after the payment of attorneys' fees and substantial community debts. The meager balance of community assets was also divided. No issue is made concerning the division of community property.

The parties have two children, both girls, age 14 and 16. Custody of the children was awarded to the wife, husband was ordered to pay the wife $100 per month, per child, for their support and also ordered to keep the girls on his company's health insurance program. Again, no issue is made concerning the custody award or the amount of child support ordered.

During the 25 years of marriage, the husband has been the family bread-winner. He is now 45 years of age, employed by Hughes Aircraft Company, and has a gross monthly income of $1,578.

In regard to spousal support, the (lower) court ordered $200 per month for two years, $150 per month for two years, $100 per month for two years, $50 per month for two years, and $1.00 per month for four years. Thereafter, spousal support is to terminate.

The wife's employment picture is bleak. She is 44 years of age and did not even complete high school. She has no apparent job skills. She has made eight efforts for employment as a salesperson, all of which were unsuccessful. She is attending a two-year junior college class, which she describes as a "guidance class for someone my age that has not had any employment, and I would like to be able to try for something if I do lose my eyes completely. The blind do work and have employment."

This latter comment refers to the fact that the wife suffers from an incurable iritis in both eyes with the possibility of becoming blind in the near future. Furthermore, she is an arthritic. Thus, the dreary picture is presented of an unemployed and currently unemployable woman, 44 years of age, facing the possibility of becoming blind, who is confronted with a court order which reduces her spousal support to a mere pittance for the next 12 years with complete termination thereafter.

Thus, when this lady is 56 years of age (and perhaps blind), there is a substantial likelihood that she will become an object of charity. The husband's only response is that an order providing for progressive decrease and termination of spousal support may be granted at the discretion of the trial court, and that such an order may only be disturbed if there has been an abuse of the lower court's discretion. There has been.

California's new Family Law Act has been heralded as a Bill of Rights for harried former husbands, who have been suffering under prolonged and unreasonable alimony awards. However, the act may not be used as a handy vehicle for the summary disposal of old and used wives. A woman is not a breeding cow to be nurtured during her years of fecundity, then conveniently and economically converted to cheap steaks when past her prime.

If a woman is able to do so, she certainly should support herself. If, however, she has spent her productive years as a housewife and mother and has missed the opportunity to compete in the job market and improve her job skills, quite often she becomes, when divorced, simply a "displaced homemaker."

In this case we are faced with a woman who, during the last 25 years, has borne two children and confined her activities to those of a mother and housewife. These activities, vital though they may be, do not qualify her to embark on a lucrative career in the highly competitive job market. Had she not been married those 20-odd years, she might now be well qualified as a typist, truck driver or tinsmith.

Opportunities for developing skills in those fields were denied her when she, and presumably her husband, decided that she would follow that most important, but somewhat non-glamorous and definitely non-salaried, occupation of housewife and mother. Assuming she does not become blind, her experience as a homemaker qualified her for either of two positions, charwoman or babysitter. A candidate for a well paying job, she isn't.

At the time this lower court order was made, Civil Code Section 4801(a), provided that the court could order a party to pay for the support of the other party ". . . any amount, and for such period of time, as the court may deem just and reasonable having regard for the circumstances of the respective parties, including the duration of the marriage, and the ability of the supported spouse to engage in gainful employment . . ."

All this language really does is to codify the thinking processes of innumerable trial judges throughout the years. A marriage license is not a ticket to a perpetual pension and, as women approach equality in the job market, the burden on the husband will be lessened in those cases in which, by agreement of both parties, the wife has remained employed or at least has had the opportunity to maintain and refresh her job skills during marriage.

However, in those cases in which it is the decision of the parties that the woman becomes the homemaker, the marriage is of substantial duration and at separation the wife is for all intents and purposes unemployable, the husband simply has to face up to the fact that his support responsibilities are going to be of extended duration—perhaps for life. This has nothing to do with feminism, sexism, male chauvinism or any other trendy social ideology. It is ordinary commonsense, basic decency and simple justice.

But, protests the husband, this order is for a "period equal to one-half of the married life of the parties." This is advanced in tones of shocked anguish as though questioning such an order is an attack on motherhood, democracy or apple pie.

However, there is nothing talismanic about the "one-half of the married life" concept which courts frequently employ nowadays. It is not an eternal verity or an immutable principle carved in legal stone or etched in judicial steel. It fits some cases, it doesn't fit others. In some cases the wife is not entitled to a dime. In other cases she must be supported for life. Each and every case must be judged on its own merits.

A judicial policy cannot be tolerated which affords blind obedience to the idea that the support order be for a period equal to "one-half of the married life." In each case the trial court must make a careful and measured judgment reflecting a sound exercise of discretion in the award of spousal support and its duration. That discretion, we repeat, must be based on facts and reasonable inferences to be drawn from these facts. A support order for "one-half of the married life" is not some kind of a universal panacea.

Insofar as this particular case is concerned, we do not hold that the husband must support wife for the rest of her natural life. Neither do we find that wife is going to be permanently unemployable. Rather, we face the fact that in seeking employment, she has substantial handicaps and the outcome is unpredictable. Under these circumstances, it was an abuse of discretion for the court to make the type of order it did re future support.

We find an abuse of discretion in that portion of the order reducing spousal support after the first two years and terminating it after 12 years. Therefore, the interlocutory judgment is affirmed with respect to the provision for spousal support in the sum of $200 for the next two years. The judgment is reversed with respect to the provision reducing payments for such support for the next 10 years and terminating them entirely thereafter. The case is remanded to the trial court for further proceedings consistent with the views expressed in this opinion.

(+250)   —end timing—   (min___sec___)

A 10

Don't Use the Law to Dispose of Used Wives—Justice Robert Gardner

SUMMARY:

COMMENT:

A 11

Comprehension Quiz

The Sea of Matrimony, Ever Stormy, Is Even Rougher in these Liberated Times

Instructions: Write the letter of the correct answer in the blank provided.

①. The main thrust of this article is to:
a) condemn the women's movement
c) fight sexual exploitation (__)
b) provoke examination of love and marriage
d) attack traditional marriage

2. The marriage Oppenheimer mourned was:
a) not terribly solid
c) a short-term trial marriage (__)
b) doomed from the start
d) none of the above

3. The author's wife originally wanted:
a) wealth
c) stability (__)
b) a house in the suburbs
d) all of these

4. After six years, the marriage was:
a) strained financially
c) lacking their society's support (__)
b) strained by children's needs
d) all of these

5. The author describes himself as:
a) chauvinistic
c) liberated and confused (__)
b) angry and condemning
d) a corporation "climber"

6. The relationship between the author and the couple's friends was:
a) helpful and supportive
c) critical and hostile (__)
b) destructive by example
d) both (b) and (c)

7. Efforts to improve the marriage included:
a) sharing chores and child care
c) marriage counseling (__)
b) sharing an occupation
d) all of the above

8. Changes in public attitudes towards marriage were caused by:
a) increased employment of women
c) a dynamic society (__)
b) birth control pills
d) all of these

9. Since the author began "pulling himself together" he has:
a) given up on marriage
c) tried to redefine love and commitment (__)
b) learned to understand new rules
d) begun to hate women

10. According to this article, men and women should:
a) return to traditional marriage
c) find steady, solid relationships (__)
b) avoid friends
d) learn to live alone

Vocabulary Preview

1. "in the *suburbs*" _____

2. "any of its *accoutrements*" _____

3. "by *conventional* standards" _____

4. "the same *stability* in life" _____

5. "sworn off *monogamy*" _____

6. "*consciousness-raising* groups" _____

7. "in debt—not *overwhelmingly*" _____

8. "for *oppressing* my life" _____

9. "attempt . . . *degenerated* increasingly" _____

10. "at an *impasse*" _____

11. "mouth such *sentiments*" _____

12. "sex *deteriorated*" _____

13. "all too *doctrinaire*" _____

14. "*impotence* became a subject" _____

15. "male *supremacy (supremacist)*" _____

16. "against the *onslaught*" _____

17. "were under *siege*" _____

18. "*heaved* its last gasp" _____

19. "a real *rupture*" _____

20. "some *consolation*" _____

THE SEA OF MATRIMONY, EVER STORMY, IS EVEN ROUGHER IN THESE LIBERATED TIMES

by Joel Oppenheimer   (from *The Los Angeles Times*, July 5, 1978)

—begin timing—

In the preceding Reading Selection, we were given a judge's view of what he felt was a miscarriage of justice in a divorce case. In this one, we are faced with the readjustments that must be made by a husband in similar circumstances. Again, we are dealing with a dynamic society where centuries-old institutions are subjected to change.

Not too many months after this article was written, newspaper headlines throughout the world described the first "test-tube" baby, a child born as the result of conception in a laboratory dish. A year or two before, British doctors made this extraordinary birth possible, a well-known American author described the "cloning"—duplication of a single parent—of another baby. Fact? Fiction? The book aroused comment throughout the world. The legal, social, and moral implications of these birth procedures are earth-shaking. The perfection and use of these techniques, if accepted by society, could eventually eliminate the need for marriage as the approved environment in which to have children.

Joel Oppenheimer, in the selection which follows, describes a tragic side of a marriage of today which was a victim of change. What happens to children?

None of us men is fool enough to blame the "women's movement" for what happened to our lives. The marriages that my friends and I mourn were not, by and large, terribly solid to begin with—or at least it seems that way from this perspective. But all of us who have gone our separate ways have a sneaking suspicion that our marriages might have lasted—might have weathered the storm and even grown stronger—in a different time.

I'm not talking about short-term, trial marriages. Those relationships that my friends and I sit around and talk about had lasted 8 or 10 or 12 years, had produced kids—and had "liberated" husbands as one of the partners. But they broke up, or down, in the mid-'70s, and we have to feel that the women's-liberation movement played at least some role.

Take my case. My wife, like many others, had come to the marriage after some experience in the world of workaday jobs; she was educated, intelligent and healthy. She wanted kids, she wanted a home. She didn't want a place in the suburbs, or any of its accoutrements, either. She knew that I was a poet—at that time I was working at a print shop—and that our life probably wouldn't be "normal" by conventional standards. But she also felt, correctly, that I wanted the same stability in our lives that she did. So we got married.

My wife tended the house, cooked the meals, had the babies, while all around her the rest of her world—the world of young women she knew—was going the other way. Every friend she had was either separated, divorced or had sworn off monogamy. Families, in the traditional sense, were out.

The new philosophy filled the air. Consciousness-raising groups popped up, and a new book came out every week, it seemed, that clearly espoused the need to find one's self, to go it alone, to make it in a man's world, and to make that world a *woman's* world.

We'd been married about six years by then; our oldest son was almost 5 when the other one came along. Two young kids aren't easy under any circumstances. We were in debt—not overwhelmingly, but enough to frighten a reasonable person. The kids' needs were frightening, too. They pulled us in two directions because the baby needed us physically 24 hours a day, and his older brother, having pretty much outgrown that kind of dependence, needed us emotionally almost as much.

These are the strains that marriages have always had to put up with, and either they survived or not. But there used to be support, history tells us— relatives to help out with the kids, friends to pour one's troubles onto. Above all, in the larger society there was a widely shared belief that what the young couple were doing—sharing, sacrificing, raising a family—was good. Life would get easier, people used to say, and generally they were right.

Now, however, there were no more families in the old sense, and now our own friends disapproved of what we were doing. So did society, at least the part that was closest to us. I was a beast for oppressing my wife; she was a beast of burden; our children were interferences. Any attempt that the two of us made to talk about all this degenerated increasingly into a clash of cultural viewpoints, I taking the old line ("it will get better") and my wife the new one ("the most important thing is for me to find myself"). We were at an impasse.

I said that we husbands were liberated, and I meant it. I believed, and still do, that women down through time have gotten the shaft; that too often men have been emotionally absent from their families; that household chores should belong to both partners; that women deserve careers—and equal pay. But expressing my views like this became another sticking point. How could I mouth such sentiments when everywhere we went she was *my* wife, and we were spending *my* money?

Okay, I said, work or go back to school so you can work later. I'll help with the children and the house. We tried it—it wasn't enough.

Sex, which had been splendid, deteriorated. Articles appeared saying that any penetration of a woman's body was rape, and that attention to tradi- tionally erotic areas of a woman's body was chauvinist. So we tried other rec- ommended approaches. I stayed passive, she took the active role. It was fun, but it couldn't help our relationship—it was all too doctrinaire.

Impotence became a subject for open concern. Men were reacting to emo- tional assault in the only way that their bodies knew how—by withdrawing. Then the pressure grew even stronger, for, if a man did become impotent, it meant that he was holding on to those worn-out ideas of male supremacy. It was a vicious circle, because if he stayed potent, that also meant that he was a supremacist.

Marriages were collapsing all around us. At times, when things were going reasonably well, we felt like the last fortress holding out against the onslaught. We were under siege, and, in fact, we too were crumbling. We tried to divvy up the house, literally—my area, her area, the kids' area. Then we split up the week and the household chores and the child care. None of this worked, ei- ther. If I played by the rules and waited for a signal, that meant that I didn't care; if I intruded myself into her space or time, that raised all the old argu- ments.

Finally, early in 1975, our marriage heaved its last gasp. She moved out; I kept the kids. Now it is three years later, and some of the other marriages that went down then have risen again; some of the people from the old marriages have found new mates; some go on alone with or without their kids. As for me, I'm still healing—and I use that term not because I was the only one who got hurt but because it was a real rupture.

I was 45 at the time. This had been my second marriage and, I thought, my last. Now I had to find out if there was a place for me in that big world out there. I did—and there was.

Then I began trying to put myself back together in terms of what I had learned. It's still a problem going out to eat with a woman—I haven't been right once about offering to pay or not. I haven't been right once about whether to pick her up at her house or meet her outside. And it took two years before I found myself able to laugh in bed, rather than worry about my performance—about where what was permitted, about being a good lover instead of a dirty old man.

The women are hurt, too. There's no trust left, or damned little. They tell me that men find them too aggressive—and sometimes they are; they tell me that they can't find men interested in a relationship—or that all we want are mothers, or sisters, or daughters.

So we're all finding our way, but the way is difficult. We have to lay a groundwork that will allow for real communication. We have to find things that we all believe in enough to make it possible to cooperate; in other words, we have to find a new definition for love, for commitment. We have to find out what family means now, what children are, and why we are pulled toward each other and toward our continuation through children or joy or work or whatever. Because, despite everything, we are pulled toward each other, still.

But the old rules have changed—that's one thing that women's lib did. A lot of it is healthy—yet I wish it had happened at a different time, to someone else. Because I'm not sure I understand all the new rules. My boys will understand them, I think, and will be better men for it, and better human beings, too. That's some consolation—but there are still nights when I realize that I don't want to just hang out, when I wish that I had someone adult to talk to at home.

It will come; I know that now. Maybe not marriage anymore, but some kind of steady, solid, giving relationship. That's, of course, what I thought we had before—and what she and I might have worked into, with a little bit of help from our friends. I guess our friends had their own problems.

(+200)   —end timing—   (min___sec___)

A 11

The Sea of Matrimony, Ever Stormy, Is Even Rougher in these Liberated Times—Joel Oppenheimer

SUMMARY:

COMMENT:

A 12

Comprehension Quiz

A Permanent and Limitless Energy Source for the World

Instructions: Write the letter of the correct answer in the blank provided.

1. This article deals primarily with unlimited sources of electrical power from:
   - a) geothermal steam
   - b) atomic *fission*
   - c) solar power
   - d) atomic *fusion*   (___)

2. For fuel, atomic *fission* plants depend on:
   - a) heavy elements like uranium
   - b) ultra-high temperature plasma
   - c) light elements like deuterium
   - d) specialized fossil fuels   (___)

3. Atomic *fusion* plants, on the other hand, would work using unlimited quantities of:
   - a) fissionable materials
   - b) radioactive wastes
   - c) a molecule found in sea water
   - d) all of the above   (___)

4. A major advantage of fusion power over fission power is:
   - a) it is available now
   - b) waste production is minimal
   - c) research required is small
   - d) plant cost is lower   (___)

5. In a fission plant, the "China Syndrome" refers to:
   - a) China's use of atomic weapons
   - b) failure of the cooling system
   - c) atomic radiation
   - d) Russian-American cooperation   (___)

6. On the basis of known world resources for energy production, the supply that will last longest is:
   - a) fission fuels
   - b) fossil fuels
   - c) fusion fuels
   - d) not mentioned   (___)

7. Research in the fusion area is international. The U.S. contributes:
   - a) 100%   b) 40%   c) 16%   d) 34%   (___)

8. On the basis of progress now being made, fusion feasibility could be proved:
   - a) withing the next year or two
   - b) as early as 1985
   - c) about the year 2000
   - d) cannot now be determined   (___)

9. Fusion research will cost billions. The one kind of ownership of the perfected technique not mentioned by the article is: (___)
   - a) government financing, industry development
   - b) combined government and industry financing and development
   - c) a consortium of private corporations
   - d) research, development, and ownership by the government alone

10. Because perfection of the process could raise worldwide living standards, the article suggests international distribution of the technology. If *we* solved the problems, American reaction to this would be:
    - a) dubious
    - b) nonpolitical
    - c) enthusiastic
    - d) all of these   (___)

Vocabulary Preview

1. "*dwindling* fossil fuel reserves" _____

2. "the force of *fusion*" _____

3. "*literally* limitless supply" _____

4. "for guarded *optimism*" _____

5. "nuclear *fission* process" _____

6. "elements or *isotopes*" _____

7. "*ionized* gas" _____

8. "found *abundantly* in water" _____

9. "kind to the *ecosystem*" _____

10. "no *noxious* products" _____

11. "*wryly* called the 'China Syndrome'" _____

12. "are virtually *inexhaustible*" _____

13. "proof of fusion *feasibility*" _____

14. "commercially *applicable*" _____

15. "on magnetic *confinement*" _____

16. "*alleviation* of scarcities" _____

17. "*supplanting* it at the earliest date" _____

18. "*magnitude* of the venture" _____

19. "magnitude of the *venture*" _____

20. "becoming the *domain* or province" _____

—begin timing—

Energy—A Crucial Issue for the Future

In this period of brownouts, rationing, and energy crises, the promise of unlimited sources of energy radiates like a beacon of hope. Certainly we are all aware of dwindling fossil fuel reserves, particularly natural gas and oil. And while we have coal reserves that may last for many years, their unlimited use may cause permanent damage to living things. Moreover, we must remember that while the U.S. is well supplied with coal, many other nations (especially the "have-not" countries) have little or none. It is hard to believe the poor nations will stand by idly while rich ones continue to raise their material standard of living. The energy crisis was not unforeseen; we simply lacked the determination and courage to do something about it. What we needed was long-range planning; what we got was short-term budget-balancing.

Other areas of power potential deserve full-fledged research. The chairman of the United Nations Committee on the World Energy Emergency, working with his counterpart for the state of Claifornia, stated that the underground steam available in the west and southwest alone could supply the U.S. with all the electricity we could consume in the foreseeable future. (Did you know that half of San Francisco, all of New Zealand, and part of Italy are powered by this source alone?)

We are getting a firm technical hold on the economical use of solar power, another possibly unlimited source. Geothermal heat, from the molten core of the earth, also has great potential.

The following article describes yet another system with enormous promise.

A PERMANENT AND LIMITLESS ENERGY SOURCE FOR THE WORLD

(from *The Center Report*, October, 1972)

For twenty years Richard Post, physicist, and his colleagues at the Lawrence Livermore Laboratory, Livermore, California, have, in one way or another, been trying to find a way to harness the force of the fusion of nuclear particles to give the world a literally limitless supply of energy. The effort at this laboratory is but one element in a worldwide research effort to achieve fusion power. Fusion research has progressed to the point for guarded [limited] optimism. A worldwide Energy Revolution may be at hand. Herewith a report based on Post's recent presentations at the Center.

WHAT IT IS

Nuclear fusion is not to be confused with the nuclear fission process which is in increasing use by electric utility companies. *Fission* energy is created by the fracturing of the nuclei of *heavy* elements (uranium and plutonium) into lighter elements and releases energy in the form of neutrons, gamma radiation and thermal [heat] energy. The *fusion* process fuses together *light* atoms (deuterium, tritium, helium 3, etc.) into other elements or isotopes which are heavier than the elements which entered the reaction. To carry out fusion reactions requires the production of an ultra-high-temperature plasma (ionized gas) composed of these elements, which would then react with the release of energy (in the form of fast flying reaction products) which can be captured and has the potentiality of being directly converted into electricity. Deuterium, the fusion reactor's main fuel, is found abundantly in water. Each gallon of sea water, for example, can deliver deuterium equal to 300 gallons of gasoline in energy. The cost of separation of deuterium from water is so low that fusion fuel would cost less than one percent of the cost of coal, on a per-unit-of-energy basis.

WHY ITS EXTRAORDINARY PROMISE

Fusion energy is kind to the ecosystem. The fusion process does not result in radioactive ashes and produces minimal radiation. It burns no fossil fuels and releases no noxious products. In contrast the fission process now being used in an ever-growing number of nuclear power plants (nukes) creates a large amount of dangerous radioactive wastes. According to present practice these are shipped by rail or truck and stored in tanks or in underground caverns. There are other dangers inherent in nuclear fission, among them the hazard, wryly called the "China Syndrome," in which a "failure of cooling" accident could occur, allowing the reactor core to melt its way down all the way to China!

According to Post's calculations there is a factor of 100,000 to a million between the biological hazard potential of the fusion reactor and the fission reactor, in favor of fusion.

Fusion-derived energy becomes a possibility at a time when the world's conventional energy sources are dwindling. Presently known reserves of fossil fuel will last no more than another 150 years at most at projected rates of usage. High-grade sources of uranium and thorium as required by the fission process will have been used up within a relatively few decades, leading to increased costs and sharpening the energy crisis for have-not nations. Fusion fuel reserves, on the other hand, are virtually inexhaustible. The deuterium in a cubic meter of sea water can provide the energy equivalent of 2000 barrels of oil; the total deuterium reserve in the waters of the oceans is good for billions of years at any conceivable rate of energy usage.

A third argument in favor of fusion-derived energy is the problem of material accountability and the possibility of sabotage. Fission reactors utilize substances which can be converted into nuclear weapons. Fusion reactors do not. Fission reactors could be sabotaged with disastrous environmental consequences. Fusion reactors could not.

WHERE IT'S AT

Controlled fusion research began about twenty years ago, in secrecy and almost simultaneously, in the U.S., the U.K., and the U.S.S.R. Secrecy was ended by international agreement in 1958. Since then an unusually high degree of international cooperation has existed in the field. The present worldwide fusion research effort is about the equivalent of $120,000,000. About 40 percent of it is taking place in the Soviet Union, 16 percent of it in the U.S. and the balance in the U.K., Western Europe and Japan. The world political effects of final proof of fusion feasibility are difficult to imagine. It might have a dramatic effect, for example, on the pricing structure of mid-East oil.

WHEN WILL IT BE COMMERCIALLY APPLICABLE?

If progress on magnetic confinement of fusion energy continues as expected, fusion experiments proving the scientific feasibility of fusion reactors could be operational by 1980. Traditionally the time lag between scientific proof and full commercial development ranges between thirty to forty years.

For fusion this time lag might be substantially shortened since many of the severe technological problems that must be solved to build a fusion reactor will have already been solved in the course of proving scientific feasibility. Among them: large-scale super conducting magnet coils, intense particle beams, good vacuums. These development-type problems have been and are being solved concurrently with the necessary qualitative preparatory research. Today fusion research is centered more on quantitative questions, questions of how to make the various processes sufficiently efficient to achieve net power release.

With high-priority governmental support an organized program of concurrent R & D toward an integrated industrial complex with fusion energy at its core could conceivably lead to early alleviation of the worldwide scarcities caused, in large part, by high energy costs. A bold and far-sighted energy policy should put fusion as the next necessary step *beyond* the fission reactor, supplanting it at the earliest possible date. The cost of exploring the remaining scientific problems of the fusion reactor (primarily confinement physics) is minimal compared to its future value as a permanent and limitless energy source for the world.

HOW TO PUT IT TO WORK

(Recent Center resident member, Scott Kelso, who heads a Texas-based fossil fuel and mineral exploration corporation, provided some ideas on how fusion energy plants will be capitalized.) Several alternatives to financing what will probably be a multi-billion-dollar effort are available. One model would be the Manhattan Project in which different facets of the project were farmed out under government financing, in large part. Another is the COMSAT model, a corporation which has brought together both private and public funding. A third model is to be found in NASA. One might see certain aerospace and oil companies as prime and sub-contractors. Finally, there could be a consortium [group of corporations].

If this is going to be a multi-billion-dollar effort, no one company, not even one the size of General Motors, could undertake it. Probably the most efficient method of getting there fast is to tap what private industry can do well and to make ownership available to everybody, COMSAT-style. Because of the magnitude of the venture there is no possibility of fusion energy becoming the domain or province of one or two or three large companies.

There is no real reason not to share the know-how. It is just as much in the U.S. interest for Chile to have inexpensive energy as it is for us to have it. Primary fuel, deuterium, is readily available to everyone. Here is an area which could bring about a new intensity of international cooperation. There's every chance that fusion energy production will be one of the very few ventures in which we can engage without international competitiveness.

Why? Because if fusion energy were to become feasible our reasons for being competitive might drop by an order of magnitude. It means that everyone would have the means to achieve wealth, namely unlimited energy resources. What would we compete for? Technically it is probably the most promising possibility for dampening destructive competitiveness in the world. *It could be the most revolutionary thing that has happened in a thousand years.*

(+300)   —end timing—   (min__sec__)

A 12

A Permanent and Limitless Energy Source for the World—The Center Report

SUMMARY:

COMMENT:

NOTES

Time-Rate Conversion—1000-Word Units (Chapters)

Locate your time in minutes and seconds in the left-hand columns. Your rate in words per minute can be found to the right in the WPM column.

TIME Min.	RATE WPM	TIME Min.	RATE WPM	TIME Min.	RATE WPM	TIME Min.	RATE WPM	TIME Min.	RATE WPM
6:00	166	5:00	200	4:00	250	3:00	333	2:00	500
5:55	168	4:55	204	3:55	255	2:55	343	1:55	524
5:50	170	4:50	208	3:50	260	2:50	353	1:50	546
5:45	172	4:45	211	3:45	266	2:45	364	1:45	571
5:40	176	4:40	215	3:40	271	2:40	376	1:40	602
5:35	178	4:35	218	3:35	276	2:35	384	1:35	633
5:30	180	4:30	221	3:30	281	2:30	400	1:30	666
5:25	184	4:25	225	3:25	290	2:25	415	1:25	704
5:20	188	4:20	230	3:20	299	2:20	429	1:20	752
5:15	192	4:15	235	3:15	308	2:15	445	1:15	800
5:10	194	4:10	240	3:10	316	2:10	461	1:10	857
5:05	197	4:05	245	3:05	324	2:05	481	1:05	933

Completion in one minute equals a rate of 1000 words per minute.

You can determine your precise speed for any article by using the formula:

$$\frac{\text{No. of words}}{\text{Time in sec.}} \times 60 = \text{WPM}$$

Time-Rate Conversion—1500-Word Units (Appendix)

Locate your time in minutes and seconds in the left-hand columns. Your rate in words per minute can be found to the right in the WPM column.

TIME Min.	RATE WPM	TIME Min.	RATE WPM	TIME Min.	RATE WPM	TIME Min.	RATE WPM
9:00	166	7:00	214	5:00	300	3:00	500
8:50	170	6:50	219	4:50	310	2:50	529
8:40	173	6:40	225	4:40	321	2:40	563
8:30	177	6:30	231	4:30	333	2:30	600
8:20	180	6:20	237	4:20	346	2:20	643
8:10	183	6:10	243	4:10	360	2:10	692
8:00	187	6:00	250	4:00	376	2:00	750
7:50	193	5:50	257	3:50	392	1:50	818
7:40	196	5:40	262	3:40	409	1:40	900
7:30	200	5:30	272	3:30	428	1:30	1000
7:20	204	5:20	282	3:20	450	1:20	1125
7:10	209	5:10	290	3:10	475	1:10	1286

Completion in one minute equals a rate of 1500 words per minute.

PROGRESS CHART

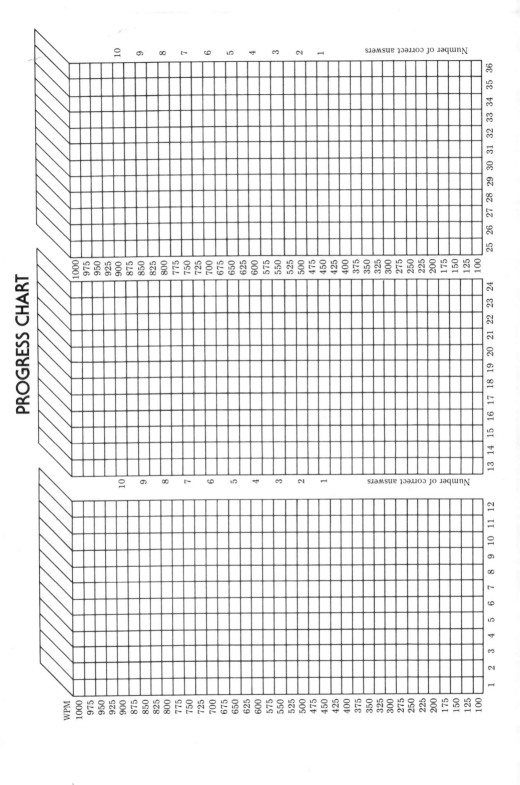

SUCCESSFUL
READING

Third Edition

Maxwell H. Norman and Enid S. Kass Norman

- A text-workbook designed to further more effective reading for information, growth—and pleasure
- 12 chapters, each including:
  - A 1000-word Reading Technique for timed reading and understanding
  - A 1000-word Reading Selection, chiefly stressing the changing nature of society
  - Vocabulary "previews" and exercises
  - Self-grading comprehension quizzes
  - Exercises to develop skill in summarizing
  - Activities structurally designed toward understanding and perfecting outlining
- Appendix of 12 articles for timed reading, each with vocabulary-building activity and comprehension quiz
- Time-Rate Conversion Chart and Progress Chart for self-recording rate of improvement

---

- Emphasizes techniques for sharpening study skills
- Introduces a fast, single, *organized approach* for mastering college-level material: OARWET—Overview—Ask—Read—Write—Evaluate—Test (Chapter 2)
- Stresses and provides for working at individual pace

Holt, Rinehart and Winston

ISBN 0-03-043126-3